ROUSSEAU'S
Social Contract

ROUSSEAU'S
Social Contract
The Design of the Argument

HILAIL GILDIN

The University of Chicago Press
Chicago and London

The University of Chicago Press, Chicago 60637
The University of Chicago Press, Ltd., London

© 1983 by The University of Chicago
All rights reserved. Published 1983
Printed in the United States of America
90 89 88 87 86 85 84   5 4 3 2

Library of Congress Cataloging in Publication Data

Gildin, Hilail.
    Rousseau's Social contract.

    Includes index.
    1. Rousseau, Jean Jacques, 1712–1778. Du contrat
social I. Title.
JC179.R88G54   1983   320'.01   82-20148
ISBN 0-226-29368-8

Contents

v

Acknowledgments

A seminar on Rousseau's political philosophy which Leo Strauss offered—in which the *Discourse on the Sciences and Arts*, the *Discourse on Inequality*, and the *Social Contract* were dealt with—kindled my interest in Rousseau. In this work I have made an attempt to repay my debt to that extraordinarily illuminating seminar. Responsibility for the use made in what follows of the light Strauss shed on Rousseau must, of course, remain mine.

Generous fellowship grants by the Relm Foundation and the Earhart Foundation enabled me to prepare and to write this book. When preparing the interpretation that follows, I sometimes found that the same point arose more than once in the course of the argument. The repetition has been permitted to remain when it serves to clarify the point.

Chapter One

Preliminary Considerations

In the *First Treatise of Government*, Locke enunciates the fundamental issue of political life as well as of political philosophy as follows: "The great Question which in all Ages has disturbed Mankind, and brought on them the greatest part of those Mischiefs which have ruined Cities, depopulated Countries, and disordered the Peace of the World, has been, Not whether there be Power in the World, nor whence it came, but who should have it" (sec. 106). All of Rousseau's major predecessors in political philosophy, whether they were ancients or moderns, had to face the "great Question" of who should rule. No less than his predecessors, Rousseau seeks to discover the true answer to this question and he communicates what he thinks that answer to be in the *Social Contract*.[1] But if the question Rousseau faces in that work is, as the quotation from Locke reminds us, at least as old as political life, there is something peculiarly modern about the answer to it that Rousseau supplies. The very terms in which his answer is formulated—the state of nature, the state of civil society, the institution of a legitimate sovereign, the concern with self-preservation from which legitimate rule is derived—all point to modern innovations within political philosophy which Rousseau makes his own, thinks through, and profoundly transforms—the innovations commonly associated with the names of Hobbes and Locke.[2]

The major works of modern political philosophy that Rousseau's book calls to mind are all larger in size and more comprehensive in scope than the *Social Contract*. Rousseau himself draws the reader's attention to the brevity of his work, as well as to

1

its less than comprehensive character, in the Foreword that precedes it. Unlike any one of Hobbes's three presentations of political philosophy, for example, the *Social Contract* is unaccompanied by an account of the nature of man or of the state of nature, although assertions that would have to be justified in such accounts are made throughout the work.[3] What the work Rousseau originally intended to write would have dealt with in addition to what he discusses in the *Social Contract* will be left an open question. Answering it would be easy if one could equate the scope of Rousseau's projected work with the content of Emile's political education. The implausibility of any such equation becomes manifest once one realizes that the *Social Contract* alone deals with matters of the highest importance—the legislator and civil religion—which are not part of the political education received by Emile in the work that bears his name.

Rousseau's "small treatise" is not the only short book to be found among the masterpieces of political philosophy. The two most famous ones that readily come to mind—Machiavelli's *Prince* and Plato's *Statesman*—are both referred to with approval in the text of the *Social Contract*. Their authors are the only major political philosophers who are mentioned without ever being criticized in this work. The theme of these other works is not the same as that of the *Social Contract*. "The Principles of Political Right," as Rousseau understands that phrase, would not be a suitable subtitle for either of them. Yet the account of human inequality and greatness contained in them, as well as that present in *That Beasts Use Reason*, a dialogue by Plutarch which Rousseau calls exactly what he called the *Social Contract*—a "small treatise" (1.2.8)*—all will shed light on how much Rousseau's egalitarianism owes precisely to his appreciation of human greatness, its supreme importance for political life, and, above all, its rareness. Both references to Plato's *Statesman* draw attention to that rareness.[4]

Although the *Social Contract* is not the comprehensive work Rousseau originally intended to write, it is said to be complete in one important respect. The subject of the work, as announced in its subtitle, is "The Principles of Political Right." At the end of the work, Rousseau affirms that he has "set down [*posé*] the true principles of political right" in it (4.9.1). By the principles of political right Rousseau means what we today might call the principles of constitutional law, although in doing so we should remember that

*References to the *Social Contract* are by book, chapter and paragraph. 1.2.8 means Book 1, Chapter 2, paragraph 8.

such principles are not necessarily embodied in written laws. Not even all constitutions are written. What is true of constitutions is still more true of the rules comprising the principles of political right. These principles, as Rousseau understands them, point out where the sovereign of a society is to be found, what its functions are, and how it secures compliance with its commands. In one respect, Rousseau's principles of political right are analogous to Thomas's definition of law in the *Treatise on Law*: both are normative. Thomas's definition explains the nature of law and in doing so sets forth the conditions which a statute must meet in order to deserve to be considered a law. If a statute is not in accord with reason or directed to the common good or enacted by the ruling authority, to mention three of these conditions, it is not a legitimate law (*lex legalis*) according to Thomas. One is not morally bound to respect and obey it in the same way that one would be bound to respect and obey a law worthy of the name. Similarly, in explaining what sovereign authority is, Rousseau sets forth the conditions of legitimate sovereignty. These conditions *are* the principles of political right. A political society by which these conditions are not met does not have a valid constitution or a legitimate sovereign, according to Rousseau, and the statutes enacted by its rulers are not, strictly speaking, laws.

If the principles of political right are the subject of the book, the question arises why it is called *On the Social Contract*. The answer to this question is implied in the way in which the entire argument of the book is presented, but Rousseau answered it explicitly in an earlier draft of the work: the social contract is "the fundamental compact which is the basis of every true body politic," and it is necessary to have "the most correct ideas [*les plus justes idées*] that one can have" concerning it and to develop them with precision and care because "for want of having conceived them clearly, *all* those who have dealt with this subject have always founded civil government on arbitrary Principles which do not flow from the nature of the compact."[5] According to Rousseau, the true principles of civil government do flow from the nature of the social compact. The social contract is the principle of the principles of political right. It is therefore not surprising that the entire treatise is named after it.

The brevity of the *Social Contract* helps make the work difficult and obscure. Rousseau was aware that this was the case. While claiming that he had written "a book for all time," he thought that it would be "suited to few readers" owing to its "arid matter [*matière ingrate*]" and its abstractness. Now, few authors can equal Rous-

Preliminary Considerations

seau in eloquence. Moreover, the question of who should rule is one that is difficult to deal with without passion. In our subsequent analysis of Rousseau's decision to treat that question in a manner directly contrary to his usual one, we will find him claiming that it was precisely the abstract character of his work which permitted him to write on political matters "with some boldness [*avec quelque hardiesse*]."[6] The brevity of the *Social Contract*, however, also reflects something of a different and even opposite character. For while acknowledging the difficulty of his treatise, Rousseau also claims that the principles set forth in it grow out of first steps that are "clear, simple and taken directly from the nature of things."[7] In an earlier draft of the work, Rousseau promised to show the reader "with what ease the entire political system is deduced from [the principles] I have just established."[8] He finds it possible to sum up the politically most important points of his treatise in four lucid pages of a later book.[9] Emile, who is assumed not to be unusually gifted, is taught the chief political conclusions of the *Social Contract*.[10] The professed difficulty of the work can be reconciled with its professed clarity and simplicity. If one wishes to understand fully the nature of political life it is not enough to understand what is transcended by the city and deserves to be under the authority of the city; one must also understand what transcends the city. To the extent that the *Social Contract* contributes to that understanding, it is a difficult work. On the other hand, there is a clarity and simplicity—some may feel, an excessive clarity and simplicity—about the politically pertinent conclusions it comes to. A short work is an appropriate vehicle for such conclusions as well.[11]

The epigraph for the work—*foederis aequas Dicamus leges* ("let us declare the fair laws of a compact")—is taken from the *Aeneid*, Virgil's great epic about the founding of Rome. Rome, in turn, is the most admirable republic that ever was, for Rousseau, in spite of the fact that he found much in its constitution to criticize. The speaker of these lines—Latinus—is not himself a Roman. He is the head of a people that is described (by him) as living righteously without coercion or laws. Latinus's description of his people reminds one of the happiest period in the state of nature, as Rousseau speaks of it in the *Discourse on Inequality*. Latinus reluctantly finds himself in conflict with the founders of Rome. He utters the words of the epigraph in the hope of replacing that conflict with bonds of peace. His hope is not fulfilled.

Book 1 of the *Social Contract* opens with three brief paragraphs which immediately precede the first chapter. The first of these paragraphs outlines the subject matter of the work. Although the terms in which this outline is couched are quite innocuous, the major difficulties which Rousseau will seek to overcome in the sequel are indicated by them.

Rousseau begins by declaring his intention to determine whether there can be, within political society, any legitimate and dependable rule for managing its affairs. The fact that his concern extends to considerations of dependability as well as of legitimacy will prove to be decisive for the entire work. It will explain why the work deals, to the extent that it does, with questions of what can be expected to succeed politically. In other words, it will explain why Rousseau speaks, in the concluding chapter of the *Social Contract*, not only of having established "the true principles of political right" but also of having "sought to found the state on that basis."

The concern with effectiveness does not represent something external to Rousseau's conception of legitimacy. The principles of political right are only binding in character if one can rely on widespread compliance with them by one's fellow citizens ("The engagements which bind us to the social body are only binding because they are mutual" [2.4.5]). One can rely on compliance with them only where human agreements and laws with teeth in them give these principles an effective political embodiment. If one sets the question of religious sanctions to one side and attempts to limit oneself "to consider[ing] things humanly" one will find that "the laws of justice" are not self-enforcing; "lacking any natural sanction . . . they are unavailing among men; they merely benefit the wicked and harm the just when the latter observes them with everyone without anyone observing them with him." That is why *human* or political arrangements, *human* or political "conventions and laws" are needed "to unite rights to duties and bring justice back to its object," which cannot be to bind the just man hand and foot and place him at the mercy of scoundrels (2.6.2). Human sanctions must make up for the sanctions that nature does not supply. Human sanctions "alone render legitimate civil obligations which, without that, would be absurd, tyrannical, and subject to the most enormous abuses" (1.7.8). If the principles of political right lose their effectiveness, that is, if the social contract is violated, men are released from the obligation to live by these principles (1.6.5; 3.10.6). Since so much depends, for Rousseau, on the effective embodiment of his principles, it is not enough for him to provide a description of what the legitimate political order must be like. He must also consider under what circumstances the arrangements he describes can be realized. The exposition of the arrangements that confer legitimacy on political life must precede, to be sure, the discussion of the conditions under which these arrangements can be put into effect and thus become binding, but both subjects are pertinent to Rousseau's theme and both will be dealt with by him.[12]

In Book 2 of the *Confessions*, Rousseau speaks of becoming aware of a "great maxim of morality" which is "the only one, perhaps to be of practical use [*d'usage dans la pratique*]." The maxim is "to avoid situations which place our duties in opposition to our interests and which show us our good in another's harm." According to Rousseau, those who find themselves in such situations, "however sincere a love of virtue" they may be animated by, and even if they possess a "strong soul," will "weaken sooner or later without realizing it" and will "become unjust and wicked in deed without ceasing to be just and good in their soul."[13] We propose to linger briefly over this maxim because Rousseau claims to have presented it in all of his most recent writings—the reference clearly encompasses the *Social Contract*—and he complains of the public's failure to perceive it in them.[14]

In embracing this maxim, Rousseau plainly is not prepared to settle for a life consisting of noble intentions and base acts. That is precisely what the maxim is intended to prevent. The maxim reflects a concern with duty that is irreducible to a concern with one's advantage, but it also reflects an appreciation of the power that one's advantage will have over one's life. Rousseau praises the maxim as highly as he does—"Now *that*, according to me, is good philosophy, the only one truly suited to the human heart [*vraiment assortie au coeur humain*]. Every day I become more fully convinced of its profound solidity."—because it indicates how the requirements of duty can be reconciled with the exigencies of human practice. It points the way to a morality by which "men as they are" can live as well as one they can look up to. The maxim does not assume that whenever duty and advantage come into conflict, advantage will triumph over duty. What it does assume is that situations in which the two constantly remain in conflict will sooner or later lead to the triumph of advantage over duty. A perfect coincidence between duty and advantage is not called for by the maxim, but a rough correspondence between them, in the long run, is.

One encounters a political version of the maxim under discussion in the very first paragraph of the *Social Contract*. There we learn of Rousseau's intention to prevent "justice and utility from becoming separated," of his concern "to always ally what right permits with what interest prescribes." The preceding discussion of Rousseau's views regarding the need for effectiveness as well as legitimacy also reflects his adherence to the maxim. These concerns account for his determination to be mindful of "men as they are" while considering "laws as they can be."

The conclusions which Rousseau will be led to draw in seeking to apply his maxim to political life do not shine through the outline he gives. However, the outline does indicate the major difficulties that he will face, even if one only becomes fully aware of them after encountering them in the course of Rousseau's argument. His efforts to overcome these difficulties will lead him to his conclusions. Establishing laws that are both dependable and legitimate may not at first seem to be extraordinarily difficult, but as Rousseau's discussion progresses the obstacle to establishing such laws appears, for a moment, to be insurmountable. What Rousseau understands by justice insofar as it is irreducible to utility, and why he thinks it indispensable for a sound political order, is something that the reader is only gradually brought to see. Keeping justice united with utility will also be exceptionally difficult, and possible only for a limited time. In the two concluding paragraphs of his introductory remarks, Rousseau makes use of distinctions he will later draw between the prince, the legislator, and the sovereign. Understanding the difference between these three and keeping each separate from the others and in its proper place in the political arena will be very hard tasks as well.

Rousseau imagines himself being asked how he can claim to pronounce on who should rule and who should not. In response, he affirms himself, without fanfare, to be something higher than either a prince or a legislator: he is, if not the sovereign by birth, still a member by birth of a sovereign body. What follows in the work is meant to be useful to citizens of free states who, like himself, are aware of the duty to make a wise use of their sovereign authority. Rousseau's answer quietly foreshadows the most important teaching of his work.

The final paragraph of Rousseau's introductory remarks indicates that he was mindful, in writing the *Social Contract*, of the implications of his conclusions for political life in Geneva. He tries to convey the impression that a perfect harmony obtains between his conclusions and the way Geneva is governed. In the *Confessions*, however, a different account is offered. There we are told that the large work from which the *Social Contract* is taken was meant to disclose "great truths useful to the happiness of the human race, and above all to that of my fatherland, where I did not find in the trip I had just made there notions of laws and of liberty that were either correct or clear-cut enough to my liking, and I believed that this indirect way of giving its members these [notions] was best suited to spare their amour-propre and to win me their forgiveness for having been able to see further than they had been in this respect."[15] Is the difference between the criticism of Geneva implied here and the praise of Geneva with which the *Social Contract* opens due to the intervening condemnation of Rousseau by Geneva that followed the publication of *Emile* and the *Social Contract*? Does the quoted passage project onto the Rousseau of an earlier period a dissatisfaction with Geneva that he began to feel only after that condemnation? If one believes, with many careful students of Rousseau, that the chapters in the *Social Contract* on periodic assemblies were written at least in part with Geneva in mind, and if one grants Rousseau an awareness that what he required was not yet to be found in Geneva, one will not feel compelled to answer these questions in the affirmative. In the *Confessions*, Rousseau declares that the lessons he intended for his countrymen were to be conveyed *indirectly* in the work he was projecting. One way of doing this would be, for example, to show in the abstract what the role of popular assemblies should be in both establishing and restraining government, without pointing to Geneva and saying that this was not being done there. The book of the *Social Contract* devoted to the preceding subject (Book 3) is the only one in which Geneva is not mentioned. Whenever Geneva is mentioned, no breath of criticism is voiced of it. Rousseau says he thought that by proceeding in this indirect manner, he would escape the anger of his fellow citizens. He does *not* claim to have anticipated, at this early date, that his work would be greeted with open hostility though he does say that the way in which an earlier work of his had been received revealed the secret enmity towards him by members of Geneva's governing council.[16]

The remarks that precede the first chapter of the *Social Contract* are a brief introduction to the work as a whole. The first chapter itself, on the other hand, sets the stage for the most important chapter of the work, the one which presents the social contract.

Chapter 1 opens with a famous and startling assertion. If one were asked to state in one word what the end of a political society is according to the *Social Contract*, the word one would most likely choose would be "freedom." Yet the *Social Contract* opens with the denial that there can be any freedom in political society. "Man is born free and *everywhere* he is in chains," even, apparently, in the "free" state where Rousseau just told us he was born. The reader who expects Rousseau to say he will show men how to overcome this calamity is promptly undeceived. Rousseau does not promise to show men how to win release from their political bonds and regain their original freedom. He promises to show them how their chains can be made legitimate. Whether men are rulers or ruled, legitimate slavery is the best that political society has to offer them.

How is this forceful assertion to be understood, given the importance of freedom as a political theme in what follows? The freedom of which Rousseau is speaking in the present passage is natural freedom. Now, freedom is formally introduced, in the argument of the first book, as a means to self-preservation (1.2.2). The requirements of self-preservation are appealed to in an effort to justify the assertion that men are by nature free.[17] However, natural freedom is also understood in a different manner by Rousseau, who often speaks of it as a condition and ingredient of happiness.[18] The very possibility of the social contract will prove to rest on its ability to supply a solid substitute for natural freedom as a means to self-preservation, a substitute that Rousseau calls conventional freedom.[19] There can, for Rousseau, be no substitute for natural freedom as an ingredient of happiness, however (2.11.4). And natural freedom, or acting as one pleases, is not compatible with life in political society. Bearing this distinction in mind will prevent one from becoming confused by the presence both of passages which present the substitution of conventional freedom for natural freedom as an advantageous transaction and those that, like the present one, speak of the loss of natural freedom as a terrible misfortune. From a certain moment on, the formation of political societies and the renunciation of natural freedom become necessary. The *Social Contract* for the most part bows to that necessity without looking beyond it. Yet there are passages even in this work to remind the

Preliminary Considerations

reader that Rousseau has not forgotten the views he expresses elsewhere regarding happiness, views according to which happiness, now possible only to a few and aspired to only by a few, lies outside the city and requires natural freedom.

The contrast between freedom and slavery with which the first chapter of the *Social Contract* opens brings to mind the well-known thesis of the *Discourse on Inequality* according to which the savage condition of mankind in the state of nature was happier than the condition of "men as they are" or that of political man. Contrary to the impression some have received, Rousseau's description, later in the *Social Contract*, of the transformation man undergoes as a result of becoming a member of political society is not an unequivocal retraction of that thesis. After describing the impressive moral development man undergoes as a result of that transformation, Rousseau remarks that "*if* the abuses of this new condition did not often degrade him beneath that which he left he would have to continually bless the happy moment that tore him from it forever and that made a stupid and limited animal into an intelligent being and a man."[20] The understanding of this sentence depends on seeing that it contains a very important "if." Once one has noticed this, one will not be surprised to find Rousseau, later in the *Social Contract*, advising a people that has a genuine choice regarding whether or not to form a political order to remain as it is: "remain barbarian and ichthyophagous; you will live a more tranquil, possibly a better, certainly a happier life" (2.11.4). For a people to have any choice regarding whether to form a political society is unusual in the *Social Contract*. The typical condition under discussion there is one in which the alternative to forming a political order would be extinction (1.6.1). In cases where a choice exists, however, Rousseau unequivocally prefers the condition in which men are certain to be happier to the condition which leaves open some possibility of their becoming better. Rousseau does not recognize a moral obligation for men to form political societies.

Rousseau's advice to the ichthyophagous people is in harmony with the preference he manifests regarding a kindred point in the *Discourse on Inequality*. As Rousseau describes the human developments that occur during the second period in the state of nature, his canvas momentarily begins to darken. He begins to portray the rise of jealousy, vanity, contempt, shame, and envy. He shows men becoming aware of what consideration and respect mean and instantly claiming a right to them. "Thus, as everyone punished the contempt shown him by another in a manner proportionate to the importance he accorded himself, vengeances became terrible, and men bloodthirsty, and cruel." Rousseau's state of nature seems to be on the verge of becoming a state of war.

Rousseau pauses to observe that, because most known savage people are at the stage he has described, an erroneous influence has been drawn to the effect that man is by nature cruel. This error is due, according to him, to a failure to distinguish the second period in the state of nature from "the first." According to Rousseau, "nothing is so gentle as man in his primitive state when, placed by nature at equal distances from the stupidity of brutes and the fatal enlightenment of civil man, and limited equally by instinct and reason to protecting himself from the harm that threatens him, he is restrained by natural pity from harming anyone himself, and nothing leads him to do so even after he has received harm."[21] In the "first" or "primitive" state of nature the human race attains its moral peak, or at any rate its peak as regards goodness. That peak is presented as a mean equally distant from two extremes. Immediately thereafter Rousseau proceeds to describe a different mean. This time the mean is a peak not of goodness but of happiness. The men enjoying this happiness are precisely the men described above, who created the false impression that man is by nature cruel. The presence of jealousy, the desire for recognition and revenge, so far from transforming the period in the state of nature in which they appear into a condition of misery, fail to prevent that period from becoming man's happiest one:

> Thus, although man had come to have less endurance and although natural pity had already undergone some adulteration, this period of the development of human faculties, maintaining a golden mean [*juste milieu*] between the indolence of the primitive state and the petulant activity of our vanity, must have been the happiest and most durable epoch. The more one thinks about it, the more one finds that this state was the least subject to revolutions, the best for man, and that he must have come out of it only by some fatal accident, which for the common good ought never to have happened.[22]

In brief, Rousseau juxtaposes a description of two means in two adjoining paragraphs. The first mean characterizes the period of mankind's greatest goodness, the second the period of mankind's greatest happiness. Rousseau unhesitatingly prefers the period in which men are happiest to the period in which they are best. The preference expressed in the *Social Contract* is no different.

The fact that, for Rousseau, freedom in the fullest sense can be found only outside the political society does not diminish the importance, for him, of the freedom, however restricted, obtainable within it. However, the nature and the full importance of that freedom become visible only at an advanced stage in his argument. To anticipate what it will be possible to show only in the sequel, one can express the difference between Rousseau and Hobbes by saying that political freedom will occupy in Rousseau's thought the place that peace occupies in the thought of Hobbes.[23] In Hobbes, peace is, in a way, the end of political society. But it is not an end in itself. It is justified by self-preservation. One wants peace because "it can never be that War shall preserve life and Peace destroy it" (*Leviathan*, pt. 1, chap. 15). For Rousseau, political freedom replaces peace as the end. Political freedom, in turn, is justified by the "preservation and prosperity" it produces. What makes for a secure and thriving population, or "what makes the [human] species truly prosper is less peace than freedom" (3.9.4 and note). For the present, we must leave it at the remark that "prosperity," in Rousseau, points to the abundant and secure presence, for all, of the necessities of life, and not to luxuries and riches.[24]

The first paragraph of the opening chapter draws the reader's attention to the sacrifice of freedom required of rulers as well as subjects in every political order. The second and concluding paragraph outlines the various reasons that have been advanced to justify that sacrifice and indicates which of them Rousseau will reject. Force is not what makes the social order "a sacred right that serves as a basis for all other [rights]." Nor does nature do so. This leaves voluntary agreement between men, or convention, as the only remaining source. Rousseau promises to offer reasons for his rejection of nature and of force as well as to examine which conventions can and which cannot make the social order sacred.

If one places the first and the last chapters of the *Social Contract* in a class by themselves, owing to the introductory character of the one and the concluding character of the other, the argument of the first book, and of every subsequent book, falls into two parts each of which contains an equal number of chapters. In the first book, four chapters are devoted to refuting views regarding the foundation of political authority (1.2–5) and four more to establishing what the true foundation is (1.6–9). In the second book, the theme of which is law, the first six chapters treat the sovereign as a source of law (2.1–6), while the last six deal with that extraordinary individual, the legislator, as a source of law (2.7–12). Rousseau expounds his views regarding government in the first nine chapters of the third book (3.1–9), while the last nine chapters are devoted to showing what can be done to prevent what he means by government from usurping sovereign authority (3.10–18). Setting the final chapter of the work (4.9) to one side, one finds the first four chapters of Book 4 concerned with how to order the conduct of popular assemblies so as to make them beneficial to the state (4.1–4), while the last four deal with the contribution that institutions other than popular assemblies—institutions to which popular assemblies are, in a way, subject—can make to that end (4.5–8). We note that there is a certain conflict between the two parts into which each book falls.[25]

A pattern that is deeper than the one we have just outlined, although it is not incompatible with it, emerges when the course of Rousseau's argument in the first two books of the work is compared with the course of his argument in the last two. The nerve of Rousseau's argument in the first two books is his new teaching regarding legitimate sovereignty, as expressed in the new principles of political right he enunciates. The last two books, at first glance,[26] deal with the "political" laws—today we would call them constitutional laws—which bring into being the institutions in which these principles must be embodied. We will refer to the first two books as Part 1 and the second two as Part 2 of Rousseau's argument. The views Rousseau seeks to refute in the first section of Part 1 (1.2–5) have one thing in common: they all seek to derive the right to rule from the inequality between men. Each of the inequalities considered—those between fathers and children, masters and slaves, gods and men, men and brutes, the strong and the weak—had been invoked prior to Rousseau by writers seeking to justify claims to despotic rule. The grounds on which Rousseau rejects these claims will be discussed below. For the present, it is sufficient to note that the solution proposed by Rousseau is based on the equality of men and it is held to be alone capable of securing that limited, but all-important, freedom which remains possible within political society and without which, according to him, it makes no sense even to contemplate entering political society. Rousseau develops his own answer to the question of who should rule, or his teaching concerning legimate sovereignty, in a group of chapters that encompasses the second part of Book 1 and that continues through the first part of Book 2. If a fitting subtitle to the first group of chapters (1.2–5) would be Inequality, a fitting subtitle to the group we are now considering (1.6–2.6) would be Freedom and Equality.

The inequalities between men dealt with in the first section of the *Social Contract* are subordinate to the freedom and equality that are established when a legitimate sovereign is instituted. At the end of Rousseau's section on the true teaching concerning sovereignty a serious difficulty suddenly emerges. To state it briefly for the moment, according to Rousseau a people may be equal to the task of perpetuating a political order dedicated to freedom and equality, but a people necessarily lacks the wisdom needed to constitute such a society in the first place. Such wisdom is the preserve of surpassingly superior individuals whom Rousseau refers to under the collective title of the legislator. They so excel their fellows that he does not hesitate to call them gods. The effort to bring about the triumph of freedom and equality finds itself confronted, in the end, with an inequality of a wholly new kind. The superior wisdom of the legislator is not under the control of the sovereign. Yet without the assistance supplied by it, a legitimate sovereign could not come into being, according to Rousseau. A fitting subtitle to the section on the legislator (2.7–12) could well be Inequality (see especially 2.7.1).

The argument of Part 2 of the work, like that of Part 1, contains three sections. The first of these sections is made up of the nine chapters in the first half of Book 3. It deals with government in a sense of the term that is known by Rousseau to be very different from the common one (2.2.2, 3). Rousseau, as we shall see, sharply distinguishes the sovereign, whose sole function is to enact laws, from the government, whose sole function is to execute them. He is fully aware that the sharp distinction he draws between the two is not commonly made. Government introduces a new inequality into political life. Those who govern are, in a sense, superior in rank to those whom they govern. The first section of Part 2, like the first section of Part 1, deals with relations between unequals, relations that are essentially different from those between sovereign and subject but which have been mistaken for them. The price paid in political life for mistaking the government for the sovereign is the loss of freedom and equality. According to Rousseau, government ceaselessly strives to usurp the authority of the sovereign. How to keep the legitimate sovereign from succumbing to this effort is the question to which Rousseau now turns.

It is only in the second half of Book 3 that Rousseau begins to make clear what kind of a political being a legitimate sovereign must be. It is here that one first clearly learns that the sovereign body must be an assembly of the people and that Rousseau's principles require such assemblies to be held at fixed and periodic intervals. In the second half of Book 3 and the first half of Book 4 Rousseau, in fact, returns to the subject of sovereignty which he had previously discussed in the second half of Book 1 and the first half of Book 2.[27] He carries forward his earlier analyses of the essence of sovereignty and sets forth his views concerning the inner workings of the sovereign assembly. That his later discussion is pervaded by the concern to prevent the inequality inseparable from government from achieving supremacy over the legitimate sovereign is one more parallel between the earlier discussions and the later one. The inner working of popular assemblies, the prevention of the destruction of the legitimate sovereign, and the essence of sovereignty remain Rousseau's concerns in the first half of Book 4. The new section on sovereignty, like the old one, is concerned with safeguarding freedom and equality.

In Part 1 the section on sovereignty was preceded by discussion of inequalities between men, inequalities that should be under the control of the sovereign. The section on sovereignty was followed by a discussion of the legislator who transcends the sovereign and is not under the sovereign's control but who nonetheless enhances rather than diminishes the sovereign's authority. The section on sovereignty in Part 2 is preceded by a section on government, whose workings are meant to be under the sovereign's constant supervision and control. It is followed by a section on a number of institutions which are, indeed, established by an act of sovereignty but which in their working are not subject to the sovereign's command (4.5–8). These bodies are an institutional reflection of the legislator's transcendence of the sovereign and of the assistance he gives to the sovereign. The first of these institutions is called the tribunate. Its powers correspond roughly to those of our Supreme Court.[28] In an extraordinary passage it is described as being "more sacred and more revered, as the defender of the laws, than the prince who executes them and the sovereign who enacts them." It has the extraordinary power to declare an act of the sovereign null and void.

Preliminary Considerations

The second of the institutions discussed is an extraordinary power of a different and even an opposite kind. Rousseau calls it dictatorship. By this he means not what we think of when we hear the word today but what we would call emergency powers. The duration for which Rousseau permits the exercise of such powers is fixed and severely limited. For the length of that duration, however, if the emergency is grave enough, the sovereign authority may have to be suspended. The emergency authority by which it is temporarily replaced cannot enact laws, but it is permitted something that the sovereign is not permitted, namely, it may act contrary to the laws that have been established. The third institution in the series we are discussing—Rousseau calls it censorship—is intended to give official public expression to the unwritten law of a people, to their spontaneous judgments regarding what is admirable and what is base. Such opinions are not subject to direct command. Even if a people wished its opinions to be different from what they were, it could not command itself to change them. Free government requires public judgments to be of a certain character, according to Rousseau. He therefore favors enhancing and strengthening them where they are of the required character by giving them official public expression. That is the task of the institution Rousseau calls censorship. The final subject discussed by Rousseau in the final section of the *Social Contract* is religion as a political institution. A religious spirit, according to Rousseau, is indispensable for a free society. He therefore tries to see what kind of religion is compatible with republican institutions. The divinity worshiped by the citizens manifestly transcends and outranks the sovereign. Yet that divinity not only does not diminish the authority of the sovereign but first endows it with the sacred character without which it cannot effectively embody the common good.

In what follows, we will try to clarify the meaning of this outline and to show that it agrees with the articulation of Rousseau's argument. To set it forth in tabular form:

Part 1	Part 2
Introduction (1.1)	
(1) 1.2 to 1.5	(1) 3.1 to 3.9
False accounts of political authority or what the sovereign cannot be and is above.	Government, or what the sovereign cannot be and is above.
[Inequality]	[Inequality]

(2) 1.6 to 2.6	(2) 3.10 to 4.4
What the sovereign is	Assemblies of the people
and must be.	or what the sovereign is
[Freedom and Equality]	and must be.
	[Freedom and Equality]
(3) 2.7 to 2.12	(3) 4.5 to 4.8
The legislator, or what	What the sovereign can-
the sovereign cannot be	not be and is not above.
and is not above.	[Inequality]
[Inequality]	

Conclusion (4.9)

The contrast between freedom and bondage in the first chapter assumes that man is by nature free and that a condition under which men had no obligation to obey any of their fellows antedated their present condition.[29] Rousseau makes it his first order of business to dispose of an important rival view according to which men are not by nature free, because natural superiority confers on those who possess it the natural right to rule those who do not, at the same time that it imposes on the inferior the natural obligation to obey those superior to themselves. An example favored by those who thought that the right to rule is derived from natural superiority was the family and the relations of authority which characterize it. Rousseau concedes to those who bring this example forward that both the family and the authority of the father in it are natural. Following Locke, he denies that what holds true of a family the children of which are immature continues to hold true of the same family once the children become adults. The father's natural superiority to his small children is far more obvious than is his natural superiority to his grown sons and daughters. The family as a natural society is of limited duration. It therefore cannot serve as a model for the lasting association that political society is intended to be. Rousseau proceeds to discuss the family not as a temporary but as a permanent association: it now includes children after they have become adults. It is still governed by the father, but the children no longer obey him because of his natural superiority to them. They obey him because they have decided that it is advantageous to themselves to remain in the family governed by him. They have consented to a "convention" or agreement by which they have "alienated their freedom." They have done so, however, "only for their utility" (1.2.3).

The permanent family, understood in this way, can serve as a paradigm for political society. This paradigm, however, no longer

17

supports the contention that the right to rule is conferred by nature. Moreover, the degree to which the conventional family sheds light on the character of a sound political order is limited. The analogy between the conventional family and political society suffers from an important defect. In the family, the father's love for his children guarantees that the end for the sake of which they alienated their freedom will not be disregarded. The passion animating those who rule in political society—the pleasure of commanding—guarantees nothing of the kind. The suggestion that political society, like the conventional family, requires the advantageous alienation of one's freedom is not withdrawn, but the thoughtful reader cannot help wondering how that requirement can ever be met, given the passion which is said to animate rulers. The conventional family sheds light on Rousseau's understanding of the fundamental difficulty a sound political order must overcome rather than on how it does so.

The preceding discussion will remind many readers of Locke's analysis of paternal authority in the *Second Treatise*. The conclusion that a child comes to be his own master by coming of age is arrived at by both authors. However, the argument by which that conclusion is reached at first sight differs in Locke from what it is in Rousseau. The argument of Rousseau restates the nerve of the reasoning through which Hobbes deduces the natural rights of all men.[30] Rousseau's argument, unlike Locke's, is patently Hobbesian. What makes men by nature free according to the reasoning Rousseau reproduces is the concern with self-preservation: "This common freedom is a consequence of the nature of man. His first law is to attend to his own preservation, his first cares are those he owes himself: and as soon as he has reached the age of reason, as he alone is the judge of the proper means of preserving himself, he thus becomes his own master" (1.2.2). The most important step in this argument, as Leo Strauss has pointed out, is the claim that the right to preserve one's life entails the right to decide for oneself what the best means for preserving it are.[31] With this step, any claims to rule which would have traditionally been advanced on behalf of superior wisdom are ruled out in advance. This is the step which is equivalent to the assertion that men are by nature free.[32]

As is well known, the thesis that men are by nature free and equal antedates Hobbes. The innovation of Hobbes consists in his novel derivation of that thesis, a derivation that gives a new meaning to it and that predetermines his new teaching regarding the purpose and character of a sound political order. Like Hobbes, Rousseau will hold that the end of the social contract is the preservation of those who conclude it (2.5.2) and that the necessity of concluding it results from the incompatibility, at least subsequent to a certain period, between the state of nature and the requirements of self-preservation (1.6.1). Unlike Hobbes, and following Locke, Rousseau will demand that the security afforded by the social order include guarantees against oppression by the sovereign, a demand that Hobbes had repudiated as self-contradictory.[33] That is why Hobbes appears in the immediate sequel in the company of other thinkers who hold that rule over others can be by nature right, even in the absence of such guarantees, that is, even when exercised for the ruler's sole benefit.

Rousseau's whole discussion of nature as a possible ground of legitimate authority is reminiscent of Aristotle's classic treatment of the same subject in Book 1 of the *Politics*. The sequence of subjects Rousseau discusses (family, slavery) as well as the title under which he discusses them ("Of the First Societies") bring to mind Aristotle's attempt to establish the natural character of political society and of political authority. Aristotle's reflections lead him, too, back to "the first societies," which include the association between parents and children and the association between master and slave. Aristotle insists on the essential difference between the family and the city as well as on the essential difference between political authority and the authority of a master over a slave. Nevertheless, the natural character of the family is a decisive step in his argument for the view that the city is natural. Similarly, it is in connection with an analysis of slavery, an analysis which denies that it can never be by nature right, that Aristotle provides the first broad outline of his views regarding the natural right to rule. Rousseau develops an independent argument against the view that political rule can be right by nature, an argument that complements the one he makes on behalf of natural freedom.

Whatever Aristotle's reasons may have been for discussing the natural right to rule while speaking of slavery, the reason why the treatment of sovereignty is so closely linked to the theme of slavery by Rousseau is clear. Rousseau accepts the view according to which every sound political order requires a sovereign, some final authority with the right to have the last word in every dispute. To be a member of a political society worthy of the name means, among other things, to be the subject of a sovereign. The ascendency of a sovereign over his subjects is no less great than the ascendency of a

Preliminary Considerations

master over his slaves, although the two relations are essentially different. They would not be different, however, if a sovereign could be legitimate even if he did not rule for the benefit of his subjects. Rousseau will examine whether natural superiority can supply a basis for sovereignty or slavery of this kind. He will then survey the conventions which are sometimes held to justify it (chap. 4). Rousseau's views regarding the relation between sovereignty and natural superiority are expressed in the following passage:

> It is therefore doubtful, according to Grotius, whether the human race belongs to a hundred or so men, or whether these hundred or so men belong to the human race, and he seems all through his book to incline to the first opinion; this is also the sentiment of Hobbes. And so we see [*Ainsi voilà*] the human species divided into herds of cattle, each with its chief who looks after it to devour it.
>
> As the nature of a shepherd is superior to that of his flock, the nature of the shepherds of men, who are their chiefs, is superior to that of their peoples. So reasoned Emperor Caligula, according to Philo's account; inferring correctly enough [*concluant assez bien*] from this analogy that kings were gods or that people were beasts (1.2.5,6).

If a man is to be naturally entitled to rule his fellow men, the gulf separating this man from the others would have to be as great as the gulf separating gods from men or men from beasts. The view that nature has endowed some men with the right to rule over others appears to entail the absurd contention that by nature some men are not men.

For the right to rule men politically to be justified by the superiority of some men over others, that superiority would have to be as great as the superiority of gods to men or men to brutes. But Aristotle, to whom Rousseau refers here, seems to have admitted that inequalities of this magnitude were not to be found within the city. Man, according to Aristotle, is by nature a political animal because he is more than a brute and less than a god. A brute would not be able to be part of a city and a god would not need to be part of one.[34]

We can appreciate the force which Rousseau's argument for natural equality possessed for many of his thoughtful contemporaries attention if we consider an allusion he makes to Defoe's *Robinson Crusoe*: "Be that as it may, it cannot be denied that Adam was Sovereign of the world, like Robinson of his island, as long as he was its only inhabitant, and the great advantage of that empire [*ce qu'il y avoit de commode dans cet empire*] was that the monarch secure on his throne had to fear neither rebellions nor wars nor conspirators" (1.2.9).

Rousseau appears to be alluding to a specific passage in *Robinson Crusoe*. That passage occurs in the thirteenth chapter of the novel, near the middle of the book. By that stage of his life on the island, Crusoe's ingenious exertions have finally succeeded in making him reasonably well supplied with food, shelter, and various conveniences of life. Though he still longs to leave the island, he has at least begun to feel at ease on it. It is at this point that we encounter the absolute sovereign at dinner with his "family" or his "subjects."

> It would have made [even] a stoic smile to have seen me and my little family sit down to dinner; there was my majesty the prince and lord of the whole island: I had the lives of all my subjects at my absolute command. I could hang, draw, give liberty, and take it away, and no rebels among my subjects.[35]

In the immediate sequel Crusoe's security and comfort abruptly collapse. They are shown to have been a fool's paradise all along and are destroyed by a terrifying discovery that Crusoe makes: he finds the naked footprint of a man. The contrast between Crusoe's security while he believed himself to be "alone" on the island and the fear which grips him once he realizes that he might not be "alone" brings out clearly the difference between having to deal with subjects who are cats, dogs, parrots, goats, and wild animals, and having to deal with other human beings. That contrast forcefully illustrates what Rousseau means by saying that men are by nature equal, as well as how that equality is related to men's concern for their self-preservation.

Rousseau however, is only partly in agreement with the conclusion of the preceding remarks. He does hold, like Hobbes, that no man is by nature subordinate to another, both because of the natural power of the concern for self-preservation and because of how dangerous men can be to each other. However, insofar as the contrast between King Crusoe and Crusoe the cowering fugitive suggests that men cannot be as superior to each other as Crusoe is to his animals, Rousseau does not simply agree. He accepts the egalitarian conclusions that follow from making the right to self-preservation the central concern of political life. At the same time, he recognizes the existence of inequalities in merit between men that are as great as those asserted by the thinkers against whom he argues. The disagreement between him and these thinkers is not over whether these inequalities exist but over what political conclusions are to be drawn from them. This becomes clear from the passage following the report about Caligula quoted above:[36]

> The reasoning of Caligula amounts to that of Hobbes and Grotius. Aristotle before them all had also said that men are not naturally equal, but that some are born for slavery and others for domination.
> Aristotle was right, but he mistook the effect for the cause. Every man born in slavery is born for slavery, nothing is more certain. Slaves lose everything in their chains, even the desire to get out of them: they love their servitude as the companions of Ulysses loved their brutishness. If there are slaves by nature, therefore, it is because there have been slaves against nature. Force made the first slaves, their cowardice has perpetuated them.

Rousseau does not simply agree with Aristotle, but he does not simply disagree with him either. The reasoning of Caligula, and the Platonic reasoning of which it is the foolish caricature, will reappear in the work. In fact it will occur once in the part of each Book which constitutes a section on Inequality, according to the outline set forth above (1.2.6, 2.7.2, 3.6.15, 4.8.1). It will be understood somewhat differently in what follows and will no longer be scornfully dismissed. In the chapter on the legislator, we will find Rousseau joining Aristotle in acknowledging that there are human beings so outstanding in merit that they can be described as "gods among men." Rousseau will even be willing to ascribe the superiority of such men to nature (3.6.15). In a word, Rousseau acknowledges that there are differences in rank between men that are no less great than those Aristotle asserted to exist. Where Rousseau disagrees with Aristotle is in the way in which he understands these differences and their political consequences. More clarity regarding their consequences will have to await Rousseau's treatment of the legislator. What he says here enables us to understand better how Rousseau interprets the gulfs between men. These gulfs are not primarily differences in nature, according to Rousseau. Rather they are differences between nature on the one hand and a servitude that violates nature but to which one becomes attached on the other. What does he have in mind? It is difficult to believe that he is thinking of sons of despots who are destined to become despots just as the sons of their subjects are destined to become subjects. The very terms he employs in the passage we just quoted remind one of the famous opening lines of the first chapter of the *Social Contract*: "Man is born free and everywhere he is in chains. One who believes himself the master of others is nonetheless a greater slave than they." If the reference is to slaves enamored of their slavery, that description could fit the tyrant no less than it does his subjects.[37] It could also fit social man as he is described in these lines and in the *Discourse on Inequality*. For society, according to these passages, is against nature even if, from a certain period on, it becomes indispensable and remains so. But what, then, is one to make of Ulysses and the comparison between him and his companions? The incident referred to is the Circe episode in the version of it that one finds in a small work by Plutarch entitled "That Beasts Make Use of Reason." Plutarch's version, as Rousseau encourages us to read it, differs from Homer's in one curious respect, which does not by itself mean that Plutarch's point is essentially different from Homer's. In Plutarch, Ulysses asks Circe to liberate his companions as well as other Greeks whom she had bewitched and transformed into brutes. Circe refuses to do so without their consent. She restores the power of speech to one of her victims and leaves Ulysses alone to speak to him. The beast to whom he speaks argues for the superiority of his transformed condition and refuses to become a man again.

In this interpretation of the Circe story, Ulysses succeeds in preserving his nature. He resists Circe's efforts to transform him into a brute. He refuses her offer to make him a god. While retaining his nature, he is plainly as superior to his bewitched companions as men are to brutes. Contrary to what one might have thought at first, Rousseau is not denying that men can be as superior to other men as the argument of Caligula implies. He is only denying that Caligula and those like him are examples of such superiority. Ulysses points to the legislator, who, though mortal, will be declared to be as superior to his fellows as Ulysses is to his companions. He will be described as one no less concerned with glory than Ulysses is said to be. Because he is the founder of the conventions which bind society and make it possible, he understands them and transcends them as those who are simply enslaved to them and to society cannot do. It is no accident that Ulysses at the same time points to natural man, albeit to natural man with the fully developed reasoning powers that render him immune to witchcraft. To the extent that

Rousseau in the *Social Contract* can be understood, however indirectly, as engaged in legislation himself, and to the extent that Rousseau understands himself as "natural man enlightened by reason," Ulysses points to Rousseau as well.[38]

Before concluding that legitimate political authority can arise in no other way than through convention, Rousseau discusses and dismisses one additional view regarding its origin, the view that superiority in power confers a right to rule on its possessor, the so-called "right of the strongest." That view, according to Rousseau, proceeds from the weakness of the strongest. Given the natural equality of men, any superiority in power is, of necessity, temporary. Accordingly, those who enjoy it for the time being seek to supplement it with the "right of the strongest." That "right" takes the form of arguments seeking to show that one is entitled to rule because one possesses political power. The example of such arguments given by Rousseau is the contention that one should obey the powers that be because all power comes from God. The "right" of the strongest is a confession of weakness. Once this is seen, that "right" refutes itself. If the possession of power is to be taken as an infallible sign of divine favor and approval, then so must the possession of the power to disobey, to conspire, to overthrow, and to supplant be taken for such a sign. No genuine obligation can result from this state of affairs since no genuine obligation lapses whenever it can be violated.

The reader may have been struck by the omission of any reference to God in Rousseau's enumeration of the alternative ways of explaining why the social order is a "sacred right," or what makes the social order "legitimate." Its omission does not mean that religion will not finally prove necessary for making the social order sacred. The section in which the contribution of religion to political life will be discussed is the third section of each Part, the section dealing with those inequalities that transcend the sovereign. Without religion, a good political order will not be possible, according to Rousseau, but religion will not determine for Rousseau what a good political order must be. The subject will be discussed explicitly in Book 4, Chapter 8.

Neither the claim to rule in virtue of natural superiority nor the claim to do so in virtue of superior force would, if valid, require the consent of the governed for its rightful exercise. Rousseau rejects both claims and turns to what he believes to be the only remaining alternative, mutual agreement. In the course of discussing natural political authority, Rousseau had already indicated that he thought the institution of political society requires an agreement in which future subjects alienate their freedom. Accordingly, when he begins to discuss agreements as a source of political authority, he limits his discussion to agreements in which men alienate their freedom, or to slavery as well as to its political counterpart, absolute monarchy resulting from the agreement of a people to alienate its freedom to a king. He proceeds to inquire into whether such agreements can ever be valid and concludes that they never can be. This leaves one wondering how a legitimate political society is possible.[39]

In discussing the family based on agreement, Rousseau had referred to a difficulty which marred the parallelism between the conventional family and political society. The father's natural affection for his children afforded some guarantee that the advantages for which they had alienated their freedom would be secured. It proved difficult to see what the political counterpart of such a guarantee could be, but without such a guarantee there could be no reason, according to Rousseau, for subjecting oneself to the rule of others, or for alienating one's freedom. He examines various attempts to show in what way conventional slavery could be advantageous to a slave and thus valid. In reply to these attempts he argues that even if alienation of freedom could be advantageous in an individual case it could never be advantageous for an entire people. Moreover, he denies that future generations could be bound by agreements to alienate freedom and concludes that no lasting political arrangement can result from it. Finally, Rousseau brings forward considerations which withdraw all the concessions he had made to the opposing view for purposes of argument. He now denies that slavery based on agreements can ever be just under any condition, whether for individuals or peoples, whether temporarily or permanently:

> To renounce one's freedom is to renounce what makes one a man, [to renounce] the rights of humanity, [and] even [to renounce] its duties. There is no possible compensation for anyone who renounces everything. Such a renunciation is incompatible with the nature of man; and to take away all freedom from one's will is to take away all morality from one's actions. Finally, a convention which stipulates absolute authority on the one hand and limitless obedience on the other is vain and contradictory. Is it not clear that one is committed to nothing towards someone of whom one

has the right to demand everything, and does not this condition alone, without equivalent, without exchange, nullify the act? For what right can my slave have against me, since everything he has belongs to me and, his right being mine, this right of mine against myself is an expression which has no meaning? (1.4.6).

The agreement to become a slave is incompatible with the rights and duties of man or with morality. It cannot possibly be advantageous to make such an agreement. In addition to this, Rousseau claims that such an agreement contradicts the very notion of a compact or contract and that it therefore cannot be valid.

The agreements Rousseau deals with in the present context all pretend to be compacts or contracts of various kinds. It is noteworthy that he avoids the very words "compact" and "contract" in his argument, until he treats of the social contract, the first contract that is both "legitimate and reliable" with which his argument meets, and the contract that first makes other "legitimate and reliable" contracts possible.[40] Now a contract cannot be "legitimate" for Rousseau unless it is mutual (just as, in order to be worth executing, it will also have to be "reliable"). Each party must incur an obligation to the other, and each must acquire certain rights over against the other. To derive slavery from contractual agreement means, then, at one and the same time to concede rights to the slave over against his master and to deny that the slave can have any such rights. Rousseau comments on this:

> [T]he right of slavery is null, not only because it is illegitimate, but because it is absurd and meaningless. The words, *slavery* and *right*, are contradictory; they are mutually exclusive. Whether from a man to a man, or from a man to a people, this speech will always be equally senseless. *I make an agreement with you [that is] wholly at your expense and wholly to my profit, which I will observe as long as it pleases me, and which you will observe as long as it pleases me* (1.4.14).

The question might arise whether the foregoing objection can be disposed of by adopting a somewhat less strict view of contractual slavery, a view that would permit the slave to have at least certain claims against the master. The summary of the *Social Contract* in *Emile* addresses itself to this possibility:

And if there is any reserve, any restriction in the deed of slavery, we shall discuss whether this deed does not then become a true contract, in which each of the parties, having no *common superior* in this capacity, remains his own judge as to the conditions of the contract, [and whether] each consequently [remains] free in this respect and master of breaking it, as soon as he considers himself injured.[41]

Now a slave who retains the right to repudiate the agreement which reduces him to slavery, who is, in Rousseau's words, "master of breaking it," has not been effectively reduced to slavery. What makes this contract "legitimate" is what keeps it from being "reliable." How a contract could be both legitimate and reliable is far from being clear. To anticipate the objection of a reader who might want to know why the assumption is made that there would be no common superior to see to it that the terms of the contract are adhered to, Rousseau appends the following note: "If they had one, this common superior would be none other than the sovereign, and then the right of slavery based on the right of sovereignty would not be its principle." The entire point of discussing contractual slavery in the first place was to see whether sovereignty could be based on it, not whether it could be based on sovereignty.

Rousseau opened the first chapter of Book 1 by calling political society a condition of bondage. What he meant by this becomes clearer as one begins to realize that for him the subjects of even free political societies cannot act as they please but must obey the public will. Even they must alienate their freedom. However, for Rousseau, there can be no sound political order without a sovereign, without some authority possessing the right to have the last word regarding any disputes that may arise. However different sovereignty as Rousseau understands it is from sovereignty as Hobbes understands it, it is no less absolute.[42] The argument up to this point has arrived at the conclusion that sovereign authority must arise from a contract. Here the dilemma that confronted us in the preceding paragraph reappears. If the agreement irrevocably subjects the people to an absolute monarch, it contradicts the very notion of a contract. If it confers rights and imposes obligations on both the king and the people, each party remains free to declare it void whenever that party thinks it has been violated. Neither party is effectively bound by such a contract. Moreover, such a contract contradicts the very intention of establishing a sovereign, if by that one means a "common superior" with the right to have the final say in all disputes. Once again it proves difficult to see how a contract establishing a sovereign can be both "legitimate and reliable."

Rousseau ridicules slavery and absolute monarchy based on mutual agreement by putting into the mouth of the master the speech quoted above. Rousseau says that such a speech will always be nonsensical, whether made by a man to a man or made by a man to a people. Rousseau remains silent on whether the speech is nonsensical if it is made by a people to a man. The omitted possibility points to the social contract. In the immediate sequel, Rousseau begins to explore what it means to be a people in the politically relevant sense of the term. To understand political affairs, he argues, means to understand what makes them "public" affairs—affairs of an entire people—even in an absolute monarchy. That, in turn, means to understand the origin of a people in the political sense of the term as well as the origin of the public good and above all the origin, at some definite time, of the people's right to make decisions that are binding on its members. Rousseau's explanations lead him to a solution which, he feels, supplies such an understanding and which possesses other properties as well. That solution—the social contract—will establish a sovereign which is absolute (2.4.1, 2.4.9), a sovereign people on whom the contract by which he—or it—is brought into being imposes no explicit obligations. At the same time, Rousseau will argue, that solution will not be exposed to the criticism previously directed against contractual despotism or slavery. It will be the only solution which complies with conflicting requirements that, at first, appear impossible to satisfy.[43]

Chapter Two

The Social Contract
Sovereignty and
the General Will

The requirements of self-preservation originally supplied a rationale for natural freedom in the *Social Contract*. The very same requirements dictate the abandonment of natural freedom in the conditions that prevail prior to the rise of political society. In the *Social Contract* Rousseau simply assumes that these conditions will prevail once a certain point has been reached in the development of the human race. For the defense of this assumption one must study the *Discourse on Inequality*.[1] Once men need the help of others in order to survive, they must find a way to join forces, a way which will guarantee that their united strength will be used for the same ends for which they had previously employed their own strength and freedom. Rousseau's solution will attempt to find a substitute for natural freedom which will serve the same end natural freedom would have served but have at its disposal a power far greater than one's individual power. This substitute—conventional freedom— will only be able to come into being through the alienation of natural freedom. That does not imply, as we saw, any abandonment on Rousseau's part of his teaching that natural freedom is an indispens- able ingredient of happiness, and that the formation of political society, even of one which fulfills Rousseau's requirements, makes the attainment of the highest happiness impossible. The reason this fact alone does not invalidate his solution, in Rousseau's opinion, is that, for a variety of causes which are set forth at length in the *Discourse on Inequality*, men as they are and as they will continue to be, once they require political society, have irrevocably lost the inner tranquility, the simplicity and the independence which are no

29

less indispensable for happiness than natural freedom is. As we will see, Rousseau will not claim that the foregoing is true of all individuals without exception. Some of these exceptions will even prove to be of great political importance.

The title Rousseau chose for the present work points in particular to the chapter in which the social contract is set forth. The rest of the book can be viewed as devoted to developing and clarifying the content of that chapter. The most perplexing difficulty that makes its appearance in that chapter is one that cannot help confronting the reader from the first, even though Rousseau's efforts to clarify and resolve it are found throughout the work. The difficulty results from what appears to be a startling conflict between Rousseau's account of the problem that the social contract is meant to solve and his account of how the social contract is supposed to solve it. It is best to let the passages in question speak for themselves. The "fundamental problem to which the social contract provides the solution" is said to be the following:

> To find a form of association which defends and protects the person and goods of each associate with all the common force, and by which each uniting with all yet obeys only himself and remains as free as before.

The essence of the solution to this problem is said to consist, "properly understood," in "the total alienation of each associate with all his rights to the whole community." The obvious question is how one can possibly be free if one totally alienates oneself and all one's rights. As we will see, the answer to this question will depend on understanding what Rousseau means by "the general will" which takes the place of "the whole community" in the formal enunciation of the social contract that follows this analysis of its essence. In spite of the obscurities that remain to be elucidated, the outline of Rousseau's solution does come into view in this chapter.

The views Rousseau sought to refute in the opening half of Book 1 all attempted to base the right to rule on the inequality between men. Now, as we have seen, Rousseau denies that there can be any incontestably manifest and dependably recurring inequality in merit, within political society, of the magnitude of the inequality in rank between a sovereign and those subject to his rule.[2] Any superiority in rank of this magnitude would be as great as, though essentially different from, the ascendency of a master over his slaves. In the absence of sufficient merit to justify it, such a superiority in rank could only come into being through voluntary agreement, but no such agreement, we have seen him argue, could possibly be advantageous to subjects and hence valid. Given the inadmissibility of inequalities of this magnitude on the one hand, and the necessity for an authority of this rank on the other, Rousseau concludes that only society as a whole can be sovereign. His answer to the question, who should rule, is society as a whole should. In more contemporary terms, Rousseau's conclusion is that self-government is the only legitimate form of government.

Two strands may be distinguished in the foregoing argument for a sovereign consisting of free and equal citizens. The one derives from a tradition that goes back to the classics and is based on considerations of merit. Rousseau will hold, with the Eleatic Stranger in the *Statesman*, that the absence of human "king bees" possessing manifestly surpassing merit and outshining all unkingly rivals is enough by itself to make the sovereignty of the truly deserving—at first glance the most reasonable solution— unworkable. Nor is this the only objection that one finds in these authors to the feasibility of this solution. Rousseau will declare (and the Stranger suggest) that the proper place for kingly individuals in political life is to be legislators or founding fathers.[3] The rejection of the sovereignty of an individual does not, however, lead without further ado to a collective sovereign every member of which is equal to every other. Even if inequalities of the magnitude and manifestness of which we have been speaking are not a normal feature of political life, it does not immediately follow that the remaining inequalities are of no political importance and that everyone is entitled to an equal share of sovereignty. To arrive at that conclusion, one needs the assumption supplied by the second strand in Rousseau's argument, the strand that ultimately derives from the conclusions of Hobbes that Rousseau made his own. The fundamental freedom and equality of men based on the concern for self-preservation and the need for an absolute sovereign—as distinguished, say, from any mixed regime—are also pre-supposed by the argument for self-government outlined above. If one discards the Hobbesian assumptions, without losing touch with political life, the doctrinaire character of Rousseau's solution is discarded as well. Self-government ceases to be the *only* legitimate form of government no matter what the circumstances may be and whether or not self-government is conceivable under them. What remains is an illuminating analysis of the conditions under which the case for

Sovereignty and the General Will

self-government is compelling and of the proper way to order a self-governing political community. Some of Tocqueville's most incisive perceptions regarding American democracy owe much to what he learned from these analyses.

Let us return to what Rousseau regards as the nerve of the social contract: "the total alienation of each associate with all his rights to the entire community." In what way does this contract differ from the agreements previously discussed and declared invalid? In the previous agreements all the obligations were on one side and all the rights and advantages on the other. For a contract of the seriousness of the one under discussion to be valid, according to Rousseau, each of the parties to it has to derive some advantage from it and each has to be obliged by it to confer some advantage in return. The earlier agreements violated this requirement. The social contract does not. Under the social contract, *all* are equally subject to the obligations it imposes and *all* enjoy the rights it confers. The social contract is therefore valid or legitimate. Furthermore, it cannot be terminated whenever any of the parties to it thinks that its terms have been violated:

> [Since] the alienation is made without reservations, the union is as perfect as it can be and no associate has anything more to claim. For if some rights were left to private individuals, as there would be no *common superior* who could judge between them and the public, each [man] being his own judge on some point would soon claim to be so on all, the state of nature would subsist, and the association would necessarily become tyrannical or futile [*vaine*].[4]

In requiring the total alienation of oneself and all one's rights, Rousseau is following Spinoza, who had already argued that if the sovereign is indeed to be the final arbiter in all conflicts individuals have already, in effect, transferred all their rights to it. Failure to require this explicitly, according to Rousseau, would lead to the very difficulty he drew attention to in discussing mitigated slavery based on contract: the absence of a "common superior" and the resulting ineffectiveness of the contract. Without a "common superior," the social contract would not be effectively binding. The association it is intended to create could not be a lasting association, but would soon give way, he suggests, either to despotism or to the continued anarchy of the state of nature. The total alienation that Rousseau requires is meant to provide for a collective "common superior" capable of seeing to it that the social contract is observed. Thanks to that collective common superior, the social contract is not only legitimate but reliable.

What assurances does Rousseau offer that the "common superior" to which one alienates all will be beneficial to all? The guarantee is stated succinctly and will require much discussion. As stated here, it derives from the equal effect that the decisions of the common superior are to have on each associate and on the fact that the common superior *is* all of the associates. Later elucidation will reveal, at least provisionally, that every valid act of their common superior, or of the "general will," must be a law that treats all equally and that all take part in enacting. Such laws, to be sure, will oblige men to act differently than they otherwise would have acted and will even compel men to do so, if necessary. Nevertheless, such laws will be advantageous to all rather than oppressive. An inkling of what Rousseau means is conveyed by the following passage from a work which was not written with either him or his teaching in mind.

> The distinction between the public good and private self-interest is basic to law. Examine, for instance, the law requiring new automobiles to have pollution-control devices. Everyone, no doubt, is in favor of clean air. However, it is not necessarily in the self-interest of each individual to install such a device on his or her car. A person might reason this way: "Pollution-control apparatus will cost me extra money, so I will not buy one unless it is in my personal interest. I agree that it is in my best interests to have clean air. But if no one else buys a pollution-control device, my having one will not do any good, so I'll just be out the money. On the other hand, if everyone else buys one, then my not having one will not do any harm, so there is no point in my purchasing one." This logic is sound, but if everyone reasoned that way we would never get rid of pollution. Therefore, a *law* is needed to serve the public good.[5]

To complete the analogy between the example and what Rousseau has in mind one need only make the additional assumption that the law spoken of is enacted by the individuals concerned. It would be wrong to say that the conduct required by the law is no different from that which private self-interest would dictate. Yet it would also be wrong to say that what the law requires is contrary to the self-interest of the individuals concerned. We can begin to see from this example how Rousseau will seek to prevent "justice and utility from becoming separated," even if the public good and private self-interest will never be simply one and the same thing. Rousseau will try to show that rule by a legitimate sovereign, or by the general will, *means* rule by laws like the one we have been discussing. Being ruled by laws such as these is a very different thing from being oppressed.

But is it the same thing as being free? Can it be said to meet that requirement? Rousseau forcefully states this difficulty in another one of his works and at the same time reminds us of what his other requirements are:

> Seek the motives which have promoted men united by their mutual needs in the large society to unite more closely through civil societies; you will find none other than that of assuring the goods, life, and freedom of each member through the protection [of them] by all: but how can one *force* men to defend the freedom of one of them without violating that of others? and how can public needs be provided for without infringing on [*sans altérer*] the private property of those whom one forces to contribute to them? Whatever sophisms one may color all this with, it is certain that, if one can constrain my will, I am no longer free, and that I am no longer master of my goods, if someone else can lay a hand on them [*peut y toucher*].[6]

Rousseau's answer to the question concerning freedom is formulated succinctly in the last of the three explanatory remarks he appends to his statement of the nerve of the social contract. The first two remarks briefly spelled out why the alienation had to be total. The last one spells out why it has to be made to all. The assumption on which the exposition of the social contract is based is that men no longer have any choice regarding whether or not to form a political society. The only choice they may have is whether to make society as a whole sovereign rather than some individual or individuals. Only in the first case can the result be called freedom. Again, understanding what he indicates will require realizing that rule by society as a whole, or by the general will, means rule by equitable laws enacted to assure the security of each. The choice will then be between being at the mercy of some arbitrary sovereign will or obedience to equitable laws of the kind we have mentioned, combined with freedom from subjection to men. It is the latter condition that Rousseau will call "conventional freedom." The following passage, from a later work by Rousseau, sheds light on what we have been speaking of:

[Independence, or doing exactly as one pleases, and freedom] are so different as to even be mutually exclusive. When everyone does as he pleases, what displeases others often is done, and that is not what one can call a free state. *Freedom consists less in doing [whatever is] one's will than in not being subject to that of another; it consists also in not subjecting the will of another to our own.* Whoever is master cannot be free, and to rule is to obey. Your Magistrates, who like Otho leave nothing slavish undone in order to command, know this better than anyone. I know of no will that is truly free [other] than one to which no one has the right to oppose any resistance; where there is common freedom [*dans la liberté commune*] no one has the right to do what the freedom of another prohibits him [from doing], and true freedom is never self-destructive. Thus freedom without justice is a true [*véritable*] contradiction. . . .
    There is therefore no freedom without Laws, nor [is there any freedom] where anyone is above the Laws: even in the state of nature man is only free thanks to the natural law which commands all. A free people obeys, but it does not serve; it has chieftains and not masters; *it obeys the Laws but it obeys only the Laws, and it is by dint of the Laws that it does not obey men.*[7]

Summing up the social contract in the work from which this quotation is taken, Rousseau points out that "it binds the contracting parties without subjecting them to anyone."[8] He adds that in giving them no other rule than their will, the social contract leaves them as free as they were before. This collective freedom, which expresses itself exclusively in laws, will concern us later; it will prove to be an important ingredient of Rousseau's understanding of the freedom possible within political life. Our present analysis has been concerned with the relation between the individual freedom of the contracting parties and the general will by which each of them agrees to be guided, rather than with the collective freedom of the general will itself. The importance of equitable "laws" as a theme in the remarks we have just made calls to mind the mention above of both "compact" and "fair" (or "equitable") laws in the epigraph for Rousseau's work.[9]

Rousseau's formulation of the social contract immediately follows his analysis of its content: *Each of us puts in common his person and all his power under the supreme direction of the general will; and as a body we receive each member as an indivisible part of the whole*. The second portion of the contract draws attention to the fact that no one is left out of the social order it establishes; that social order will not consist of "insiders" and "outsiders."[10] The social contract, to return to the question that preceded Rousseau's analysis of it, first creates a people in the political sense of the term, a people with a common self, a common life, and, above all, a common will with the right to make political decisions that are legitimately binding on all its members. Moreover, it first creates, according to Rousseau, something that deserves to be called a state, a sovereign, citizens and subjects in the strict and *normative* sense of these terms. Where the social contract has been violated, for example, there can only be a so-called state, not a genuine state constituted by a genuine obligation to obey those who rule. One important consequence of the definitions Rousseau offers on the basis of his account of the social contract is that the city, or the republic, or the body politic on the one hand and the people on the other become indistinguishable, or, rather, one and the same. This charge proved to be highly influential. It has been noted, for example, that when Hegel translates passages from Plato and Aristotle in his "Wissenschaftliche Behandlungsart des Naturrechts," the word πόλις is rendered *Volk* ("people").[11]

Rousseau leads up to the exposition of the social contract with the observation that "before examining the act whereby a people [according to Grotius] elect a king it would be good to examine the act whereby a people becomes a people [with a right to make political decisions by which its members are bound]" (1.5.2,3). That act proves to be the social contract. Is the reader to gather from this that, according to Rousseau, wherever a people and a political society are found, a tacit or express enactment of the social contract must be presumed to have taken place? Two considerations make it difficult to accept this view. In the first place, Rousseau freely admits that he does not know how the transition from the state of nature to political society took place (1.1.1). Furthermore, he will later note that "the most instructive part of the annals of peoples, which is the history of their institution, is the one most lacking to us. Experience daily teaches us from what causes the revolutions of empires spring: but since peoples are no longer being formed, we

Chapter Two

have hardly anything but conjectures to explain how they [once] were formed" (4.4.1). These remarks scarcely testify to any certainty on Rousseau's part regarding how they *must have been* formed. The epigraph for the *Social Contract*, it must be remembered, is taken from a fabulous tale concerning the founding of Rome.[12]

In an earlier version of the *Social Contract* Rousseau declared himself regarding the question under discussion as follows:

> There are a thousand ways of assembling men, [but] there is only one [way] to unite them. That is why I give in this work only one method for the formation of political societies, although in the multitude of aggregations which presently go by that name, perhaps no two were formed in the same manner, and not one in accordance with the manner I establish. But I seek right and reason and am not quarreling over facts.[13]

In the definitive version, however, an entirely different impression is created:

> The clauses of this contract are so determined by the nature of the act, that the least modification would render them null and void; so that, although they may never have been formally declared, they are everywhere the same, everywhere tacitly admitted and recognized; until, on the violation of the social compact, each one regains his original rights and recovers his natural freedom, thereby losing the conventional freedom for which he renounced it (1.6.5).

One can attempt to explain away the conflict between these two passages by observing that in the first version of the work the exposition of the fundamental contract was not preceded by an analysis of false views regarding the origin of political society. It was preceded by an attack on the belief, expressed in Diderot's article on Natural Right in the *Encyclopédie*, that men should take their fundamental moral bearings by the general will of humanity conceived as one vast society. Rousseau raises doubts regarding the being of such a universal will, regarding the ease with which its decrees can be identified, and regarding the sanctions by which these decrees are supported. The social contract and the general will created by it are understood, in the original version, as an answer to Diderot's general will, an answer capable of doing effectively what the general will of the human race cannot do at all. In the definitive version of the *Social Contract*, on the other hand, Rousseau presents his own solution as tacitly implied in the erroneous views he is attacking, insofar as these views suggest the existence of a people for which they fail to account. One might go even further and say that wherever a political order is a government of the people and claims to be a government for the people, the being of a people and a public good, as well as the preeminence of the public good over the private good, are all assumed, which is tantamount to saying that these assumptions are made "everywhere." Now, for Rousseau, to grasp clearly what is implied in these assumptions means to understand the social contract. This is what permits Rousseau to say that the clauses of the social contract are "everywhere tacitly admitted and recognized."

Nevertheless, the matter cannot rest there. In the second of the two passages we quoted, Rousseau speaks of a time subsequent to the enactment of the social contract, a time at which the social contract is violated with the result that those who violate it no longer have a claim to rule that is entitled to the respect of their subjects. This manner of speaking goes beyond the contention that governments everywhere claim to be legitimate and at least suggests that governments everywhere once were legitimate. Why does the man who announced that he did not know how political rule and subjection had arisen now ascribe a legitimate origin to political orders everywhere?

The manner in which Rousseau describes the enactment of the social contract is more favorable to the possibility that most existing regimes are legitimate than are the views he expresses later in the work. As we shall see, he goes on to point out just how difficult it is for a legitimate social order to come into being and, as a consequence, how rare such societies are. This is only one of a number of cases in the *Social Contract* in which Rousseau appears more favorably disposed to the common political practices of men than his strict doctrine would require or, indeed, would permit: for example, one will find him speaking as though all forms of government, including hereditary monarchy, are capable of being legitimate (2.6.6; 3.18.2). Careful students of the *Social Contract* have seen, however, that the chapter devoted to monarchy in Rousseau's discussion of various forms of government is not intended to show how hereditary monarchy can be made legitimate but rather why this cannot be done.[14] When one has followed to the end Rousseau's discussion in Book 3 of the danger that sovereignty will be usurped by government and of the measures that must be taken to protect the sovereign against that danger, one sees clearly that the scope of governmental arrangements which are compatible with his principles is far narrower than one might at first expect (3.17.7; 3.18). Moreover, there can be no doubt that, according to Rousseau's strict doctrine, if the people are kept from exercising their sovereignty, the social contract is violated and the individual regains his natural freedom. Yet Rousseau fails to apply this principle clearly to the subjects of large monarchic states: on the contrary, speaking of Rome, he dates the usurpation of sovereignty not from Caesar or Augustus, whom he calls "monarchs," but from Tiberius, whom he calls a "despot." Those readers who would prefer to call Caesar or Augustus "tyrants," as Rousseau himself does in his other writings, find themselves confronted with a distinction between tyrants, who usurp governmental authority but govern in accordance with "law," and "lawless" despots (3.10.3n,9,10). From Rousseau's strict doctrine of law it follows, as he remarks (in an aside), that "if one examined things carefully one would find that very few nations have laws" (3.15.8). Nevertheless, he frequently chooses to speak of law in a much looser and more commonsense way, and as a consequence the line separating legitimate from illegitimate government is far vaguer than it need be, given his doctrines.

Rousseau's *Social Contract* is his least eloquent and impassioned work dealing with moral and political matters. The restraint Rousseau exhibits at least in that work is caused by his reluctance to incite men living under illegitimate rulers—that is, most men—to throw off their chains. If the conditions conducive to a just society are, of necessity, rare, as he says, illegitimate regimes are a necessary evil for the overwhelming majority of men— necessary because the incompatibility between natural freedom and self-preservation forces men to form political societies even when the conditions favorable to legitimate government are absent.[15] Rousseau clearly wishes the management of public affairs to be entrusted to men who are law-abiding in his strict sense of the term, but where this is not feasible, where only illegitimate rule is possible, he prefers illegitimate rulers who are "law"-abiding in the usual sense of the term, if not in his own sense, to rulers who are utterly lawless and arbitrary. He thinks that revolutions against "law"-abiding but illegitimate rulers tend, on the whole, to replace such rulers with others who, in addition to being illegitimate, are "law"-less and despotic, a change which he does not regard as an improvement. Rousseau, given his teaching, cannot deny subjects the right to remove their rulers when the terms of the social contract have not been observed, but he obviously did not think that it is always wise for men to exercise this right, and he did not wish to be guilty of inciting men to acts which he regarded as unwise. This accounts for his relative tolerance of certain political practices which he saw no way to avoid. At the same time, he is careful to show societies fortunate enough to be law-abiding, in the strict sense of the term, the dangers they face and the means to overcome them. Accordingly, his analysis of government is as much concerned with how to protect the sovereign against the usurpation of its authority by those who govern as it is with determining what kinds of government are compatible with the sovereignty of the people, to use these words in his sense. He makes his preference for small and free republics clear in the *Social Contract* but does not wish to encourage men whose societies cannot be of this character to overthrow the societies in which they *do* live merely because those societies are not small and free.

If Rousseau had believed that thanks to the beneficent workings of the invisible hand of progress legitimate political orders either were or would have become possible under most circumstances, he might well have written a revolutionary manifesto instead of, or in addition to, the *Social Contract*. However, Rousseau did not believe in progress. He did not think that the world was becoming ever more hospitable to legitimate government. The work that made him famous was an attack on the view that intellectual progress, and the diffusion of its results, tends to be accompanied by moral and social progress. It was only when Rousseau's doctrine was combined with a belief in progress, a belief incompatible with it, that it became a revolutionary call to arms. Since that combination was, so to speak, rejected in advance by Rousseau, there is nothing surprising about the fact that he did not encourage upheavals that presupposed its validity. In the *Social Contract*, at any rate, he communicated his views regarding a subject's obligation to obey his rulers in such a way as not to encourage such upheavals but also in such a way as not to detract from the usefulness of his book in the Europe that would survive the revolutionary storm which he saw coming regardless of any precautions that he might take.[16] For Europe will, later in the work, turn out to be a "climate" of which freedom has been and might well again be the "fruit."[17]

Rousseau's account of the social contract has often been criticized for being "unhistorical." His depiction of prepolitical men gathering together to form political orders in accordance with his prescriptions would seem to be a perfect example of the kind of error into which one can be led if one does not have a sufficiently developed sense of history. We have already discussed why Rousseau was not as clear in the definitive version of the *Social Contract* as he had been in the earlier version regarding the small chance that any society of his time had been formed in the manner he prescribes. His immediate objective is to show how a sovereign political authority can originate in a contract which is neither illegitimate nor unreliable. In his effort to do this, he limits himself to the barest essentials of the social contract and to the barest essentials of the situation out of which it arises. This does not mean he will never face the question of under what precise circumstances and in which precise way the social contract can be made the foundation of a given political society. Rather than ignore that question he simply delays discussing it until more clarity has been achieved regarding the political implications of the social contract or until it becomes clearer what a society based on the social contract would be like. Once that is clear, the problem of how to establish such a society is raised without any attempt being made to conceal or mitigate the enormous obstacles that must be overcome in order to solve it. In dealing with that almost insoluble problem, Rousseau displays the highly developed sensitivity to times and circumstances that he is sometimes criticized for lacking.

Rousseau's description of the act through which private individuals become members of political society has often been compared to the accounts of Hobbes and Locke. Rousseau claimed in a later work to have used exactly the same principles as those of Locke when treating political matters in the *Social Contract*. All the more striking is the frequently noted absence of any reference to natural right or to natural law in Rousseau's account of the social contract. This, in turn, has led to considerable debate over whether or not Rousseau's teaching implies a repudiation of the notion of natural law.[18] In reflecting on this, it is important to keep in mind something that bears not only on how Rousseau understands natural law but also any other notion his precise definition of which differs from the common understanding of it. The rule Rousseau follows in such cases is not always to adhere to his new, precise sense of the term when using it. After setting forth the social contract, for

41 41 Sovereignty and the General Will

example, he distinguishes between several closely allied expressions and notes that "these terms [which have just been distinguished] are often confused and mistaken for one another; it is enough to be able to distinguish between them when they are used in all their precision" (1.6.10). Rousseau does not say that he will always use them in all their precision and it is not his habitual practice to do so. Examples of this are found throughout the *Social Contract*. A striking one is supplied by his new definition of law. The book in which this definition is arrived at closes with a classification of the various kinds of law. Of these, the one mentioned last—the law governing morals, customs, and opinion—although it is said to be the most important of all, is only a law in the usual sense of the term and not a law at all in Rousseau's new and precise sense. The natural law, it has been remarked, is not mentioned at all in Rousseau's classification.[19] The reason for this cannot be that it is not a law in Rousseau's precise sense since that did not prevent the unwritten law from being included and assigned the greatest importance.

When Rousseau speaks of natural law elsewhere he sometimes does so in the usual sense and at other times in the strict sense of the term. What he means by natural law in the strict sense is made clear in his Preface to the *Discourse on Inequality*. After surveying the controversies surrounding natural law since ancient times, he draws the following conclusion: In order to deserve to be called a law, natural law must be addressed to a rational being capable of obeying and disobeying it (only reason can apprehend universal prescriptions), while in order to deserve to be called natural, natural law must speak with the voice of nature. Now since, according to Rousseau, the development of reason stifles the voice of nature, there is no place strictly speaking in his doctrine for natural law. As he himself delineates it, natural law is a square circle. While discussing the meaning of natural law, Rousseau also speaks of natural right or natural justice. In contradistinction to the laws of nature, the rules of natural right do not have to be rationally apprehended by the being over whom they hold sway. Nor, judging from the principles which engender those rules according to Rousseau—pity and fear, or self-preservation and compassion—need the being over whom they hold sway be capable of disobeying them. Once the development of reason brings passions into being that destroy the simple workings of pity and of the desire for self-preservation, it becomes necessary for reason to lay a new foundation for the rules

Chapter Two

of conduct which formerly sprang from them. Let us call these new rules together with their foundation the law of reason. We may note that neither natural right nor the law of reason are self-contradictory for Rousseau in the way natural law, strictly understood, is. Natural right is not addressed to a rational being. The law of reason does not speak with the voice of nature.[20]

While the law of reason cannot be equated with either natural law or natural right in the sense these terms have for Rousseau, the contents of the law of reason, as described by him, are clearly not arbitrary. Now the traditional understanding of natural law was not what Rousseau understood it to be. Traditionally, it was held to comprise the rules of conduct which set forth the difference between right and wrong and whose validity did not depend on human arbitrariness. Rousseau's new account of natural law sums up his criticism of the traditional view. To the extent that natural law as traditionally understood makes the awareness of right and wrong depend on the sound exercise of natural reason it is guilty of vastly overestimating the power of natural reason over human thought and conduct. The defect of all previous natural law teachings— including that of Hobbes, whom Rousseau credits with an awareness of this difficulty—consisted in their inability to explain convincingly how the moral law came to be known and its authority came to be recognized by the overwhelming majority of men through the workings of natural reason. From the standpoint of the traditional understanding of natural law, Rousseau's principles of political right and, more generally, his law of reason would be natural-law teachings. Since Rousseau, in keeping with his usual practice, talks of natural law in the usual and traditional sense as well as in his novel sense, one can find him speaking as though there is and as though there is not a natural law, without contradicting himself. Insofar as the principles of political right set forth valid, nonarbitrary rules of conduct, they can be understood as laws of nature in the traditional sense, as can the rules regarding which kinds of contracts are valid and which are not that guide Rousseau in framing the social contract. Insofar as these rules are discovered by reason rather than being simply dictated by the voice of nature, they are not laws of nature in Rousseau's new sense.

The *Social Contract* testifies to Rousseau's belief that there are nonarbitrary principles of right and wrong. The work is devoted to setting forth the true principles of political right. These principles, however, stand in a different relation to Rousseau's sovereign than

Sovereignty and the General Will

Hobbes's natural law does to Hobbes's sovereign. In Hobbes, the sovereign is instituted to give effect to preexisting rights and laws of nature. In Rousseau, the politically pertinent parts of his law of reason—such as the natural freedom and equality resulting from men's concern with their self-preservation, and the conclusions concerning what kinds of agreements can and what kinds cannot be valid—determine the character of the social contract and are, so to speak, built into it. They govern the workings of the sovereign created by it—the general will—from within rather than from above. The following explanation for this difference has been suggested.[21] In order to dispose of the dangers of anarchy and civil war, Hobbes wished to establish a sovereign from whose will there could be no legitimate appeal, practically speaking. Yet, in spite of his efforts to show that the sovereign, as it were, absorbs the natural law, that law remains a standard independent of the sovereign, by which the sovereign's conduct can be measured, and which can supply grounds for resisting him. Rousseau's account claims to establish a sovereign—the general will—that can be depended upon to make a sincere effort to secure the common advantage and that can alone be depended upon to do so; it can therefore command the loyalty even of citizens who might feel, in a given case, that it has made a mistake.

The general will, as we will learn, is not infallibly wise. That is not how we are finally meant to understand the claim that "the Sovereign, by the mere fact that it is, is always what it should be."[22] The simple notion underlying this strong claim is that the common advantage is the self-interest of the entire people. That is why the people, if sovereign, can be relied upon to secure it. With "men as they are," reposing sovereignty elsewhere, for Rousseau, means running an unacceptable political risk. As his argument progresses, however, things do not remain so simple. He soon has to face the two questions which have confronted all thoughtful friends of dem- ocratic republics, the question of whether the people is as apt to discern the common advantage as it is to desire it, and the question of how to prevent unjust, tyrannical, and oppressive majorities that will not even desire it from forming. Rousseau will face both ques- tions, and it would be best to delay further discussion of the reliabil- ity of the general will until we reach the portion of his work in which he does so. For the moment let us leave it at saying that the strong claim we have quoted will have to be both qualified and elaborated.

To be effective, the laws enacted by the general will must be enforced. Rousseau expresses this by saying that "whoever refuses to obey the general will shall be compelled to do so by the entire body; which means nothing other than that he will be forced to be free" (1.7.8). Some interpreters have cited this passage in support of the view that Rousseau's teaching is totalitarian, at least by implication. We do not claim that the following remarks suffice to dispose of this view. They are merely intended to show that this passage can be understood in the light of what we have already said and that such an understanding lends no support to the accusation in question. The only political alternatives as Rousseau presented them in the passages quoted and discussed earlier, were, on the one hand, a freedom which is inseparable from obedience to equitable laws and, on the other, subjection to arbitrary and oppressive rule. The sanctions that make the rule of law possible thus make freedom possible as well. Rousseau adds that "this [enforcement of the general will] is the condition which, by giving each Citizen to the Fatherland [*Patrie*], guarantees him against all personal dependence" (1.7.8).[23] We will have to see later how Rousseau understands the relation between freedom, rule of law, and patriotism. The mere reference to patriotism, however, does not justify the inference that Rousseau is a totalitarian, since patriotism and totalitarianism are not the same thing.

Immediately after describing the coercive sanctions that are tacitly implied in the social contract, Rousseau proceeds to discuss how the contract transforms the individuals who enact it. The proximity of the two discussions is not altogether accidental. The social contract, by making it impossible for an individual to exploit, for his own private advantage, the collective force instituted by it, puts the individual in a position in which he cannot seek his self-interest except by transcending himself. It thereby teaches him the meaning of duty and justice. "Then only is it that the voice of duty takes the place of physical impulse and right [the place] of appetite; [and that] man, who until then thought only of himself, finds himself forced to act on other principles, and to consult his reason before listening to his inclinations" (1.8.1). If the self-mastery that transcends appetite and inclination in order to act in accordance with duty can be described as freedom, one may say that the social contract forces man to be free in more senses than the most obvious one. Taken in connection with the description of self-legislation given later in the work, Rousseau's view of moral freedom obviously influenced Kant profoundly. The differences between Rous-

Sovereignty and the General Will

seau and Kant are no less profound, however. There is an important distinction, according to Rousseau, between legislating for oneself and legislating for a whole of which one is part, since, as he concedes, one is not bound by promises one makes only to oneself (1.7.1,2). The first discussion in this work of the kind of sovereign authority the social contract brings into being stresses the importance of this distinction. Moreover, as we have already noted in another connection, political society has both an ennobling and a degrading effect on man.[24] Does the ennobling effect outweigh the degrading one? The sentence with which he concludes his description of how the social contract contributes to the development of the human soul is perfectly ambiguous in this regard. It contains an all-important "if." That man should bless the happy moment that brought him into political society is not affirmed. What is affirmed is that he would have to bless it *if* the abuses of his new condition did not often degrade him beneath the condition he was previously in. As if to underscore in how undecided a state this question is left, Rousseau immediately proceeds to suggest that it be restated in terms which would make it easier to decide (1.8.2). The terms of the comparison now are rights, and in particular property rights, before and after the social contract. Although Rousseau does not explicitly declare his conclusion favoring the condition produced by the social contract until he has shown why sovereign authority can never be oppressive, his promise to show this, together with the manner in which he explains the problem the social contract is meant to solve, clearly foreshadows that conclusion. In order not to be misled by Rousseau's conclusion, it is important to bear the following point in mind. Rousseau reaches a conclusion favorable not to political society as such but only to political societies in which the social contract is observed. The conclusion is reached by contrasting such a society not with the state of nature as such but with the final phase in the state of nature, the phase just prior to the rise of political society, a phase in which men are a threat to each other's lives and property. Finally, the contract is limited to considerations of self-preservation, security, and property. To the extent that freedom is an indispensable means to the foregoing, one can say that the social contract leaves man not only as free as he was before but even more free. If freedom were viewed in its relation to happiness, the entire issue would have to be reopened on a broader basis.

Book 1 is devoted, directly or indirectly, to the exposition of the social contract. The book ends with a chapter that indicates the moral limits of the solution achieved by the social contract. That

Chapter Two

solution, it becomes apparent, is only binding within the confines of the society formed by the social contract. Rousseau makes this point in the course of a discussion of property rights. He rejects the view, put forth by Locke, that property rights antedate the founding of political society. Or rather, while conceding a certain weight in the state of nature to the right of the first occupier, Rousseau regards that right as less fundamental than the right all men naturally have to all things necessary for their self-preservation. The conflict between these rights was the chief source of enmity in the state of nature during its last phase, according to the *Discourse on Inequality*. Both rights are surrendered when the social contract is enacted. The arrangements regarding property, by which they are replaced, are the outcome of positive law.

The law that regulates property relations between members of a society governed by the social contract is not binding on other societies. The question therefore arises whether the situation from which the social contract rescued individuals continues to obtain between societies or whether a commonwealth's claim to its territory is any more deserving of respect by other commonwealths than an individual's claim to his possessions in the state of nature is by other individuals. Rousseau's first inclination appears to be to answer this question in the negative. While a commonwealth is better able to defend its territory than an individual, its claims to its possession are not more legitimate to foreigners than those of an individual in the state of nature are to other individuals. Rousseau does not leave the matter at this, however; according to him, thanks to the social compact political man acquires a respect for property rights of a certain kind, a respect that transcends the positive law of his own commonwealth and that bears on property claims made outside his society. The property right in question is the right of the first occupier. With the abandonment of the right to whatever one deems necessary to self-preservation, the right of the first occupier, whose claims were drowned out rather than absent in the state of nature, can finally make its voice heard, even beyond the confines of one's own society. Civil man, accustomed to having his rights defined and limited, is open to the claim that something is not his in a way that natural man is not likely to be. Rousseau spells out the conditions under which that claim can be persuasive and in accordance with those conditions requires of a just conqueror at least as scrupulous a respect for the lives and property of the vanquished as do Locke and Montesquieu.

Few societies or their members could live up to the conditions

Sovereignty and the General Will

laid down by Rousseau for invoking the right of the first occupier if these conditions were interpreted strictly. In particular the condition that requires the absence of any previous occupant would be difficult for many nations to meet. Rousseau stresses the third condition: labor and cultivation. The difficulty of meeting all the conditions leads him to speak of how the social contract transforms "usurpation" by individuals into property rights and also to speak of men who possess nothing first uniting and subsequently "seizing a territory sufficient for all." In spite of this, there remains a difference between not fully complying with all these conditions in the claims one makes and flouting all of them: a qualified claim is still a claim. An example given by Rousseau of what it means to flout these conditions is the claim to vast territories in America made by explorers on behalf of their kings. An example of what it means to ignore even the qualified claims that are entitled to one's respect would be a conqueror who plunders and massacres those who are at his mercy.

Rousseau momentarily speaks as though all possible arrangements regarding the ownership of land were equally compatible with the social contract: the general will could decree with equal right that there shall be no private ownership of land or that one class of society will be permitted to own a larger proportion of the land than another. These theoretical possibilities are on a par with Rousseau's later claim that hereditary monarchy and hereditary aristocracy are, as forms of government, perfectly compatible with the social contract.[25] Both assertions serve to establish the preeminence of the sovereign, in the one case over property in land and in the other over forms of government. In both cases the genuine possibilities prove to be narrower than the theoretical ones, when due attention is paid to the conditions required for the embodiment of the principles of political right. In the case of private ownership, Rousseau makes fairly clear in the concluding paragraphs of the chapter on property and in the footnote designed to clarify them, as well as elsewhere in the work, that it will be strengthened rather than abolished. In the small society of which he is thinking, practically all will be haves, practically none will be have-nots, and vast inequalities in wealth will be avoided for as long as possible.[26]

On the basis of this one can understand the way in which the founding of political society is described in the *Discourse on Inequality*. That work seems to present political society as a swindle perpetrated by the haves on the have-nots. The fraudulent speech

Chapter Two

through which the haves seduce the have-nots into forming a political order is:

> Let us unite to protect the weak from oppression, restrain the ambitious, and secure for everyone the possession of what belongs to him: Let us institute regulations of justice and peace to which all are obliged to conform, which make an exception of none, and which compensate in some way for the caprices of fortune by equally subjecting the powerful and the weak to mutual duties. In a word, instead of turning our forces against ourselves, let us gather them into one supreme power which governs us according to wise laws, protects and defends all the members of the association, repulses common enemies, and maintains us in an eternal concord.[27]

What is the difference between the proposal in this speech and that in the social contract? What makes the one a change for the better and the other a swindle? In both, men abandon their natural right to whatever they think they need for their self-preservation. In both, possession based on claims that are open to question even when they are sound is transformed into secure property rights. Both solutions obviously favor haves rather than have-nots. The whole difference is that the social contract is assumed to be enacted by men practically all of whom are haves, whereas the swindle is assumed to be perpetrated in a situation in which there are gross inequalities between a few haves and many have-nots. The solution proposed by the haves abolishes natural freedom and "assures to each the possession of what belongs to him." It is definitely more in the interest of the few who possess than of the many who do not. The swindle is a caricature of the social contract. The social order Rousseau is proposing is intended to be, in this regard, an overwhelmingly middle-class society. Tocqueville, depicting American democracy, describes a social order that may be very different in other respects from the one envisaged by Rousseau but in this respect is very much the same.

Rousseau did not need the enlightenment about the possible limitations of equality under the law contained in the quip that the rich and the poor are equally forbidden to sleep on park benches at night. He reveals himself to be fully in possession of that profound insight. His understanding of inequality is not limited to that insight, however. He also thought that the relation between those who are politically powerful and those who are not is a kind of inequality. In

Sovereignty and the General Will

fact the most extreme and oppressive kind of inequality of which he knew is that found between absolute political rulers and those subject to their tyranny. He would never have described this condition as one of equality without freedom, not even if those ruling claimed to be serving the cause of equality, because he would have been at a loss to see how an inequality of that glaring magnitude could conceivably be understood as a kind of equality. If the entire *Social Contract* is directed against any single thing, that thing is arbitrary government, which can be exercised by a group of men as well as by one man and which Rousseau regards as no less oppressive, to say the least, when it is exercised by a group. The equality which Rousseau is concerned to safeguard is inseparable from freedom and cannot be increased at its expense. Equality so understood is the cornerstone of the political edifice Rousseau seeks to erect. Preserving it in its fundamental character in spite of the inequalities that will continue to be found among men, and in spite of those that will result from satisfying the need, soon to be acknowledged, for a legislator, a government, and a civil religion will be the chief difficulty with which Rousseau will have to struggle throughout the work.

The almost insoluble conflict between what is required to make the convention through which political authority arises legitimate and what is required to make that convention viable binds into one the critical and constructive parts into which Book 1 is divided. The parts into which Book 2 is divided are also linked by a seemingly insoluble conflict. The first part of Book 2 (Chapters 1–6) continues the discussion of the second part of Book 1. The purpose of the discussion is to make clear the character of the sovereign general will instituted by the social contract. The conclusion reached is that the general will is society as a whole prescribing laws for all its members. Every act of the general will is an act of self-legislation by society as a whole. The general will is society as a whole as legislator. Rousseau, as we shall see, means this much more literally than some of his nineteenth-century successors will. Every valid law will have to be enacted by the sovereign people in person and every valid act of the sovereign people will have to take the form of a law. In the very last paragraph of his discussion of the general will, however, Rousseau begins to raise certain difficulties the point of which is to make one distrust the people's ability to enact at least the most important of the laws that it requires. Once these laws are in place, that is, once the political framework of the society has been established, the people may well be equal to the task of legislating, provided that the framework has been established properly. The difficulty is to see how the laws of which that framework is composed ever came to be enacted in the first place in a manner that is compatible with the principles that Rousseau is at such pains to establish in his account of the general will. Contrary to what his critics sometimes have alleged, Rousseau does not ignore the question of how the kind of society envisioned in the *Social Contract* could have had a believable beginning in time. He delays raising this question for reasons we discussed earlier. When he finally does raise it, however, he presents it with such clarity and force that it appears, for a moment, as unanswerable as did the central question faced by him in Book 1.

Let us examine the argument through which Rousseau seeks to establish that every act of the general will is a law enacted by the sovereign people. The first point he attempts to settle is that the general will cannot delegate or part with its sovereignty. His reasons for this have been found obscure by some.[28] His argument seems to be based on the alleged inability of the will to be represented. The general will can, and even must, entrust the management of the common force of society to another. But it cannot let anyone else do its willing for it. Since every individual who took part in enacting the social contract has done precisely what the general will is here declared incapable of doing, one might wonder where the alleged impossibility lies. The difficulty would be a false one if the will of those concluding the social contract could be said to coincide with the general will, but it is precisely that coincidence which Rousseau questions: "if it is not impossible for a particular will to agree with the general will on some point; it is at least impossible for the agreement to be durable and constant, for the particular will tends by its nature to partiality [*aux préférences*] and the general will to equality" (2.1.3). The particular will—the will of private individuals—and the general will may and do overlap to some extent. Without some overlap the formation of political society would not be to the common advantage of all. But they do not coincide. Becoming a member of political society means submitting to the rule of a will that is other than my own. Why should the general will be held to be unable to do what every individual had to do in order to bring it into being?

We will not find Rousseau's argument obscure if we pay attention to the attribute of the will that is decisive for him in this context:

Sovereignty and the General Will

"no will can consent to anything contrary to the good of the being that wills" (2.1.3).[29] What is important about the will for Rousseau is its necessary directedness to the good of the willing being. It is this necessary directedness to the good at which the general will aims that cannot be transferred to or grafted onto any other will, since that other will must have *its* own good as its necessary correlate. Now, it was precisely the good at which the general will aimed that made alienating one's natural freedom to the general will something that one could safely and advantageously do. It was precisely because that good was constituted by everyone's good as an equal and inseparable part of the common good, that the contract through which one submitted to the general will was not open to the objections which made contractual slavery and despotism invalid. If the general will were to abdicate its sovereignty in favor of the wills of some private individuals, the old objections to alienating one's freedom would return: "the second there is a master there is no longer a [legitimate] sovereign, and from that moment on the body politic [in the strict sense of the term, which requires that there be a valid obligation to obey those who rule] is destroyed" (2.1.3). Rousseau's argument may not be perfectly convincing, particularly after one learns that not even he can completely dispense with a certain amount of "grafting," at least on the part of subjects (2.7.3). Nevertheless it does carry some weight and is by no means obscure.

Even if one were to grant the cogency of Rousseau's argument, however, the question would still remain whether he has shown more than that the general will can be depended on to desire what is in the common interest. One would still want to know if the sovereign people can be depended on to discern how to achieve the common interest. The difference between the two is, or at least can be, as great as the difference between desiring to be free of cancer and discovering a cure for it. Rousseau had earlier asserted that the sovereign, by the mere fact that it is, is always what it should be. Now he makes it clear that in saying this he was referring to the intention of the sovereign alone: "It follows from what precedes that the general will is always right and always tends toward the public utility: but it does not follow that the deliberations of the people always have the same rectitude. One always wants [wills] one's good, but one does not always see it. The people are never corrupted but they are often deceived, and only then does it seem to want [will] what is bad" (2.3.1). The chapter in which these matters are discussed raises a question in its title, but the title does not indicate how the question will be answered. The chapter is entitled "Whether the general will can err." In raising this question Rousseau is in fact addressing himself to the classical issue of the relation between wisdom and consent in political life. One of the two works referred to by title and author in the text of the *Social Contract*—Plato's *Statesman*—deals at length with this issue. In Plato's work, it was to wisdom alone that any social arrangement owed its respectability. The undiluted, absolute, and unconditional rule of wisdom is the only solution to the political problem that is simply just and simply respectable. However, owing to the presence of rival aspirants to high office and to the difficulty of distinguishing apparent or sham wisdom from genuine wisdom, the simply just solution is not safe or workable. For all practical purposes one must settle for a second-best solution—the rule of laws prepared by a wise legislator to which a society consents.[30] The justice of the second-best solution is of a diluted character, however, and it therefore no longer commands unqualified respect. Rousseau's subsequent discussion of the legislator in Book 2 will show that his views coincide to a remarkable degree with those suggested in the *Statesman*. Regarding one important point, however, Rousseau's views are opposed to those of Plato (and, one might argue, even to those of Aristotle).[31] Rousseau believed that undiluted justice was politically possible and necessary, since for him, as for Hobbes, establishing the feasibility of a simply just social order was equivalent to ascertaining whether any social order could be unequivocally entitled to the obedience of its members. The source of legitimacy for Rousseau was, as we have seen, not superior wisdom but a voluntary agreement entered into out of a concern for one's self-preservation. In other words, the source of legitimacy is consent. Yet Rousseau will also have to acknowledge that, without wisdom, the goal for which men institute political society will not be achieved.

In attempting to show that the general will can be relied on to arrive at the right decisions, Rousseau proceeds in stages. His first concern is to make clear what guarantees the general will against errors due to unfairness rather than to ignorance. He appears to suggest if one can only guarantee the fairness of the general will, its sagacity will also be guaranteed. This suggestion proves to be only provisional however. The question of how to guarantee the availability of wisdom will reappear clearly and forcefully after Rousseau has elaborated his reasons for relying on the fairness of the general will.

To follow his explanation of how the totality of particular wills is transformed into the one general will it is important not to misunderstand the difference between the two wills. The fact that the general will has regard only to the common interest does not mean that it is unconcerned with what is in one's private interest. Similarly, the fact that a particular will is concerned with its private interest does not mean that it is concerned with it to the exclusion of the public interest. As we pointed out previously, there is a partial overlap between the private interest and the common good. The public or common interest is a part of the private interest. Rousseau explains how this comes to pass in a later passage describing an individual in a corrupt society where the general will has been mastered by private interests in the management of public affairs. "Each one, detaching his interest from the common interest, sees clearly that he cannot separate the one from the other entirely, but his share of the public misfortune seems like nothing to him next to the exclusive good which he means to appropriate for himself. With the exception of this private good, he wants the general good for his own interest, just as strongly as anyone else" (4.1.6). The public interest continues to be part of the private interest even in a corrupt society where the general will has been silenced. Let us now consider a society where the general will is still in command but let us abstract from all considerations except those suggested by interest and calculation. Each citizen will bring to the sovereign assembly both his desire for the common advantage and his desire to be spared the burden which he wishes others to shoulder in order for the common advantage to be achieved. At that assembly he finds that his own desire coincides with the desire of every other citizen regarding the first point, but that his desire is at variance with the desire of every other citizen as regards the second. Under conditions which Rousseau will specify, that settles the issue in favor of the common good of all. A man may wish not to pay his taxes and he may feel the total good that he will derive from not paying them manifestly outweighs the small portion of the harm that he will suffer from the fact that he has not paid them. But this does not mean that he wishes to see taxation abolished.

The manner in which Rousseau explains the emergence of the

general will from the will of private individuals has sometimes been criticized for its obscurity:

> In the third chapter of Book II of the *Social Contract*, Rousseau distinguishes "the will of all" from "the general will," saying that the first is a "sum of particular wills," and the second the "sum of differences" remaining when the "pluses" and "minuses" of the particular wills cancel each other out. Now, this account of the general will, if we take it literally, is sheer nonsense. What can the "pluses" and "minuses" of particular wills be except what is peculiar to each of them. Let John's will be $x + a$, Richard's $x + b$, and Thomas's $x + c$; x being what is common to them all, and a, b, and c, what is peculiar to each. If the general will is what remains after the "pluses" and "minuses" have cancelled each other out, it is x; but if it is the sum of the differences it is $a + b + c$. Whichever it is, it cannot be both; and the second alternative is too absurd to be considered. Beware of political philosphers who use mathematics, no matter how simple, to illustrate their meaning! God will forgive them, for they know what they do, but we shall not understand them.[32]

The passage about which this complaint is voiced is important and terse, but it is not hopelessly obscure, in our opinion. It makes use of a mathematical metaphor which furthers Rousseau's exposition provided one remembers that it is not meant to be more than a metaphor:

> There is often a great difference between the general will and the will of all; the former looks only to the common interest, while the latter looks to private interest, and is only a sum of particular [private] wills: but take away from these same wills the pluses and minuses which cancel each other out [*qui s'entrédetruisent*], [and] the general will remains as the sum of the differences.

In order to explain this passage let us revert to the example, given on page 33, of pollution-control devices and clean air. Let us assume that every member of the sovereign assembly is a driver and let us label them $D_1, D_2, D_3, \ldots, D_i$. Let $+Dx$ express the desire that Dx install a pollution-control device while $-Dx$ will express the wish that Dx not install such a device. Let us further assume that all drivers want clean air and regard the installation of pollution-

Sovereignty and the General Will

control devices as necessary to achieve it. The following are the particular wills, *if* one takes interest only into account, that each driver brings to the assembly. As we will see, no two of them are the same as each other and none is the same as the general will.

Driver	Particular Will of Driver
D_1	$-D_1 + D_2 + D_3, \ldots, +D_i$
D_2	$+D_1 - D_2 + D_3, \ldots, +D_i$
D_3	$+D_1 + D_2 - D_3, \ldots, +D_i$
.	
.	
.	
D_i	$+D_1 + D_2 + D_3, \ldots, -D_i$

The "differences" between the particular wills are "small" and the areas of overlap great, assuming the absence of collusive voting arrangements (2.3.3). Taking the "sum" of the "differences" means no more than adding together these differing particular wills and letting the pluses and minuses cancel each other out. The result of doing this is, by an overwhelming margin:

Driver	Particular Will of Driver
D_1	$-D_1 + D_2 + D_3, \ldots, +D_i$
D_2	$+D_1 - D_2 + D_3, \ldots, +D_i$
D_3	$+D_1 + D_2 - D_3, \ldots, +D_i$
.	
.	
.	
D_i	$+D_1 + D_2 + D_3, \ldots, -D_i$
General Will	$+D_1 + D_2 + D_3, \ldots, +D_i$

i.e., all drivers shall install pollution-control devices.

The example we have chosen is a simplified one in that there are only burdens to be shared and no benefit to be apportioned (clean air is, so to speak, self-apportioning). The point of the example is not affected by this simplification, however. On the other hand, the abstraction from any considerations other than interest, on which the preceding exposition has been based, will soon have to be abandoned. In particular, the easy transition made in the argument to a universal rule of conduct will require extensive discussion.

The passage we quoted contrasts the general will with the will of all. In later thinkers who sought to clarify and further develop Rousseau's teaching, both expressions came to be important technical terms. In Rousseau only the former expression—the general will—is a technical term. The latter expression—the will of all—is not. When the latter expression occurs in the writings of Rousseau, what it means depends on whether the word "all" is understood distributively or collectively. If it is understood distributively, as in the present passage, the will of all refers to the particular will of every one of the citizens before any public deliberation and voting have taken place. If "all" is understood collectively, the will of all is indistinguishable from the general will and can be found occurring in its place in the writings of Rousseau.[33] The present passage may be said to show how the will of all understood distributively becomes transformed into the will of all understood collectively.

The most Rousseau could claim to have established by the foregoing is the rectitude, in his sense of the term, of the decision at which the citizen assembly arrives. This is far from being an unimportant result however. In Aristotle's analysis, two things are required for good conduct: moral virtue which assures that the goal is right and practical wisdom which assures that the means to it are appropriate. Rousseau's account of the general will, at least up to the present point, has attempted to show that the just intention can be supplied without presupposing moral virtue. Since moral virtue, according to Aristotle, is not something one readily finds among "men as they are" the general will comes to sight as a "realistic" substitute for the virtues the classic writers thought necessary for a sound political order. The general will is a kind of justice one need not despair of ever seeing effectively govern the conduct of imperfect men. This result will have to be somewhat qualified: the general will will prove to be in need of some support of a moral character, but that support will still fall far short of the virtues required by Aristotle and Plato for a good society.[34]

We are still left with the question of what in Rousseau's opinion guarantees the wisdom of the decision at which the citizen assembly arrives. His first answer appears to be that by guaranteeing the rectitude of the result one has at the same time guaranteed its wisdom: "If, when an adequately informed people deliberates, the citizens had no communication between themselves, from the large number of small differences the general will would always result, and the deliberation would always be good" (2.3.3). Rousseau obviously assumes that the assembly will include members with the ability to enlighten their fellow citizens and that no secret agreements will deter them from doing so.[35] This answer is, for a number of reasons, not Rousseau's last word. Even if the general will were to be the spontaneous outcome of the free play of particular wills when secret agreements are absent, there is nothing spontaneous about the absence of such agreements. Their absence, which first makes sound deliberation in a sovereign assembly possible, is attributed to the artful contrivances of extraordinary individuals whom Rousseau will later refer to as legislators. By speaking of the extraordinary contributions of Lycurgus, Solon, Numa, and Servius, Rousseau indicates the limits within which he has answered the question regarding the wisdom of the sovereign assembly. He has observed that, in a properly ordered society, enough intelligence will be available to guide its deliberations. What remains to be explained is where the wisdom needed to order a society properly will come from and what the relation between this wisdom and the sovereign people will be. Rousseau will face this issue in the second half of Book 2. Facing it will mean discussing how a legitimate political order can have a believable beginning in time.

It was noted previously that "the will of all" is not a technical term in Rousseau. In particular, rule by an oppressive and unjust majority cannot be described as an example of rule by "the will of all" as distinguished from the general will. The factional intrigues which lead to the formation of unjust majorities involve compromises or modifications in what Rousseau here calls the will of all, just as the formation of the general will does. Rousseau believes no less than "Publius" and Tocqueville do, that a decision can be unjust even though it enjoys majority support. When this happens, it no longer embodies the general will. In order to prevent this from happening, he suggests measures similar to those proposed by "Publius": If the formation of partial societies cannot be prevented, their number should be multiplied and they should be kept relatively equal.[36] The fact that not every majority decision expresses the general will does not mean that anything other than a majority decision can express it. Rousseau is categorical regarding this point: once the majority cannot be trusted any longer, there is nothing else that can be trusted (4.2.9).

The fact that all particular wills, in the absence of intrigue, coincide in wishing to deny to everyone else the exceptional status that each would like for himself tells us more about what an undistorted vote in the sovereign assembly would prohibit than it does

Chapter Two

about what it would command. Rousseau proceeds to shed additional light on the content of such commands, light which makes clear what his previously expressed claim that these commands *cannot* be opposed to private interest is based on. In the course of doing so he shows why he believes that the demand for total alienation to the entire community and the doctrine that the commands of the general will are always legitimate pose no threat to the individual. Only after explaining this does Rousseau explicitly and unequivocally declare political society to be more advantageous for self-preservation than the state of nature (2.4.10).

The situation Rousseau assumes to obtain in the sovereign assembly is one where the rectitude of the general will is safeguarded from unjust partiality to the self-interest of any one citizen by the self-interest of all the others. It is in this way that what is unjust in the self-interest in each is checked in each, in turn, by all the others. Checking that self-interest, however, is not the same as destroying it. Rousseau does not wish to see self-interest stamped out. On the contrary, it is the survival of self-interest as an ingredient in the general will that guarantees the rectitude of the general will in yet another sense. The demand that a man surrender himself and all his force unconditionally to a larger power whose help he needs in order to survive calls up the fear that this power will be used to oppress him rather than to help him. The ineradicability of self-love is the basis for Rousseau's confidence that once true equality had been secured, the general will simply could not oppress the entire citizen body. If Rousseau believed it possible for man to become completely socialized, then the issue of guaranteeing the individual from oppression by a sovereign to whom he had alienated all without any reservations would become far more serious for him than it is. As far as he is concerned, nature has already seen to it that this difficulty will not arise. All that needs to be done is to guarantee true political equality. Natural self-love can be relied on to do the rest, in keeping the demands of the sovereign within proper limits. That self-love guides the deliberation of the sovereign. Once it has become clear that the social contract makes it impossible for any citizen to benefit himself at the expense of his fellow citizens and that any scheme that benefits him must benefit all the others, just as any scheme that harms any of the others must harm him as well, explicit limitations on the authority of the sovereign cease to be necessary. These limitations are built into what Rousseau requires of a decision before it can claim to be a genuine act of the general will. It is precisely in this context that Rousseau's most emphatic reference in the *Social Contract* to natural right occurs. He speaks of it in a sense that is completely at variance with what he had said earlier and he indicates to the reader that he is aware of doing so (2.4.2 and note). He distinguishes the citizen from the sovereign—earlier he had equated the sovereign with the citizen body—and he distinguishes within citizens between the duties they must fulfill as subjects and the natural right they must enjoy as men. This emphatic reference serves to accentuate the fact that Rousseau feels he has attended to the difficulty Hobbes and Locke tried to face by rendering certain contractual rights inalienable more successfully than they did, and that he has done so without having recourse to measures which would create doubts regarding where obedience is due.

Rousseau feels that he can afford to refrain from placing explicit restrictions on the rights of the sovereign. As long as *all* citizens are equal and mutually independent, that is, free, the workings of self-interest can be relied on to keep the burdens imposed by the sovereign on the subjects within reasonable bounds. If the citizens are not all equal and free, that is, if the common force is in fact controlled by some to the exclusion and hence to the detriment of the rest, if the vote in the assembly reflects secret factional arrangements rather than the sincere opinions of each voter, a legitimate sovereign is no longer in being. For Rousseau, therefore, it is not a question of limiting the authority of the sovereign but of seeing to it that a legitimate sovereign exists. If there is a legitimate sovereign, then by the mere fact that it is, it always is what it should be at least as far as the rectitude of its decisions is concerned.

For Rousseau, then, the nonoppressive character of the general will is not guaranteed by the disinterestedness of citizens but precisely by their "interestedness" under proper circumstances. Their interest moves them to strive for freedom and equality as a guarantee against being at the mercy of the common force they helped to create. Their interest also keeps the commands of the sovereign within moderate bounds. The sovereign can be trusted with absolute authority because it is composed of individuals naturally independent of it and prior to it. It is interest that directs the sovereign assembly in its deliberations (2.4.5). If the matter under discussion in that assembly were not of concern to all, if the interest of every citizen were not affected by it, it would not be a proper matter for discussion in the sovereign assembly. Just as the will of a private individual has that private individual's interest or good for its object, so the general will has the general or common interest as its object, and what is not of universal concern is not a proper subject for the sovereign's commands. What makes the general will *general* is not only the fact that every citizen without exception has the right to participate in its formation but that the matter with which it deals directly concerns every citizen without exception and does so equally. A perfect, though impossible, example of the kind of commonwealth for which Rousseau is seeking would be one in which all citizens were identical and would be affected identically by every action the sovereign took. Rousseau is well aware of the fact that this state of affairs cannot be realized (1.9.8). Bearing in mind his recognition of the need for unusual political astuteness in the sovereign assembly, we cannot be certain that he would wish to see it realized from every point of view. He certainly wishes to see it approximated, however, or, to put the matter more precisely, he wishes the respects in which it can be realized to be more important and powerful politically than the respects in which it cannot. How this can be accomplished will become clearer when we turn to his discussion of the nature of law.

The manner in which the general will has been explained up to this point is useful insofar as it discloses how the general will and the equality it imposes is derivative from particular wills and the preferences by which they are characterized. The fact that the general will derives its being from the wills of particulars, the fact that it does not have a natural being of its own of the kind individuals have, the fact that, from a certain point of view, the sovereign disappears into the individuals out of which it is made up, all serve to guarantee that the interest of each citizen will be attended to in the least burdensome manner possible: what makes Rousseau's sovereign moderate is the fact that it does not possess existence in its own right. The account given up to this point explains how the general will continues to be guided by the natural selfishness it transcends and modifies. It explains how the particular will is preserved in the resulting general will. It does not shed sufficient light, however, on how the particular will is transcended by the general will. What information it has supplied regarding this subject could be profoundly misleading if it were not supplemented by the clarifications contained in Rousseau's discussion of law.

The inadequacy of the way in which the general will has been described up to this point is reflected by the fact that the formation of the general will still appears to be an exercise in coalition politics

Sovereignty and the General Will

on the basis of that description. The general will seems, as it were, to be the resultant of an interaction in a field of forces, an interaction in which everyone else vetoes the desire of each to be spared having to bear his share of the common burden or to receive more than his share of some common benefit. This view of the general will is explicitly repudiated, however, by passages in which Rousseau points out that no general will can result from an interaction of particular wills in which one or a few are opposed by all the rest. Such a division suffices to show that the subject under discussion is not general in the sense required and is therefore not a matter regarding which the sovereign has a right to pronounce (2.4.6; 2.6.4).[37] The general will can only be concerned with matters that affect everyone equally. What this means begins to become clearer in Rousseau's discussion of laws that require risking one's life in combat as well as of laws that impose the death penalty (2.5).

The end of the social contract is the preservation of those who enact it. To preserve them the general will must take measures to protect them against foreign enemies and criminals. Such measures, to be effective, require endangering the very thing that one seeks to preserve, either through combat duty or through capital punishment. This fact, Rousseau thought, would not lead the assembly to water down the effectiveness of the measures it would adopt. The members of the assembly, it is assumed, will think of themselves as potential victims of murder rather than as potential murderers. In order to preserve their lives they will agree to forfeit them under certain conditions, and they will do so without hesitation. Without ceasing to be individuals, they will think of themselves as parts of a whole and seek to benefit themselves by benefiting that whole. Domestic security and security against foreign attack can only be enjoyed if they are shared. They can only be effectively supplied by organized society. In these cases, it is manifestly in one's interest to, as it were, transcend one's interest by seeking the common interest. It is manifestly in one's interest not to permit the effectiveness of the measures taken to secure the common interest to be diluted out of the desire to be treated gently if one should ever become a murderer oneself. In a word it is manifestly in one's interest to seek a universal solution. That solution undoubtedly entails a risk to one's life. The examples we have been discussing illustrate what Rousseau means by the general will and how he understands its relation to the particular will. The general will must be universal. It must be a law. There is no place for raw particular wills in the general will. Their absence is indicated in the example we are considering by the absence both from the discussion and from the thoughts of those in the sovereign assembly of how to make the prohibition against murder as tolerable as possible to murderers. If the particular will makes its voice heard in that assembly, it does so only insofar as it has transformed itself into a universal measure proposed for adoption by the entire citizen body regarding how the entire citizen body shall conduct itself for the good of all its members.

The foregoing example points in the right direction, but it suffers from an important defect. To see what is wrong with it one need only reflect on the difference between death in combat and capital punishment. Rousseau seeks to explain how laws enacted with a view to the self-preservation of all can have as their effect the death of some of those who wholeheartedly voted for them. To that extent, the two cases are parallel. But there is an important difference between them which the principles we have considered cannot yet account for. An army whose soldiers went into combat with the same spirit of resignation with which someone who accepts his punishment because he believes he deserves it goes to his execution would not be likely to win many battles. In order to be effective, a citizen army must be animated in addition by a public-spirited concern for the common good of the city, a concern that cannot be reduced to self-interest and to which self-interest may have to be, on occasion, completely sacrificed. Unless self-interest is supplemented by a bond higher than itself, the social contract will not be able to provide the security that the self-interest of each of the contracting parties enacted it to provide. That bond—the public-spirited love of the common good of one's city or one's people—is not intended by Rousseau to be habitually in conflict with self-interest, since such a conflict would sooner or later detract from its effectiveness. As long as the conflict is not a lasting one, the city can, in emergencies, command its citizens to risk their lives for it and depend on them to do so with vigor and spirit. For the most part, however, self-interest and public spiritedness coexist and modify each other. Self-interest moderates the burdens that the general will imposes on all citizens. Public spiritedness leads citizens to avoid seeking their advantage at the expense of the common advantage, something that requires a concern for the common advantage which is not reducible to the concern for one's own advantage and an acknowledgment that the common advantage is higher in dignity than one's own advantage. In the city as a whole, the higher bond

Sovereignty and the General Will

and the lower bond cannot exist without each other. Although neither can be reduced to the other, each influences the content of the other.

It is not only in relation to national defense that the need for a higher bond emerges clearly. Without a higher bond, the sovereign assembly would find it difficult to consider properly the laws it must enact. The requirement that the general will must concern itself only with matters that affect all equally cannot always be met as obviously as it is met by the prohibition against murder. Many laws must be enacted which do not literally affect all citizens in the same way. The law which establishes a police force introduces a distinction between citizens. So, too, do the laws which establish magistracies of various kinds and which engross Rousseau's attention in Book 3. As if to underscore the need to better understand the requirement that the sovereign must limit itself to matters of universal concern, Rousseau proceeds to give some curious examples of measures that meet it (2.6.6). The example he chooses—the institution of a hereditary monarchy or of class distinctions—are not selected because he favors them. They are chosen to illustrate the fact that a measure can be of general concern even though its adoption results in treating some individuals very differently from others. The only possible justification for adopting any such measure, however, is because it benefits the citizen body as a whole and each citizen as a member of that whole. When he deliberates on such laws, the citizen is intended to think of how they will affect him as a member of the citizen body rather than of how good his chances are, say, to be named to some high office that has been created. A public-spirited concern for the common advantage is necessary if the citizens are to deliberate soundly about such laws.

The sovereignty of the general will means the sovereignty of law. To qualify as a law, a decision must be genuinely universal. It may not concern itself with individuals except as nameless members of a general class. It may not even concern itself with certain matters that affect the entire citizen body at a given time. A declaration of war, for example, cannot be an act of sovereignty because it cannot be a law. Laws which are genuinely universal, may, as we have seen, command that some individuals are to be treated very differently from others. As long as they are considered and adopted because of the benefit they confer on the citizen body as a whole and on each citizen as a member of that whole, as long as no determination is made of the individuals who are to be treated differently, they are valid laws according to Rousseau's account.

The proper work of the sovereign assembly is to enact laws. In order to do it well it must be enlightened by its politically more able members. The soundness of its decisions depends on the soundness of their advice. They are therefore in a decisive position. Among the laws regarding which their advice will have to be sought will be those that establish the magistracies that are meant to execute and administer the decision of the general will, magistracies to the most important of which the politically most able are likely to be named. One of Rousseau's major concerns is to keep these magistracies— which he will discuss under the title "government"—subordinate to the sovereign. The assistance of the politically most able is needed to devise properly the measures that will assure the subordination of the politically most able to the general will. If the higher bond is effective, if the politically most able are animated by a public-spirited concern for the common good of their people, that assistance will be provided both with regard to such measures and with regard to other laws.

Adopting the social contract commits all the contracting parties to follow the direction of the general will; "however in order to follow it one must [first] know what it is."[38] Appropriate positive laws must be enacted before the general will can be obeyed. What these laws should be is not self-evident to those who have enacted the social contract merely because they have enacted it: "for the primitive act by which this body [i.e., the body politic] is formed and united does not as yet determine anything about what it must do to preserve itself" (2.6.1). That is why Rousseau's chapter on law (2.6) opens with the observation that although the social contract has given the body politic "existence and life," it still needs to be given "motion and will," that is, the capacity to act (cf. 2.12.1; 3.1.2) through "legislation." The continued and effective exercise of the general will depends on the adoption of suitable positive laws that will determine, for example, when and how it will conduct its deliberations and arrive at its decisions. The measures which first give rise to the higher bond of which we have been speaking will also have to be adopted by the sovereign assembly if the sovereign assembly is to do its work properly. Here a difficulty presents itself. The situation in which all these positive laws must be enacted is one in which the higher bond does not yet exist. The manner in which

Rousseau had previously responded to the question of whether the general will could err presupposed its presence. It assumed that the politically able would, out of public-spiritedness, help the general will discern what is to the common advantage. It assumed a harmony between political understanding and the common advantage that cannot be taken for granted in the absence of the higher bond. Accordingly, Rousseau reopens the question of whether the general will can err (2.6.10).[39] His previous answer to it breaks down in the hypothetical situation that immediately follows the adoption of the social contract. The harmony that had been assumed to exist is now assumed not to exist. The politically able may see what needs to be done, but one can no longer depend on their advice because the will of the politically able tends to favor rule by the politically able while the general will favors rule by the society as a whole. Yet without the advice of the politically able, the general will remains blind: "private individuals see the good which they reject; the public wants [wills] the good which it does not see" (2.6.10).

It is only after the reader has been prepared to appreciate the need for a higher bond that he is ready to face, in all its acuteness, the question of how a sound political order can have a legitimate origin. Since the coming into being of such a social order requires that the public spirit, which results from the enactment of certain measures, be present before they have been enacted and influence the workings of the assembly which enacts them, the reader can be forgiven if, to begin with, he finds the question unanswerable.

On the basis of the foregoing, the laws on which the effectiveness, and hence the legitimacy, of a legitimate sovereign depends, and which become binding only if they are enacted by a legitimate sovereign, are laws which it lacks the ability to discern and hence cannot enact. Once again the requirements of legitimacy are confronted with a difficulty which for a moment appears insurmountable. In Book 1 the difficulty that made its appearance there was overcome by means of the egalitarian social contract. Rousseau attempts to overcome the difficulty that he raises in Book 2 through his highly inegalitarian teaching concerning the legislator.

Chapter Two

The Legislator

Rousseau's recourse to the divine-human figure of the legislator (2.7.1 [and note], 2.7.2., 2.7.11) should force readers to reconsider any hasty conclusions from Rousseau's earlier discussion of natural equality (1.2) which appeared to suggest that he did not think men could surpass each other as much as gods surpass men. As we tried to show earlier, a careful reading of that discussion would have prevented an attentive ready from drawing any such conclusion. According to the view Rousseau now presents explicitly, the assistance of individuals whose superiority is precisely of that magnitude is necessary for the success of the social contract. In raising the question of how the framework which first makes it possible for the general will to go about its business properly comes into being in the first place, Rousseau is in fact facing the very difficulty some critics accuse him of ignoring, the difficulty of supplying a believable account of how a legitimate social order, in his sense of the term, can begin to be. The difficulty he faces is even more acute than that which his critics think he should face because Rousseau, unlike some of them, does not believe that social orders which fully live up to the requirements of legitimacy can simply drift into being. He thinks that they require, for their appearance, not only an appropriate "growth" but also the presence of extraordinary political understanding at the decisive moment or moments—understanding so extraordinary as not to be available merely because a need for it exists. This is not to deny that, once a social order of the required kind exists and can serve as a model, the imitation of it by other societies which find themselves in similar circumstances does not require political abilities that are as remarkable or as rare.

The question which compels Rousseau to turn to the legislator is a fact a more radical version of the questions he faced when discussing whether the general will could err: how can one secure the concurrence of wisdom and consent in political life? Resorting to the legislator might seem like evading the question by having recourse to a deus ex machina. One need only read the chapter on the legislator for this impression to be dispelled. Acknowledging the need for a legislator means acknowledging the need for political wisdom of a very high order at least at some time if there is to be any hope of founding sound political societies. If one could dispense with that requirement it would be easier rather than more difficult to found them.

The question of wisdom and consent, as Rousseau faces it, when discussing the legislator, has two poles. The first pole concerns the likelihood that wisdom equal to the task of founding a just social order will be available at the inception of society. The second pole concerns the likelihood that the members of a nascent society, without whose consent the dictates of wisdom cannot acquire the force of law, will be wise enough to discern the beneficial effects of the burdens and sacrifices they will be asked to make before experiencing those effects and before acquiring the habit of considering the common advantage as higher in dignity than their private advantage. In the transition to the discussion of the legislator with which he concludes his analysis of the general will (2.6.10) Rousseau seemed to take it for granted that at least some members in the sovereign assembly would see what measures were needed to enable it to do its work well. Once the discussion of the legislator begins, discerning what is in the common interest reveals itself to be far more difficult than Rousseau had hitherto supposed. To assume the ready availability of intelligence equal to the task of maintaining an inherited social order is one thing. There can be no basis, however, for making the same assumption regarding the task of first creating a legitimate social order where no social order existed previously. Furthermore, it may have been plausible to suppose an effective desire for the common good on the part of the people if one assumed an established social order to be in being. In describing the task confronting the legislator, Rousseau now explicitly rejects the supposition that public spirit can already be presumed to be present among a people that is first establishing a social order (cf. 2.6.10,

2.7.9). To add to all these difficulties, it remains to be seen why the very same consideration that earlier kept Rousseau from trusting the men of political ability in the assembly that is first forming a political society should not also keep him from trusting the legislator.

Rousseau does not ascribe a love of the common good for its own sake to the legislator any more than he had previously ascribed such a love to the politically perspicacious at the dawn of political life.[1] The public-spiritedness which makes the common good desirable owes its being to the work of the legislator, according to the hypothesis of Rousseau's discussion. What prompts the legislator to give that public-spiritedness existence is the desire, one might almost say, for divine glory (2.7.1 and note; cf. 2.7.2, 10, 11). Does the coincidence between the desire for glory and the common good not indicate, however, that at least in the legislator's case an exception must be made to Rousseau's rule that it is impossible for the agreement between the general will and the particular will to be constant and durable (2.1.3)? The example of the legislator confirms that rule rather than refutes it, according to Rousseau. While the glory the legislator seeks can only be achieved by serving the common good, his creation must have begun to decay before he can begin to receive the glory. Rousseau does not explain this. He limits himself to asserting that a people becomes famous only after it has begun to decline, and he implies that the legislator is well aware of this. What he has in mind is partly elucidated by the following passage of *Emile*:

> One of the great vices of history is that it paints men's bad sides much more than their good ones. Because history is interesting only by means of revolutions and catastrophes, so long as people grows and prospers calmly with a peaceful government, history says nothing of it. History begins to speak of a people only when, no longer sufficing unto itself, it gets involved in its neighbors' affairs or lets them get involved in its affairs. History makes a people illustrious only when it is already in decline.[2]

The glory desired by the legislators whom Rousseau calls fathers of nations cannot be conferred on them by their own people. These legislators had to "honor the gods with their own wisdom." They had to pretend that the code they were bringing their people was the work of the gods rather than their own work. They cannot receive

The Legislator

the glory they seek until they and not the gods are honored for their wisdom. This cannot happen among their own people as long as it remains faithful to their code. "The continuing existence of the Judaic law and the law of the Child of Ishmael, which for ten centuries has governed half the world, still proclaims today the great men who dictated them; and though proud philosophy and blind partisanship see them only as successful imposters, the true states- man admires in their institutions the great and powerful genius which presides over durable establishments" (2.7.11). Only those not under these laws can do justice to the genius of their authors. The divine glory sought by the legislator and the common good cannot both be at their peak at the same time. The good of the legislator and the common good not only do not coincide, they are, in a sense, incompatible. At the same time, however, the good of the legislator and the common good are, in another sense, insepar- able because the legislator cannot achieve his goal without achiev- ing the common good and the common good cannot be achieved without the legislator's services. The most one can say is that the particular will of the legislator and the general will are not in opposition. One cannot say that they coincide.[3]

According to Rousseau, a legislator is needed to establish a people and render it fit to be sovereign. In order to do this the legislator must "so to speak change human nature." To fulfill that task means not so much to produce citizens who constantly stand ready to sacrifice their private good for the common good and who always seek opportunities to demonstrate their readiness to do so, so much as to create public-spirited citizens who habitually seek their interest as part of the public interest and who do not seek it at the expense of the common good. The general will entails an egal- itarian republic which, in turn, cannot exist without a civic-minded citizen body. Rousseau imposes on the legislator, whose job it is to transform natural individuals into members of such a body, the requirement that they comply with the principles of political right as they have been elaborated up to this point. He draws attention to the fact that he has gone out of his way to repeat, in the context of the discussion of the legislator, the contention that no proposal can acquire the force of law unless it is enacted by the free votes of the people (2.7.7). The legislator can only advise. He cannot legislate.

In order to acquire the force of law, the suggestions of the legislator must be enacted by the general will. Before it can enact any laws properly, however, the citizen body must already be possessed of the public-spiritedness and the basic political arrangements that are supposed to first result from obedience to the laws devised by the legislator. The social contract, it would appear, would have to exist already, in order to first begin to be. By the principles which Rousseau has enunciated up to this point of his argument, and the validity of which he reasserts in the present context, the legislator is prohibited from imposing his views on the people by force. He must persuade the people to adopt his views. Under the assumption that governed Rousseau's first discussion of the formation of political society, and that he never explicity repudiated, the legislator must do this at the very dawn of political life as well as on subsequent occasions. Yet for the legislator to do this at the inception of political life does not appear possible. "In order for a nascent people to be able to appreciate the sound maxims of politics and to follow the fundamental rules of reason of state, it would be necessary for the effect to be capable of becoming the cause, for the social spirit, which must be the work of the institution, to preside over the institution itself and for men to be, prior to laws, what they must become as a result of them" (2.7.9). Rousseau proceeds to describe what legislators at the dawn of the social order *did* do when confronted with this difficulty. They resorted to fraud, according to Rousseau's blunt assertion. More precisely, they presented the proposals they wished the people to adopt, as divine commandments which they had been instructed to transmit. As described by Rousseau, the first founders, the founders of nations and peoples, were farsighted statesmen who disguised themselves as prophets bearing new religious codes.

> This sublime reason which rises beyond the capacity of common men is that whose decisions the legislator puts in the mouth of the immortals in order to sweep along by divine authority those whom human prudence could not sway. But it is not every man who can make the Gods speak, nor gain credence when he proclaims himself their interpreter. The great soul of the legislator is the true miracle by which his mission must be justified (2.7.1).

Rousseau's chapter on the legislator both begins and ends with the discussion of legislators whom Rousseau calls fathers of nations. The assumption on which that chapter is based is that the gods do not legislate. That assumption had already been stated and defended in the chapter which precedes and introduces the discussion of the legislator:

The Legislator

All justice comes from God, and he alone is its source; but if we knew how to receive it from so great a height, we should need neither government nor laws. Undoubtedly there is a universal justice derived from reason only; but this justice, to be admitted among us, must be mutual. From a human standpoint, the laws of justice are inoperative among men for lack of natural sanctions; they are but the fortune of the wicked and the misfortune of the just, when the latter observes them toward everyone and no one observes them toward him. Conventions and laws are necessary, to unite rights and duties, and to accomplish the purposes of justice (2.6.2 [Watkins]).

Up to the chapter on the legislator, all the laws that were discussed were human laws that did not claim to be anything other than human laws. The manifest need for man-made laws and agreements was what first provided the social contract with its reason for being. Now it appears as though, even if the gods do not legislate, the pretense that they do cannot be avoided, at least at the origin of nations and peoples. But is that pretense compatible with the principles of political right Rousseau has set forth? Can a society based on a code which a people has been duped into accepting because they believe it to express the divine will, and which a people would not dare to modify for that very reason, be a society in which the people regards itself as the only legitimate source of law? Can a people which believes the gods to be its rulers believe itself to be sovereign? Rousseau will return to this question in the chapter on civil religion and he will answer it in the negative. The first governments were theocratic. In the beginning men did not believe that their rulers could be human and they would not have consented to be ruled by themselves or any other human beings (4.8.1).

Although it begins and ends with reflections on the original inception of society and on the founders who presided over that inception, Rousseau's chapter on the legislator is not limited to founders of this kind. Also discussed are legislators who devised codes for peoples that were already in being, legislators who were lawgivers of cities rather than of nations or countries. Though many examples of such legislators are given, the foremost example is Lycurgus, who, unlike Moses and Mohammed, is mentioned by name in this chapter. Lycurgus is first presented to illustrate the principle that the legislator must not rule or hold any political office in the society for which he is drawing up laws. It is doubtful whether

Moses and Mohammed could be said to exemplify this principle. Republics which invited foreigners to draw up their codes of law, a practice which Rousseau cites with approval, are another example of adherence to this principle.

While discussing legislators of free peoples and fatherlands, Rousseau takes for granted the prior being as well as the freedom of the people in question. The Decemvirs—it is worth noting that for Rousseau a number of men can also be a legislator—serve as Rousseau's chief example of the dangers that result from failing to observe his rule.[4] What Rousseau calls Lycurgus's abdication is an example of how a legislator must proceed if what he does is to be compatible with the sovereignty of the people. On the other hand, the dangers of tyranny inherent in suspending the people's sovereignty on behalf of the legislator is illustrated by the Decemvirs. Yet the Decemvirs themselves are presented as forced to recognize that the people alone possess the sovereign right to make laws. When Rousseau speaks of legislators of free peoples, legislators who recognize and respect the sovereignty of the people, he is not speaking of legislators through whom a people is first born. When he speaks of legislators who first beget the people, he does so without referring to the sovereignty of the people. The conclusion would appear to be that the inception of society is a poor time for enacting the social contract. Not a people that is first forming but only one that is formed already is capable of embodying the principles of political right. The earlier presentation which made it appear for a moment as though the social contract first produced organized societies proves to have been an oversimplification. Beginning societies cannot live up to the principles Rousseau expounds. Only later in its development can a people hope to comply with them and then only under certain conditions.[5] What these conditions are is the subject to which Rousseau now turns (2.8-10).

Rousseau's discussion of what kind of people is suited to receive good laws takes it for granted that a wise legislator will be drafting laws for a preexisting people. In deciding the "age" or stage of development at which the people is best suited to receive good laws (2.8) Rousseau dismisses not only old age but infancy as well. At first glance, his solution appears to require a mean between infancy and old age, which mean he calls maturity as well as youth. His thought seems to be the following: a people that is too young will as yet lack the social spirit which must already be there for the legislator to work with if he is to do his job properly. A people that is

The Legislator

old and set in its ways, on the other hand, lacks the pliancy or the desire for a new code of laws. In the course of this discussion Rousseau explicitly distinguishes between two kinds of founders. First come those founders who create everything out of nothing (the phrase is Rousseau's). They make a nation proud of its distinctiveness and courageous. They are differentiated from legislators who can only appear later and whose job it is to provide political codes. Peter the Great of Russia is explicitly criticized for trying to act as a political legislator when he should have limited himself to being a legislator of the first kind. Because of his mistakes, Peter made it impossible for a subsequent legislator to build on what he had done. The recognition that two legislators are needed rather than one and that the first must not make the work of the second impossible is tantamount to an admission that a sound political order cannot be brought into being at a single moment. The spirit needed to make good laws work must already somehow be present in the people for whom these laws are intended. The simultaneous creation of a good political order and of a public-spirited people is rejected as impossible except, perhaps, in the case of colonies.

As Rousseau's discussion progresses, one encounters a small but important change in the answer he gives to the question regarding the age in which a people is fit to receive good laws. At first he advises the legislator against framing laws for a people that is either in its childhood or in its old age. The legislator must content himself with a people that is neither as pliable as a new people nor as cohesive as an old one. However, in restating his views on this point while summarizing his entire discussion of a people's suitability for good laws, Rousseau modifies the solution we have just outlined, and stiffens his requirement (2.10.5). Just before remarking that "what makes the work of legislation hard is not so much what must be established as what must be destroyed," Rousseau requires a people fit for legislation to combine the cohesion of an old people with the docility of a new one. One can readily understand why Rousseau should have been tempted to change his mind. He obviously preferred a solution in which the greatest docility was combined with the greatest cohesion, to a solution in which middling docility was combined with middling cohesion. But how could he expect any people to meet his new requirement, given the preceding analysis? Would not a people, in order to meet it, have to be old and new at the same time? Does he not himself remind us in this very paragraph of "the impossibility of finding the simplicity of

74   *Chapter Three*

nature combined with the needs of society" (2.10.5)? Can the later version of Rousseau's requirement be met, given this "impossibility"? Rousseau does not deny that meeting it is difficult and affirms that it can be met only rarely, but how meeting it can even be possible is far from clear.

In the course of explaining why a legislator should avoid framing laws for an old people, Rousseau had drawn attention to a striking exception. That exception is an old people which experiences rebirth as the result of a revolutionary crisis which threatened to destroy it. Such a people will prove to be both old and new. It will combine the pliability of infancy, the vigor of youth, and the solidity of old age. Every political order which Rousseau found admirable and whose prospects he found promising turns out to have been a member of this exceptional class:[6]

> This does not mean that, just as there are illnesses which throw men's heads into confusion and make them forget the past, there may not sometimes be violent epochs in the lifetime of states during which revolutions do for peoples what certain crises do for individuals, when horror of the past takes the place of oblivion, and when the state, consumed by civil wars, is reborn so to speak from its ashes and recovers the vigor of youth as it leaves the arms of death. Such was Sparta in the time of Lycurgus, such was Rome after the Tarquins, and such, among us, were Holland and Switzerland after the expulsion of the Tyrants (2.8.3).

Rousseau declares the kind of revolutionary crisis described in the quoted passage to be extremely infrequent. It can only occur once in the lifetime of a people, and only occur among a people which has not yet grown completely accustomed to a fully developed code of political law. Even under these conditions, in order for anything good to come of the crisis, it must be followed by a period of calm during which men enjoy "abundance and peace" (2.10.3). Should that calm give way to a storm provoked by war, famine, or sedition, the opportunity for establishing a sound political life vanishes. In a paragraph that points to the one we have just quoted by beginning with the same phrase and ending with the same word ("Tyrants"—"Tyrants"), Rousseau declares:

> This does not mean that many governments have not been established during these storms; but then it is these

governments which destroy the State. Usurpers always bring about or choose these times of trouble to get destructive laws passed, under the cover of public fear, which the people would never adopt when calm [*de sang-froid*]. The choice of the moment for legislation is one of the surest marks of which one can distinguish the work of the Legislator from that of the Tyrant (2.10.4).

Given the difficulty of meeting these as well as other conditions (2.10.5,6), it is clear why he did not wish a rejuvenating revolutionary crisis to be viewed as a model for imitation. On the other hand, one cannot help being struck by his examples of political societies that arose as a result of such crises: it is difficult to think of a free people that he praises which is not included (for the Corsicans, see 2.10.6). Can one infer that Rousseau believed such a crisis to be the only way in which a sound political order could arise? To draw this conclusion would be to ignore the difference between a situation in which no model of the social order he desires is to be found or in which the principles he teaches have not had any influence and a situation in which both a model and widespread recognition of the principles it embodies are present. In the later case, a gradual replacement, as circumstances permitted, of the discredited principles by the true ones might well be the more likely and certainly the more desirable course of events. If one bears his long-range goal for Poland in mind, his later writing on that nation offers one example of how he thought gradual change in the right direction could be effected under the proper circumstances.[7] To the extent that the foregoing presupposes that Rousseau believed his teaching to be true, it requires no comment. If he had believed some other teaching to be true, that is the one he would have taught instead. To the extent, however, that what has been said suggests confidence on his part that its truth would be recognized by posterity and have beneficial political consequences, we will soon have to face the question of whether this confidence is compatible with his repudiation of belief in progress.

What the original founder must do if the political legislator is to be able to later build on his efforts is to invest the common good with a sacred character by having recourse to religion. He imposes codes which the people do not feel free to alter, because they believe them to be divine in origin. The religious founder establishes what Rousseau will later call a theocracy. The question is how to reconcile theocracy with the only kind of political order Rousseau regards as legitimate, one is which the sovereign people is publicly held to be the only source of valid laws. The revolutionary crisis Rousseau describes shows one way in which the question can be resolved. The crisis does not destroy the piety and patriotism of a people. It does, however, focus that people's attention on political life, and in particular on its freedom. An awareness emerges that what has been destroyed must be replaced by new arrangements more conducive to freedom. To the extent that a people exhibits such a readiness and need for new institutions it is new or "reborn." Finally, the enthusiasm for freedom that results from such a crisis, when combined with patriotism, creates a condition conducive to the success of these new institutions if the people has the good fortune to meet with a wise legislator, and this means a legislator properly enlightened by the true principles of political right.

The early legislators whom Rousseau calls fathers of nations are presented as being men of "sublime reason." The codes they impose are conceived in reason. The end for which Rousseau affirms that they act—their desire for a distant but far-reaching glory among foreign peoples including their own, after it too has become foreign, so to speak—presupposes a successful appeal to reason for its attainment. The means through which Rousseau's early legislator attains his reward among foreign people are opposed to those he had to employ to win acceptance for his code among his own. To persuade his people to adopt his proposals, the legislator could not appeal to reason. According to Rousseau he had to deceive his people into believing that these proposals were the will of the gods, with the result that the gods and not he received the honor he desired. The early legislator can gain only from foreigners the admiration for which he seeks and he can gain it only by rationally persuading them to bestow it. The projects of the first legislators both begin and end in reason although the realization of their projects depends on a deceitful invocation of divine authority. It appears from Rousseau's discussion that legislators subsequent to the earliest ones were not under compulsion to have recourse to the gods. Political legislators frequently were foreigners to begin with. The initiative in approaching them lay with the cities for which they were asked to devise codes. The proposals of these foreigners were presented for adoption on rational grounds. Calvin is mentioned as one example of such a foreigner, and his political service to Geneva is clearly distinguished from his work as a theologian, work in which appeals to divine authority were of course not absent. Plato is later named as another foreign legislator. In Plato's case, however, it is not easy to separate his political philosophy from whatever actions he may have taken under its guidance. To the extent that a political philosophy convincingly calls for action and for cities of a certain kind, the author of that philosophy is also a legislator in a sense, even if he does not draw up a detailed code for this or that people. From the standpoint of reason, he is a legislator in the higher sense in that both the content of his teaching and the means through which he gains acceptance for it are universal or rational. From this point of view, Rousseau himself, as a teacher of "the true principles of political right" who "attempts to found the state" on the basis of these principles (4.9.1), is a legislator in the higher sense. The early legislators of whom Rousseau speaks are, as it were, proto-philosophers who point beyond themselves to political philosophers like Plato, Machiavelli, and Rousseau himself.

Did Rousseau in the end revert to the belief in the triumph of reason in human affairs which he had attempted to refute in his first political writings? After having denied that the perfection of reason as well as enlightenment tend to be accompanied by beneficial political and social effects, was he compelled to embrace some version of such a belief himself? Comparing Hobbes's views on this subject with Rousseau's will make it easier to arrive at an answer.

Hobbes faces the question concerning the power of reason in human affairs in a striking passage with which he concludes the second part of *Leviathan*:

> And now, considering how different this doctrine is, from the practice of the greatest part of the world, especially of these western parts, that have received their moral learning from Rome and Athens; and how much depth of moral philosophy is required, in them that have the administration of the sovereign power; I am at the point of believing this my labor, as useless, as the commonwealth of Plato. For he also is of opinion that it is impossible for the disorders of state, and change of governments by civil war, ever to be taken away, till sovereigns be philosophers.

The reasons that prevent Hobbes from drawing this discouraging conclusion are given next:

> But when I consider again, that the science of natural justice, is the only science necessary for sovereigns and their principal ministers; and that they need not be charged with sciences mathematical, as by Plato they are, farther than by

good laws to encourage men to the study of them; and that neither Plato, nor any other philosopher hitherto, hath put into order, and sufficiently or probably proved all the theorems of moral doctrine, that men may learn thereby, both how to govern, and how to obey; I recover some hope, that *one time or other*, this writing of mine may fall into the hands of a sovereign, who will consider it himself, (for it is short, and I think clear,) without the help of any interested, or envious interpreter; and by the exercise of entire sovereignty, in protecting the public teaching of it, convert this truth of speculation, into the utility of practice.[8]

Considerations of a more general kind on the part of Hobbes shed additional light on what he thought the prospects for the widespread acceptance and implementation of his doctrines would be. On numerous occasions he criticizes his predecessors in political philosophy for failing to produce a political teaching the truth of which would be beyond dispute and whose appearance would end the dangerous conflict between rival political doctrines. Hobbes traces the defect of his predecessors, in part, to their failure to recognize the importance of mathematical science as the paradigm of indubitable knowledge. Mindful of this paradigm, he claims to produce the first clear, exact, certain, and demonstrated science of political affairs. In keeping with this claim, Hobbes ranges himself with such giants of the new science as Copernicus, Galileo, and William Harvey. Hobbes affirms political philosophy or science to be no older than his first published work on the subject. From this it might appear as though no more were necessary for the universal acceptance, at least one day, of the truth about political life than for that truth to be set forth with great clarity and precision. Nevertheless, Hobbes is perfectly aware that such clarity and precision by themselves are incapable of producing such agreement. Not even the demonstrations of mathematics would be beyond dispute if they did not consist "in comparing figures and motion only; in which things truth and the interest of men oppose not each other." But in the doctrine of right and wrong "there is nothing not disputable, because it compareth men, and meddleth with their right and profit; in which, as oft as reason is against a man, so oft will a man be against reason. And from hence it cometh, that they that have written of justice and policy in general, do all invade each other, and themselves, with contradiction." Hobbes tries to avert this difficulty by developing a doctrine which is in conformity with the interests and rights of the overwhelming majority of men as well as in

The Legislator

conformity with the interests and rights of all sovereigns. "To reduce this doctrine to the rules and infallibility of reason, there is no way, but first to put such principles down for a foundation, as passion not mistrusting, may not seek to displace."[9] The passion which Hobbes believes to be the most powerful force in human affairs is fear, and in particular fear of violent death. His doctrine is intended to free men from the fear of mutual slaughter and to alleviate their insecurity and discomfort as much as political life can.[10] Mathematical precision and clarity, in other words, is not enough. The ingredient one needs in addition for Hobbes's project to succeed is realism, a doctrine in conformity with the most powerful passion by which "men as they are" are driven. It appears, then, that mathematical clarity and exactness can have their desired effect only after the realistic ingredient in Hobbes's doctrine has succeeded in eliminating or overcoming opposition to it based on interested motives and has enlisted the support of such motives. One could leave matters at this, if it were not for Hobbes's acknowledgment that the irrational fear of invisible powers is a stronger fear than rational fears are. Until fear of invisible powers is abolished, or at least weakened, the harmony between Hobbes's teaching and the most powerful rational fear, the fear of mutual slaughter, cannot be expected to overcome the obstacles to the rule of reason.[11] Hobbes, it would seem, must succeed in persuading men of the truth of his teaching before that harmony can be relied on to enhance the persuasiveness of his teaching. We are then compelled to return in a sense to the priority of the rational, mathematical ingredient in Hobbes's teaching; even if the fear of powers invisible could be overcome through public instruction of the proper kind, orders would first have to be issued for such instruction to be given, that is, rulers would first have to be persuaded of the merits and validity of Hobbes's teaching themselves. On the basis of this, one begins to understand somewhat more clearly why Hobbes thinks that the change to the kind of society which he calls for will be more likely to be made from above than from below, particularly if the interest which sovereigns, who find their authority challenged by those who know how to inflame men's "fear of spirits invisible," might have in making this change is remembered. Hobbes explains to such sovereigns why they can reasonably expect a willing acceptance from their subjects of the changes that they would be instituting.

Rousseau frequently expressed confidence that posterity would do justice to his work. That confidence was based on a belief in progress of a certain kind. In his *Discourse on the Arts* and his *Discourse on Inequality* Rousseau clearly repudiated the belief that there was any harmony between intellectual progress and its diffusion on the one hand, and moral and social progress on the other. If anything, he thought intellectual progress and the popularization of its results tended to be accompanied by, if they did not actually produce, morally and politically harmful effects. He did not deny, however, that intellectual progress of a kind had taken place. He calls Bacon, rather than, say, Socrates "perhaps the greatest of the philosophers." He refers to Bacon, Descartes, and Newton, but to no ancient philosophers, as "preceptors of the human race." In his *Discourse on Inequality*, Rousseau's authority on natural philosophy or science is Buffon rather than Aristotle. The account of the development of the human race given in the *Discourse of Inequality* is in large part an account of the progress of human reason—as well as of the devastating effect of that progress on human life. That progress is assumed to take place in spite of the constant revolutions to which human affairs are necessarily subject. The assumption governing Rousseau's account of the progress of human understanding is that, since the growth of language, advances in human knowledge have tended on the whole to be preserved for posterity and to be added to previous advances. This tendency to preserve previous gains in understanding has been enhanced by the discovery of printing.

Rousseau believed, on the whole, in the intellectual progress of the human race, and in particular in the superiority of modern natural philosophy or science to the natural philosophy or science of the ancients. However, he thought modern Europe to be incomparably inferior, morally and politically, to republican Rome and Greece. He had far more respect for ancient statesmen, legislators, and historians than for modern ones. As regards the fine arts, they were no more part of any long-range ascent, in his opinion, than were the political affairs of mankind. With reference to the fine arts and taste, Rousseau explained why he thought it would be impossible for them to form part of any such ascent: the fine arts make their appearance and flourish only where luxury is present; yet luxury ultimately undermines and corrupts the taste which makes it possible for the fine arts reach to their peak: periods of high artistic excellence are necessarily ephemeral.[12]

The depiction of the rise and progress of human knowledge with which the first part of the *Discourse on the Arts* opens presents man as "coming forth as it were out of nothing through his own

The Legislator

efforts." It shows man rising above himself and acquiring a Promethean stature enabling him to survey the entire universe. It then specifies a still greater and more difficult task: for man to come back into himself and learn to understand his own nature, duties, and end.[13] Rousseau leaves no doubt, however, that in his opinion the latter goal has not yet been attained. His account of the rise and progress of science and his conclusion regarding what still needs to be done are very similar to those in Hume's Introduction to the *Treatise On Human Nature*. For Hume, just as in ancient times the rise of natural philosophy was followed roughly one century later by the rise of moral philosophy, so too the rebirth of natural philosophy in modern times has been followed by the rebirth of moral philosophy after the lapse of about the same amount of time. For Hume, as for Rousseau, the new science of nature is superior to the old and it demands, as a complement, a new and superior moral science. Both men claim to be satisfying that demand. Both express shock, as Hobbes had done a century earlier, at the lack of unanimity among moral philosophers, and both seek to remedy it by advancing a teaching that does justice to the importance of sentiment in moral matters.

Rousseau thought that the task he had set himself was a greater and more difficult one than the one which Bacon, Descartes, and Newton had faced. Posterity, he believed, would preserve his achievements and recognize their importance. Given his belief in the intellectual progress of the human race, the expectation that his political teaching would have some influence over future events would not have appeared to him as altogether illusory. However there were absolute limits set for Rousseau to how much benefit his teaching could confer. The description of the typical condition of social man in the *Discourse on Inequality* makes clear that for Rousseau sound political orders must always remain exceptional. Freedom cannot be the fruit of all climates. To the extent that it is the fruit of some climates, that Europe is one of these climates, that an age of revolution is approaching in Europe, and that revolutions can sometimes be followed by the institution of legitimate regimes, there was *some* hope for *some* restoration of freedom in Europe.[14] Thanks to his teaching, there was less likelihood in the future that opportunties favorable to freedom would be wasted. It is by no means fanciful, then, to view Rousseau's own teaching, insofar as it is meant to guide political action, as performing a task similar to the one the legislator is required to perform. This meaning of "legisla-

82   *Chapter Three*

tor" complements rather than excludes the more usual sense of the term: Rousseau's writings on political philosophy were what led him to be invited to make detailed proposals for the constitution of Corsica. They did not take the place of such detailed proposals.

What has been said about Rousseau's views regarding the progress of reason would be incomplete if one did not take the following passage from *Emile* into account:

> In general, Emile will get more of a taste for the books of the ancients than for ours, for the sole reason that the ancients, since they came first, are closest to nature and their genius is more their own. Whatever La Motte and the Abbé Terrasson may have said, there is no true progress of reason in the human species, because all that is gained on one side is lost on the other: all minds always start from the same point, and since the time used in finding out what others have thought is wasted for learning to think for ourselves, we have acquired more enlightenment and less vigor of mind. We exercise our minds, like our arms, by having them do everything with tools and nothing by themselves. Fontenelle said that this whole dispute about ancients and moderns comes down to knowing whether the trees in the past were bigger than those today. If agriculture had changed, it would not be impertinent to ask this question.[15]

It should be noted that Rousseau does not deny, in this passage, that intellectual progress has taken place. He does not deny that "we have acquired more enlightenment." What he denies is the inference that "we" therefore have more powerful and independent minds or even minds *as* powerful and independent as those "our" predecessors possessed. Moreover, what Rousseau denies to his educated contemporaries as a whole, he does not necessarily deny to every single one of them.[16]

Rousseau declares freedom and equality to be ends at which every system of legislation should aim. These are in turn justified by the fact that they help to make possible a state in the strict sense of the term or a political society genuinely ruled by valid laws. Obedience to the general will or to law requires that no one owe anyone else any obedience that could conflict with the obedience all owe the law. It requires that citizens be relatively independent of each other, that they enjoy secure property rights, security of person, and security from oppression, that is, it requires civil liberty as well as civil equality or the absence of institutions such as slavery and serfdom. Freedom and equality are held necessary to produce the greatest good of all. The greatest good of all is not to be simply equated with the greatest happiness of all, however. That happiness, as a remark Rousseau makes in passing reminds us, remains the preserve of prepolitical peoples (2.11.4).

Freedom and equality are distinguished, as general objects of legislation, from various other objects which are said to be appropriate to different peoples owing to their peculiarities. Significantly, religion and virtue are listed among the peculiar objects of legislation rather than among the general ones. Rousseau clearly sets himself apart from the thinkers who made fostering virtue or inculcating true religion the highest tasks of political society. Not but that both virtue (in the sense of public-spiritedness) and religion will also prove to be indispensable for every properly framed political order according to Rousseau as well (3.4.6; 4.8.14, 31). However, they will make their appearance in his argument as necessary means to the end of political life rather than as ends in themselves. But are not freedom and equality also explained as being necessary means to the sovereignty of the general will or of law? If so, why should they be treated any differently from virtue and religion? The answer appears to be that their presence is more immediately and directly implied by the sovereignty of the general will, or by the rule of law, than are the presence of virtue and religion. One might add that freedom and equality stand closer to what the end of political society is later declared to be—preservation, prosperity, and flourishing population (3.9.4 and note)—and that they suggest that end more than do virtue and religion. Rousseau will later argue that without the support of religion and virtue the city will not be able to rely on the willingness of its citizens to obey the general will when doing so does not coincide with their private advantage. When Rousseau speaks of the need to "so to speak" change human nature if one wishes to make men into citizens he has in mind achieving a preponderance within the individual of the common advantage over the private good. To change human nature or to denature man means to foster public-spiritedness and piety, thereby endowing the common good with a sanctity that can overpower nature if necessary. Without the help of virtue and piety the social order will not secure the self-preservation which it was instituted to secure. Yet piety and virtue cannot be experienced as being in the service of self-preservation without losing the ability to serve it. The reasoning which leads the legislator to have recourse to piety and virtue cannot

Chapter Three

be the basis on which they are embraced and continue to be embraced within the society he founds.

The chapter with which the section on the legislator concludes (2.12) classifies the various kinds of laws which the legislator will have to prepare for a people ("To set the whole in order, and give the best possible form to the republic, different relations have to be considered" [2.12.1]). The laws governing the first of these relations—the obedience of the entire society to its own commands, or the relation of the sovereign to the state—are called political laws. They will be Rousseau's theme in the second half of the work (Books 3 and 4). We will return to them shortly. Rousseau distinguishes political laws from civil laws, whose purpose it is to preserve the relative independence of citizens from each other by guaranteeing their civil liberties, as well as from the penal law which enforces the two previous kinds. It is of the fourth kind of law that Rousseau speaks in a remarkable manner:

> To these three kinds of law is added a fourth, the most important of all; which is graven not in marble, or bronze, but in the hearts of the citizens; which forms the true constitution of the State; which gathers new strength every day; which, when the other laws grow old or are extinguished, revives or replaces them, preserves a people in the spirit of its institution, and imperceptibly substitutes the force of habit for that of authority. I am speaking of morals, customs, and above all of opinion; a part [of the laws] unknown to our political men, but on which the success of all the others depends: a part with which the great Legislator is concerned in secret when he seems to be limiting himself to particular regulations which are only the sides of the arch, while [customary] morals, of slower birth, are in the end its unshakeable keystone (2.12.5).

What was previously said about the distinction between fathers of nations and political legislators might have given rise to the impression that Rousseau believed there to be a kind of division of labor between them: the fathers of nations provide the unwritten laws, the customary morals and beliefs, which make it possible for the political legislator later to provide a code of written laws suited to a free, self-governing people. While there is some truth to this impression, it is misleading insofar as it suggests that framing the unwritten law appropriate to the political order he is instituting is not a major concern of the political legislator because what is needed along these lines has already been provided by the father of the nation. On the contrary, it appears that framing the unwritten law properly is the legislator's most important task. Unless he succeeds in it, everything else he does will fail. The legislator must frame a code of unwritten laws suited to the written laws he proposes. These are the most important laws he devises. Yet they are not, strictly speaking, laws. They are not acts of the general will. They do not come up for action by the sovereign assembly, although the measures from which they arise may. The "great Legislator" concerns himself with them "in secret" when he proposes various "children's games" and other "trifling institutions in the eyes of superficial men," institutions which he knows "form cherished habits and invincible attachments."[17]

Book 2, the main subject of which is law, ends by discussing a kind of law which never comes before the sovereign assembly and which does not owe its being and validity to an act of the general will. This kind of law—customary morals and opinion—is called the most important kind. The way in which Book 2 ends forces on the reader's attention the limits of law in the strict sense of the term as it has been defined there. Something similar occurred at the end of Book 1. We will find something similar occurring at the end of Book 3 as well.[18]

The legislator does not proceed inconspicuously in influencing the political, civil and penal law of a mature people. He can proceed inconspicuously in molding its unwritten law only because much of what he wishes to introduce is already present in a crude form. His task is to refine and reinforce what is already there rather than to create it out of nothing. This confirms the distinction to which we were previously led between the early legislator who first makes appeals to the sacred character of the common good possible and the later legislator who establishes a political order. It is because "men at first had no other kings than the gods" that sound political laws become possible later, and it is for the same reason that they become possible *only* later. The laws that determine the constitution of a political society are necessarily posttheocratic because they presuppose the rule of human beings by human beings rather than by gods.

That the political legislator must also concern himself with framing the political law of a people does not diminish his dependence on the proper preparation of the ground by the earlier legislator. What it means to prepare the ground properly is a question Rousseau does not attempt to answer coherently until his chapter on civil religion, where he discusses the beneficial and harmful effects of various kinds of established religions on political life. Generally speaking, the precise political institutions in which the principles of political right must be embodied and the detailed positive laws that create them are the theme of Part 2 of the work (Books 3 and 4), while the principles to be embodied by these institutions are the theme of Part 1. The entire subject of the legislator arises as the result of the need for a code of detailed positive laws. The discussion of the legislator, however, does not consider these laws in any detail. It confines itself to the most general considerations of what the legislator should be, what he may and may not do, and what kind of a people he should attempt to benefit. It is only the Section 2 of Part 2, for example, that one learns what kind of political institutions sovereign assemblies must be (3.10–4.4). Again it is only in Section 1 of Part 2 (3.1–9) that one learns what different kinds of governmental bodies there may be subordinate to these assemblies. The final section of Part 2 (4.5–8) parallels the final section of Part 1 (2.7–12) in that it describes institutions that are intended in their own way to accomplish what the legislator was called upon to do. The two things chiefly required of a legislator were extraordinary political understanding and the creation of a higher bond. The institutions corresponding to the legislator's extraordinary political understanding are what Rousseau calls the tribunate (4.5), which is akin to the American Supreme Court, and what he calls dictatorship (4.6), by which he means what we would call emergency powers. The extraordinary character of these institutions is reflected in the fact that, according to Rousseau, the one must and the other should have only an intermittent existence. Rousseau's censorship (4.7) and his civil religion (4.8) are intended to embody and to strengthen the higher bond of the social order.

Although it is tempting to understand the relationship between Part 1 and Part 2 of the work as that of principles to their institutional embodiment, it would be an oversimplification to do so. Part 2 does attempt to embody the principles laid bare in Part 1 but new principles come to light in the course of discussing the positive laws required to bring into being the institutions that embody the principles of Part 1 (e.g., 3.17; 4.8.31). One comes upon new principles of political right in Part 2, but it is in the course of attempting to realize the principles of Part 1 that one does so.

If Rousseau sharply distinguishes between the early legislator and the later, political one, it is puzzling to find him referring to

The Legislator

Lycurgus as an example of both the first and the second kind (2.7.1; 2.7.5). The puzzle deepens when one learns that Lycurgus also later appears as an example of a "liberator" who brings about the rebirth of a people (2.8.4, 3). We have seen that it is possible, according to Rousseau, for a people which has undergone the crisis of a revolutionary rebirth to be simultaneously new, mature, and old. It would also seem to be possible, according to him, for one and the same individual to preside over that crisis and that rebirth and so to be the liberator who helps bring about the revolutionary crisis, the early legislator who presides over a new people's birth, and the political legislator who supplies an existing people with a code. Lycurgus is all three. It should also be remembered that Rousseau's Lycurgus was *the* ruling authority in the regime which he supplanted with his new code.

Instead of speaking of the early and the late legislator, one can also speak of the old law and the new law. Rousseau invites us to think in these terms by opening his chapter on the legislator with a description of that extraordinary figure which employs language that believing Christians would regard as appropriate only to Christ. The chapter ends with a paragraph which refers to Christianity and which follows remarks concerning Moses and Mohammed. One rapidly sees however that the old law and the new law of which Rousseau is thinking are not the same as those to which these phrases traditionally refer. One also sees that the last part of the description of the legislator in the opening paragraph—the legislator's love of the glory that is to result from universal recognition of his political wisdom—makes that paragraph utterly inapplicable to Jesus as understood by the Christian tradition and that the last paragraph refers to Christianity only to warn against applying to it what has been said in the chapter about other religions and other legislators. Both the old law and the new law dealt with in the chapter are emphatically political. The new law is openly so. The old law disguises the fact that it is so behind the appearance of religion. The religion in question is ministerial, not autonomous. Later in the work genuine Christianity will be asserted to be the autonomous religion par excellence. The new law with which Rousseau's discussion of the legislator deals is essentially different from the new law in the traditional sense. It is a political law and ultimately it is the new law the principles of which are expounded by Rousseau himself. Lycurgus appears to be the prephilosophical legislator par excellence. He relies on the past to the limited extent of having himself all but declared a god by the Delphic oracle. None of this prevents the new law he brings from being wholly new. Finally, according to Plutarch, he seals his new law by choosing to suffer an extraordinary death. He deliberately starves himself to death after leaving Sparta on a voyage and making the Spartans promise not to make any changes in his law until he returns. If one puts these observations together it is difficult to escape the impression that Rousseau is inviting the reader to contrast the founder of Sparta with the founder of Christianity. The chapter on the civil religion will confirm this impression.

Rousseau declares political laws to be the only kind of law—the laws which make it possible for the whole body politic to act on itself, that is, to execute its commands to itself—pertinent to his subject (2.12.6). The question of what positive laws are needed to make the body politic capable of acting was already raised in the chapter that preceded and introduced the theme of the legislator (2.6.1, 10).[19] The discussion of the legislator dealt with the conditions necessary to put the correct answer to this question into effect—the extraordinary collaboration of exceptional wisdom and legitimate political authority—and it explored the circumstances under which these conditions were likely to be met, but the question itself remained unanswered. The concluding chapter of the section on the legislator reminds one of this question again and indicates that the remainder of the work will contain Rousseau's own answer to it (2.12.1, 6). In answering the question that he declared one needed a legislator to answer, Rousseau in the *Social Contract* is, in a sense, acting as a legislator himself. In another sense he is not acting as one since he cannot be said to perform one all-important task he assigns the legislator, the task of forming the unwritten law of the people he is legislating for. It would be safer to describe the Rousseau of the *Social Contract* as a legislator in the narrower but higher sense in which the philosophical teacher of legislators can also be declared to be one.

Political laws are the positive laws that enable the sovereign to act. They govern the relation between the entire body politic as commanding and the entire body politic as obeying or of the sovereign to the state, as Rousseau had defined these terms. That relation is said, by Rousseau, to be made up of relations between intermediate terms. What this means is spelled out in the course of Book 3. To state it briefly, every valid act of sovereignty is a law and every law results from an act of sovereignty. Because to be sovereign means to legislate, the sovereign cannot directly act on those subject to its laws. It cannot carry out its own laws. This function must be entrusted to an essentially different body that is created by the sovereign and is subordinate to it, a body that has to be permitted to deal with particular cases and circumstances. That intermediate body is what Rousseau calls government. The legislative authority is utterly excluded from executing the law. The executive authority is utterly excluded from enacting it. The action of the people as sovereign, on the people as subjects, is composed of the action of the legislative authority on the executive authority and the action of the executive authority on the subjects.[20]

Political laws determine what Rousseau calls the constitution of the state or the constitution of the republic (2.12.2; 3.13.1; 2.7.4)—expressions which do not have different meanings in the *Social Contract* as far as I am aware. Political laws determine the inner workings of the bodies without which the state cannot exist— the sovereign and the government—as well as the relation of these bodies to each other and to the people as subject (4.5.1, 2, 3). They decide how the legislative authority will be exercised. For even if, as Rousseau claims, "sovereign authority [is] everywhere the same" (3.4.6), one must still have ways of knowing when a large number of people listening to a discussion concerning public affairs is a public meeting and when it is a sovereign assembly. One must know what conditions have to be fulfilled for a decision to be considered a declaration of the general will. A simple majority, we will learn, may not be enough if the matter is weighty (4.2.10, 11). Moreover, the criterion of citizenship, that is, of membership in the sovereign assembly, must be settled if the sovereign is to do its work without confusion. Political laws determine which of the various possible forms or constitutions of government (3.1.15, 20) a political society will have. Rousseau, it is true, insists on the importance of distinguishing the constitution of the government from the constitution of the state—"One must remember here that the constitution of the State and that of the Government are two very distinct things and that I have not confused them."[21]—but the point of that distinction is to avoid the common error of confounding governmental and sovereign authority (2.4.6 end). The constitution of the government differs from the constitution of the state in the same way that the constitution of the human hand differs from the constitution of the human body. The constitution of the government is *part* of the constitution of the state.[22] The tribunate and the legislator are said not to be parts of the constitution of the state because the state can exist in their absence (2.7.4; 4.5.3,8). On the other hand, the civil religion described in the *Social Contract* will be said to be, in a later work by Rousseau, part of the constitution of the state because the civil religion will be, by positive law, the established religion of the state—it will be a most unusual established religion—and because Rousseau will hold that the state cannot exist without it (4.8.14). Part 2 as a whole (Books 3 and 4) will deal with political laws insofar as they establish or reinforce the constitution of the state.[23] The first section of Part 2 (3.1-9) discusses government as a component of the constitution of the state. The second section, which contains the second half of Book 3 and the first half of Book 4 (3.10–4.4), treats of the sovereign as a component of that constitution. The third section of Part 2 (4.5-8) deals with other institutions by which the constitution of the state is sustained.[24]

Government

Rousseau was fully aware of how novel his teaching regarding government was. In an earlier version of the work he declared: "Just as in the constitution of man the action of the soul on the body is the abyss of philosophy, so the action of the general will on the public force is the abyss of politics in the constitution of the State. *That is where all legislators have gone astray.*"[1]

The exposition of Rousseau's views regarding government is preceded by a prefatory remark which draws attention to the novel character of his opinions much more clearly than did the introductory remarks he made at the opening of Book 1. The exposition proper begins with a warning to the reader that suggests Rousseau's awareness of the difficult character of the chapter that follows (3.1.1). This warning is echoed on two subsequent occasions within the chapter: on both occasions Rousseau seeks to avoid a misunderstanding of a mathematical metaphor he chooses to employ to express his views on government briefly (3.1.12; 3.1.16).[2]

Rousseau compares government as he understands it to the middle term B of a proportion in which A is to B as B is to C; the sovereign is to the government as the government is to the subjects. The sovereign commands but does not obey. The people taken as subjects should obey but not command. The government must both obey the people as sovereign and command the people as subjects. Rousseau's interpretation of this proportion is political rather than mathematical even though some of its mathematical consequences furnish him with apt metaphors.

Each of the three terms of the proportion signifies an essentially different function: legislation, execution, and obedience (3.1.9). When, in keeping with Rousseau's instruction, one substitutes numbers for these terms, the meaning of the ratios that result will depend on the terms whose relation to each other is being considered. As we will see, 10,000 to 1 will mean one thing when it represents the relation of sovereign to subject and something entirely different when it represents either of the relations of which that relation is composed (sovereign to government and government to people).

The first application Rousseau makes of this proportion reads as follows: "The Government receives from the Sovereign orders which it issues to the people, and if the State is to be well balanced, there must be equality, everything adjusted, between the product or power of the Government taken by itself and the product or power of the citizens, who are sovereigns on the one hand and subjects on the other" (3.1.8).

The first part of this passage is readily intelligible. To understand the second part it is necessary to remember two things: (1) in Rouseau's time the power of a quantity usually meant—if qualifying words like third or fourth were not added—its square power; (2) Rousseau describes the task of government as that of bringing about the proper relationship "of the whole to the whole" (2.12.1, 3.1.8). In the proportion sovereign (people) is to government as government is to state (people), it is not only the government that appears twice. The people appears twice as well, first as sovereign then as subject. This state of affairs lends itself to Rousseau's speaking of the "power" of government as well as of the "power" of the citizens. Just as the will must match bodily power in order for bodily action to take place, so too the "power" of the citizens as a whole must be matched by the "power" of the government in order for the body politic to act. Rousseau makes two additional observations regarding this proportion. The first is that each place in the proportion must be occupied by the appropriate member. The sovereign people must not, as sovereign people, govern; the government must not legislate; the subjects must obey government. The second is that one can see from the proportion the infinite variety of governmental arrangements which can be desirable in a state as well as the unique character of the best government for a state under a given set of circumstances. What he means by this is made clear only when he begins substituting numerical quantities for the terms of his proportion.

According to Rousseau, the citizens as sovereign are to be taken collectively. The number to be substituted for them is, roughly speaking, the number of them that there are. The people as subject, however, that is, the people considered as consisting of diverse private individuals to whom the commands embodied in the law are addressed, are to count as one individual. On that understanding, the metaphor chosen by Rousseau ceases to be utterly baffling.

The first ratio explained by Rousseau is that between the quantity to be substituted for the sovereign and that to be substituted for the subjects. What that ratio expresses is *not* the power of the sovereign over the subjects. It expresses the *disparity* between the will of the individual subject and the sovereign will. The larger the assembly the greater the disparity will be because the less of a voice the individual will have in the decisions of the assembly. Rousseau, however, does not ascribe the dissimilarity between the will of a private individual subject and the general will simply to the difference between the private and the common advantage. Rather he describes that difference as one between morals and laws (3.1.13). We are no longer dealing with the difficulty, discussed in the second half of Book 2, of how to derive the public interest from the interests of private individuals. That difficulty made clear the need for a bond different from self-interest to supplement the bond supplied by self-interest. The unwritten law of the people, its customs and beliefs, are assumed, in Book 3, to be already present and to have modified the simple workings of self-interest. The assumption underlying Rousseau's description of the first ratio he discusses is that a sovereign assembly which is smaller tends to be relatively closer to the wishes of a people that has already been rendered fit for political life by morals of the right kind. The commands of a smaller assembly are apt to be far less in variance with morals and spontaneous public opinion than the commands of a larger assembly (4.1.1). It seems to be Rousseau's view that once a political order grows past a certain size one cannot even meaningfully speak of its morals (3.9.3) or expect any support from morals for its laws.[3] On the other hand, not even the best morals make laws superfluous. Enacting sound laws and carrying them out remains a task to be accomplished even where it is habitually accomplished. Laws and their execution were "almost" unnecessary in the Sparta of

Lycurgus; that is, they were necessary even there. The need for some government cannot be avoided.[4]

The greater the disparity between morals and the general will, the less one can expect conformity to the general will to take place spontaneously and the more coercive power must be granted the government for carrying out the general will. The very fact, however, that this power must be placed in hands other than those of the sovereign lays that power open to abuse.[5] Only of the sovereign did Rousseau say that by the mere fact that it is, it is always what it ought to be. Accordingly, the greater the power of action of the government becomes, the greater the power of the sovereign over the government must become in turn in order to hold the government in check.

The proportion with which Rousseau confronts the reader in his introductory chapter on government is a metaphor, and it is intended to be understood as a metaphor (3.1.16): "if, to express myself in fewer words, I borrowed geometrical terms for a moment, I am nevertheless not unaware that geometrical precision is not to be found in moral quantities." This is not to deny that some disputes can be settled by measuring and calculating (3.9), but it does suggest that such cases are not typical. The first relation Rousseau's metaphor invites us to consider is that between the size of the citizen body and the individual member of it. The greater that relation is, the less "relation," the more disparity, there will be between the will of individual citizens and the general will. The greater that disparity, the more powerful government will have to become. The first relation expresses lack of relation (3.1.12). The second relation expresses power of action, that of the government on the subjects. The third relation, that of sovereign to government, also expresses power of action. As the second relation increases, the third must also increase to balance it. The comparison of government to a mean proportional between two extremes is a fine metaphor for this complex state of affairs, provided its metaphorical character is borne in mind. The reader is given some explanation of why government is necessary and why it must become more powerful as the gap between the general will and morals widens. One does not learn in the general chapter on government how government becomes more powerful or how the power of the sovereign over the government is augmented. The power of government is one of the chief topics of the first nine chapters of Book 3, while the power of the sovereign over the government is one of the chief topics of the last nine chapters. It is not only in Book 3 that one finds this proportion discussed, however. An important institution for preserving the correct proportion, an institution external to that proportion, will be discussed in Book 4 (4.5).

In classifying law, Rousseau had attributed to political law the regulation of the relation (or ratio) of the sovereign to the state or of "the whole to the whole." However, as we have seen there, can be no direct relation (or ratio) of whole to whole, or of the people collectively to the people distributively. For there to be such a relation, a middle term is required whose relation (or ratio) to the people collectively on the one hand and to the people distributively on the other constitutes the desired relation between the two, even though it itself is not the people in either sense. This suggests to Rousseau the metaphor of a continued proportion. In this proportion not only are the intermediate terms the same although seen from different points of view (the government as issuing commands and as receiving commands) but the extreme terms are also the same although seen from different points of view (the people collectively and the people distributively). The people must be too weak distributively to disobey the government and too strong collectively to be disobeyed by it. The power of government must exceed the power of the people and it must in turn be exceeded by it. That the proportion is destroyed unless each of its terms does its proper work needs no further comment. Finally, the proportion metaphor brings out, for Rousseau, the great variety of governments which are good for different peoples and for the same people at different times. Almost every change in the extreme terms brings about a change in the middle term. It is at this point that Rousseau seeks to make clear what different kinds of relations can be found to obtain between the extreme terms. The number of people is chosen by him not because it is the only source of disparity between the general will and morals but because it easily lends itself to the illustration of what he means.

In a paragraph remarkable for its terseness, Rousseau extends the preceding analysis of the relation between government, sovereign, and subjects to the administrative workings of government itself (3.1.17). The following interpretation of it is tentative. The government, Rousseau says, resembles political society in miniature. By this he means that the difference between arriving at decisions and carrying them out is to be encountered here as well, even though the difference is not one of principle. Only where there is no difference between the body authorized to reach a decision and the body which executes it can the need for a new middle term be avoided. The typical situation Rousseau appears to have in mind is one in which there are a number of magistrates who belong to collective bodies, which bodies are alone authorized to make governmental decisions. The carrying out of these decisions may in turn require the making of subordinate decisions by subordinate bodies, until one finally reaches an individual magistrate with the authority both to reach the appropriate subordinate decision and to act on it. He is the "unity" to which Rousseau, in my opinion, refers here. The "series of numbers" is the ascending hierarchy of collective bodies to which he belongs. The series of fractions, I believe, refers to the subordinates whom the magistrate employs to help him carry out his decisions, subordinates who have no right to a voice in the decision reached, and whose authority derives entirely from his. The relation of the magistrate to his subordinates or of the series of fractions to "unity" is comparable to the relation of a monarch to his ministers and advisors. Finally, nothing hinders the existence of a descending hierarchy of committees of subordinates, just as in a nonmonarchical government there can be an ascending hierarchy of "numbers," that is, of collective governmental bodies.

One traditional way of classifying governments had been to distinguish them by the number of those who rule and by whether they do so justly or unjustly. Rousseau conforms to this tradition in speech but reinterprets it in the light of his own principles. Since all governments by definition must be legitimate, according to him (3.1.7), whether or not they are cannot be the source of difference between them.[6] The number of magistrates who could count as "units" in the sense we have just discussed, proves to the decisive consideration for determining the various forms of government, the relative force of each, and the conformity of its will to the general will (3.1.17: "magistrat suprême"; 3.3.8: "magistrats supremês"). He arrives at this principle of classification by pressing the analogy between government and the larger body politic. Just as the general will was not self-enforcing but required special measures for its execution, so too the decisions of governing bodies in whose deliberations a large number of magistrates have the right to participate are not self-enforcing but require the adoption of special measures for their execution. Rousseau assumes that the force at the disposal of a government, however organized, will be constant, and he infers that the more force it must expend on securing the compliance of its own members to its decisions the less it will have left to expend on enforcing the will of the sovereign. As he had earlier argued that the larger the people becomes, the more force will be needed to secure obedience to its sovereign will, so he now argues that the larger the government becomes, the more force will be needed to secure its obedience to itself. That force must be subtracted from the constant force that Rousseau assumes to be available to government. Every time a new middle term has to be introduced in implementing a governmental decision, an additional expenditure of force is required. He illustrates his point by referring to two extreme cases, monarchy and democracy. In monarchy, the right to decide and the right to act are conferred on the same individual. No intermediate middle terms are needed before one reaches an "indivisible middle term." One starts with only "one supreme head or magistrate." Accordingly no subtraction whatever of force is required. The king has at his disposal the entire public force. At the other extreme we have democracy, in which the people not only legislate as sovereign but also govern. Here the amount of force that must be expended internally by the government equals the amount of force that is required to execute the general will.

The principle to which Rousseau repeatedly appeals in discussing what makes government stronger or weaker is that the use of force depends on the intensity of will. His view is that the greater the unanimity with which the magistrates will that something be done, the more effectively they will do it. He further claims that the more magistrates there are, the less unanimity there will be. The reason for this, according to him, is to be found in the three different wills that can be distinguished within every magistrate and in the relative power of these wills. The magistrate has a will insofar as he is a private individual. He is also a member of the government and as such shares in the will which is common to all magistrates and which has the well-being of the government as a whole for its object. Finally, as citizen, he partakes of the general will. Rousseau affirms that according to the natural order the private will, directed to one's own good, is the strongest while the general will is the weakest of the three. The reason why the general will is weaker than the corporate will of the government is that the private will has less influence over the former than it does over the latter; the corporate will of government is open to greater influence by the private will. The deliberations of government are not safeguarded against private interests by the requirement that government concern itself only with matters of the utmost generality affecting everyone as a whole. Moreover, each magistrate has more weight in the deliberations of the government than in those of the sovereign, both because the governmental body is smaller than the sovereign, and because each magistrate can throw into the scales the additional weight which is conferred on his desires by the governing function he performs. The relative power of these wills required by a perfect system of legislation is the reverse of that which flows from the order of nature. The sound social order requires that the general will be dominant, the corporate will of government subordinate to it, and the will of private individuals nullified by the preponderance of the other two. It is not immediately apparent how Rousseau understands the relation between the natural order of these wills and the order required by a perfect system of legislation. On the one hand, we were told earlier that without the transformation of man's nature solitary man could never become a citizen, and that without citizens a legitimate political order would not be possible. On the other hand, in discerning what makes governments stronger and weaker Rousseau argues as though the natural order of wills were their true order, which is why the less the private will has to suffer compromise, that is, the smaller the number of those between whom agreement must be reached, the less its vigor is impaired. Does this mean that Rousseau regards the natural order as the simply true order, and the order represented by a perfect system of legislation, to the extent that anything like it is to be found, as a mere facade?

The impression one might receive is that the natural order is the simply true order for Rousseau even in political matters. That impression is created by the fact that his analysis of what makes governments stronger or weaker presupposes that the will of private individuals is still very much intact whereas that will, it would seem, would have to be "null" in a "perfect system of legislation" (3.2.6). Yet if one looks at Rousseau's full statement regarding what a "perfect system of legislation" must accomplish (2.7.3) one will find a description of it which is compatible with the survival and even the vigor of natural selfishness.

At the very opening of the *Social Contract*, Rousseau indicated that his analysis of political right would give its due to "men as they are" and to "what interest demands" and that he would seek to reconcile these with "what right permits." Rousseau adheres to this intention when he derives the one and only legitimate way of

99   *Government*

forming a political society from the requirements of self-preservation. As his analysis progresses, however, it reveals that the
concern with self-preservation and security, no matter how long-
range and how enlightened, is not sufficient to secure voluntary
compliance with the common good. If a murderer voluntarily goes
to his execution in keeping with an agreement to which he sub-
scribed wholeheartedly and without mental reservations when he
entered political society, it is no longer out of a concern with his own
self-preservation and security that he does so. Such a concern might
explain why he struck the bargain in the first place, but not why he
adheres to it to the end. Seeing to it that justice and utility are not
divided is not the same as simply reducing justice to utility. Moreover, as we saw, a soldier who goes into combat in the same spirit in
which a repentant murderer might accept his execution will not be a
very good soldier. A sound society, if not every citizen, requires a
stronger bond than that which the interest born of the concern with
security provides. The task of the legislator is to supply a bond that
transcends self-preservation even if—in cases like his own—it does
not always transcend self-interest. The public-spiritedness, the love
of country and of freedom, which the legislator seeks to foster are
intended to make man social and to lend support to the universal
laws enunciated by the general will. They do not annihilate the
particular will. Such an annihilation would not be either desirable or
possible according to Rousseau. As soon as one can be reasonably
sure that the individual will seek his interest as part of the larger
whole to which he belongs and not at the expense of that larger
whole, his interest provides an indispensable guide and test for
ascertaining what the common interest is. The workings of political
life never become automatic and effortless. Enforcement never
becomes altogether superfluous. The particular will in a perfect
system of legislation may be always surmounted by the general will,
but it is always in need of being surmounted because it is always
struggling against the general will, even if that struggle is not revealed to public view. In his most cautious and precise description of
the conditions under which "the highest perfection" has been
attained by a system of legislation, Rousseau does not require that
the will of private individuals should be reduced to zero. He requires that "the force acquired by the whole be equal or superior to
the sum of natural forces of all individuals" (2.7.3). Accordingly, we
need not be astonished to later learn that "the particular will acts
ceaselessly against the general will" (3.10.1). The fact that the two

Chapter Four

struggle ceaselessly does not mean that either of them is always victorious. In a sound political order, the general will always triumphs. In a republic so corrupt as to be on the verge of collapse, the particular will always triumphs, although there too, Rousseau will later try to show, the struggle with the general will continues even if the general will is always defeated in that struggle (4.1).

Rousseau's analysis of government presupposes the conclusion that had been previously reached regarding the proper objects of the general will. It also presupposes the necessity to instill a public-spirited love of republican freedom and equality if there is to be a sound political order. As we noted previously, when Rousseau speaks about the disparity between the private will and the general will, a disparity which increases as the number of citizens grows, he is not thinking of a raw and unformed unparticular will but rather of a particular will that has been modified by the legislator. That is why he can substitute the disparity between morals and laws for the disparity between the particular will and the general will. Unless one remembers this, the problem Rousseau poses will become simply insoluble under all circumstances. If all that ever confronted the general will were the unmitigated particular will, there would always be some disparity between the two requiring corrective governmental action. For the naked particular will (which seeks preferences) is always at odds to some extent with the general will (which seeks equality). Yet the cure would merely aggravate the disease. Nothing could prevent government and its powers from becoming instruments of the particular will. And since it is government that must secure the obedience of the particular will, it is difficult to see what could secure the obedience of the particular will that had worked its way into government and was using it for its own ends. For, according to the natural order, the particular will is stronger not only than the general will but also than the corporate will of government. The problem government is meant to solve would not only be insoluble under these conditions but a solution to it could not even begin to be approximated.

If one follows Rousseau's indication, however, and thinks of the general will as confronting public-spirited citizens who have private interests which are of concern to them but by which they are not simply dominated, matters become a good deal less simple. Not only can the unwritten law appropriate to a republic greatly facilitate the work of government, without making government or laws superfluous, but it also instills a reverence for the written law and the institutions created by it. The unwritten law lends strength to written laws which command things the unwritten law does not command. This gives the sovereign which has been compelled to strengthen some scope to enact measures which will keep government subordinate to it. As we will see, various ways to keep in check a government that had to be strengthened are proposed by Rousseau. Some concern the way the strengthened government is constituted internally (3.7.4). Others, discussed throughout Section 2 of Part 2, concern the conduct of sovereign assemblies of the people (cf. 3.13.3). Still others recommend instituting special tribunals (3.7.5; 4.5). Rousseau teaches that the rectitude of government diminishes as its power increases (3.2.12). This creates difficulties that the sovereign must face but that it also can face if certain conditions are present.

Even though government means something different for Rousseau from what it had traditionally meant, he continues to use the names monarchy, aristocracy, and democracy. It is not altogether clear why he does so, particularly since his analysis reveals that there is an almost unlimited variety of kinds of government to match the unlimited variety of circumstances with which these governments must be paired (3.3.5, 6). The three traditional names would thus seem to be deceptive. They at best have the merit of terms like "thin," "normal," and "fat," with the difference that these terms have normative implications which Rousseau seems to renounce for the political terms (3.1.9, 3.3.7). He chooses these terms to designate an almost unlimited variety of kinds of government and he appears to refuse to say that any one of them is superior to the others. This is consistent with the impression he seeks to create that his principles of political right are compatible with all forms of "government."[7] A discussion of the three traditional forms of "government" follows. The upshot of that discussion, however, is somewhat startling given the above: Rousseau quietly rejects both democracy in the strict sense and monarchy as sound forms of government (3.4.3, 8; 3.6.16). Only aristocracy of a very special kind—elective aristocracy—will prove to be acceptable in the final analysis. The elective aristocracy of which he approves will show itself capable of accommodating all the different governmental arrangements that Rousseau will finally wish to accommodate. While the manner in which he proceeds may occasion some bewilderment unless one follows the steps of his argument with care, his results, we will attempt to show, are as consistent with themselves and with his principles as his manner is with his desire not to appear to be subverting almost all governments in existence.

Rousseau's discussion of the three forms of government often adheres to the special sense he assigns to the term "government." Yet on occasion he reverts to its common meaning. Thus, when he says that monarchy is the most common form of government (3.3.4), he is not speaking of regimes in which the people are sovereign. He is aware of how uncommon such regimes are in the world (2.10.5 end; 3.8.1). His lengthy discussion of monarchy will reveal itself to be an attack on monarchy in the ordinary sense of the term. In discussing aristocracy, he will consider examples of it some of which are incompatible with the sovereignty of the people (3.5.4; 3.5.5 note). In fact, Rousseau avails himself of the opportunity his adoption, in speech, of the traditional classification of government affords him to settle accounts with forms of sovereign authority other than the one he regards as alone legitimate and in particular with the form of sovereignty that he regards as most widespread. Even his discussion of democracy at times becomes a discussion of democratic sovereignty rather than of democratic government.

When Rousseau rejects democracy as a form of government he is speaking of democracy as a form of administration. His observation that one cannot imagine a people continually assembled to execute its own laws and that such execution cannot be assigned to a committee without changing the form of government makes perfect sense provided one remembers that government means the execution of law. The argument for democratic government on the grounds of its rectitude proves, on closer inspection, to be questionable; the impartiality of the sovereign people would be impaired if that people were to preoccupy itself incessantly with private interests. A government that corrupts the sovereign and then manages public affairs in conformity with its will is more to be feared than a government which deviates from the general will but does not destroy it.[8] Sovereignty is in at least as much danger of being usurped by a democratic government as it is by a monarchical or an aristocratic government. Rousseau therefore repudiates the strictly democratic administration of public affairs as both undesirable and impossible.

The fact that Rousseau rejects strictly democratic government does not mean that he rejects any and every role for the people in the administration of public affairs. How important the role is that they are finally required to play becomes gradually and increasingly

Government

apparent in the course of Book 3. Even in the present chapter some light is shed on this point. When he discusses the circumstances that are necessary for there to be a democratic government, far from pronouncing them to be unattainable he affirms that some of them are more or less necessary in every well-constituted state.

Rousseau's chapter on democracy both begins and ends by declaring democracy pure and simple not to be a form of government suited to "men as they are." One of the reasons for this will be that the conditions required for democracy are even less attainable than those that were necessary for the Sparta of Lycurgus (3.5.9). These conditions cannot exist without republican virtue, as Montesquieu had pointed out. On the other hand, these conditions contribute to the continued existence of republican virtue. However, rather than declaring republican virtue to be as unattainable as these conditions were said to be, Rousseau criticizes Montesquieu for failing to make virtue or public-spiritedness the principle of every sound political order. In this portion of the argument, the peculiar vocabulary Rousseau employs may make the point of his objection to Montesquieu difficult to follow. In the traditional classification the form of government depended on who wielded supreme political authority in it. For Rousseau, as we have seen, only the people in person can legitimately be given that authority. If it were stated in traditional terms, Rousseau's teaching would have to be expressed as the view that democracy is the only legitimate form of government. His views regarding the conditions under which a sound democracy in the usual sense is possible are not all that different from Montesquieu's, any more than is Rousseau's assertion that virtue must be the principle of every legitimate, that is, democratic, government. By using the word "government" in a most unusual sense Rousseau finds it possible to affirm in speech that monarchy and aristocracy are no less legitimate forms of government than democracy is. His agreement with Montesquieu regarding democracy is far greater in fact than it appears to be in speech. Rousseau can say that virtue must be the principle of every well-constituted state and not only of a democracy because by a well-constituted state he means one in which the people are sovereign, or what Montesquieu would call a democracy. The democracy Rousseau rejects in the chapter on democracy is a form of administration rather than of government. Democracy, in Rousseau's sense, is undesirable for men and, strictly speaking, impossible. Democracy in Montesquieu's sense is, with some modifications, the

104   *Chapter Four*

only legitimate political order according to Rousseau. If these distinctions are borne in mind, the apparent contradiction between Rousseau's rejection of democracy and his requiring every sound political order to meet necessary conditions for its existence need create no confusion.[9]

Rousseau begins his discussion of aristocracy as he did his discussion of democracy, with remarks linking his subject with the conclusions about government in general which he had previously reached. He notes the respect in which aristocratic government is free of an important defect of democracy because government in an aristocracy is a different body from the sovereign people. He also emphatically reaffirms that a government's right to command the people derives exclusively from its obedience to them in their capacity as sovereign.

Rousseau illustrates the various kinds of aristocracy there can be by describing how one kind changes into another (3.5.2, 3). The first societies were governed by an aristocratic council consisting of heads of families. Rousseau will call this kind of aristocracy natural. Those who wield authority in it do so by virtue of their superior wisdom and experience. He distinguishes this kind of aristocracy from the kind which sooner or later replaces it and in which superiority in wealth or political influence—a superiority which owes its very being to convention—is the basis on which one is chosen to be a member of the governing council. Finally, in hereditary aristocracies the right to be a member of the governing council becomes part of the inheritance that fathers pass on to their children.

The two brief paragraphs in which Rousseau outlines the transition from natural to hereditary aristocracy delineate a decline and fall. Natural aristocracy as practiced by the American Indians is praised. The substitution, in an elected aristocracy, of wealth and power for wisdom and experience certainly is not an evident change for the better. Finally, when political authority becomes something that certain families own, the inclination exhibited in the transition from natural to elective aristocracy is carried through to the end and a seat that was once reserved for age and experience is now filled by inexperience and youth. The views Rousseau proceeds to express regarding the three kinds of aristocracy, however, do not quite correspond with the impression of a continuous decline created by his account of the transition from one kind to another. Natural aristocracy is declared to be politically irrelevant, a result which is not surprising in view of the example chosen by Rousseau to illustrate its virtues. Nor is it altogether startling to find hereditary aristocracy described as a bad form of government, even if its description as the worst of all, and therefore as worse than despotism, may occasion some wonder. But to be told that rule by a council in which wealth and power have replaced age and experience as the criterion of membership is the best of all forms of government is, to begin with, astonishing. Also, if not equally, astonishing is Rousseau's willingness to pronounce some form of government best of all and some other worst of all. Finally, his declaration that, of the three kinds of aristocracy, elective aristocracy alone is, strictly speaking, worthy of the name, is in need of some explanation.

Rousseau characterizes the first governments on three occasions in the *Social Contract*. He first speaks of them near the beginning of the work in a chapter entitled "Of The First Societies," and he describes these governments as paternal (1.2.3). He last speaks of them near the end of the work, where one learns that "in the beginning men had no Kings other than Gods, and no other Government than Theocracy" (4.8.1). (The remarks about them being discussed here occur near one of the middle chapters of the work.) Are Rousseau's observations in the *Social Contract* about the first governments compatible with each other?

Natural aristocracy is compatible with a family ruled by its father or oldest member since the governing council of such an aristocracy is composed of these family heads. How an aristocracy of this kind could be compatible with theocracy is suggested by the indications to which Rousseau appeals in trying to show that the first societies were aristocratically ruled: he lists a series of names by which aristocratic rulers and the councils to which they belonged were traditionally known, with the intention of showing that a reference to old age was an essential part of the meaning of each of them. The first word to appear on the list is "priests." The council of elders was at the same time a council of priests. The view that emerges is that the first societies were religious in character and that their members not only did not regard the laws under which they lived as human in origin but that they would not have thought them worthy of obedience if they were merely human. (Judaism and Islam were treated as outstanding in the chapter on the legislator not because they were ruled by divine laws but because of the extraordinary character and durability of the divine laws by which they were ruled.)

That natural aristocracy is suited only to simple times might appear obvious. Less clear is Rousseau's reason for implying that natural aristocracy is not aristocracy properly speaking (3.5.4, last sentence). Since aristocracy means government by the best, and since in the simple times of which Rousseau is speaking those who are older and more experienced are likely to be better than those who are not, why should the government of the first societies not deserve to be called an aristocracy while governments, membership in which is determined by wealth and power, do deserve such a title? To answer this question we must remind ourselves of Rousseau's definition of government in the strict sense, which presupposes a society in which men realize that the laws under which they live owe their being to human enactment. Law in the strict sense, and therefore government in the strict sense, are impossible in a theocratic society. Natural aristocracy cannot be aristocratic government properly speaking because it cannot be government properly speaking.

Elective aristocracy as Rousseau describes it in his outline of the transition from natural to hereditary aristocracy is not quite the same as the elective aristocracy he calls the best of all governments. In his outline, elective aristocracy was the rule of those whose superiority was due to conventional attributes rather than to natural ones (3.5.3). The elective aristocracy he describes in the body of the chapter, however, is one in which those who are outstanding in honesty, in soundness of understanding, and in experience are chosen to manage public affairs (3.5.5). The difference between the two kinds of aristocracy the reader encounters corresponds to the difference between an ordinary elective aristocracy and the one Rousseau seeks to establish. That difference depends on the way in which aristocratic magistrates are selected. Rousseau calls attention in a note to the supreme importance of the right kind of election in an aristocracy (2.5.5 note). He does not, however explain there what the right kind of election is, in spite of the fact that whether one ends with the best or the worst of all governments depends on it. One can only surmise what his views on elections are from the fact that he rejects two ways of appointing magistrates. The magistrates of an aristocracy are not to be chosen by those whom they are to join or replace. Rousseau rejects aristocracy by cooptation because it inevitably leads to the worst of all governments. What is suggested, but not stated until later in the work, is that the magistrates in a good aristocracy will be chosen by the people (4.4). The election of this or that individual to be a magistrate will not be an act of the general will, however. It will itself be an act of government. Rousseau's omission of a discussion of those who do the electing in an elective aristocracy, his concentration on those whom they elect, blurs the degree to which the people will be part of such a government. This omission on his part will be remedied in the second half of Book 3. The more the danger of usurpation of sovereignty by the government becomes apparent, the more distinctly Rousseau enunciates the need for the people in person to play an important role as government in addition to the role they play as sovereign.

In his *Discourse on Inequality*, Rousseau praises Geneva for having a wisely tempered democratic government. The word "government" is used in its common meaning and designates the sovereign of Geneva. That it does not mean government in the sense the word acquires in the argument of the *Social Contract* is clear from Rousseau's praise of the Genevans for not imitating the mistake of democratic peoples who tried to do without magistrates altogether or who only allowed a precarious authority to those whom they permitted to exist, that is, peoples who "imprudently retained the administration of civil affairs and the execution of [their] own laws." He adds that "such must have been the rude constitution of the first government emerging immediately out of the state of nature, and such was also one of the vices that ruined the Republic of Athens."[10] In the *Discourse* itself, however, the account given of the rise of government is significantly different from the one we have quoted. Three stages in the development of political society are described, just as previously three stages in the state of nature had been distinguished. (In both cases the central stage is the one in which the greatest happiness is to be found, although in the state of nature the happiness is typical, and in the state of civil society it is exceptional.) The first political orders, in Rousseau's hypothetical account, had laws, but made no provision for their execution. The anarchy that resulted from this arrangement compelled men to institute magistracies for administering the law that had been agreed on:

> At first Society consisted only of some general conventions which all individuals pledged to observe, and regarding which the Community became the guarantor for each individual. Experience had to show how weak such a con-

stitution was, and how easy it was for lawbreakers to avoid conviction or punishment for faults of which the Public alone was to be witness and judge; the Law had to be evaded in a thousand ways; inconveniences and disorders had to multiply continually in order that men finally thought of confiding to private persons the dangerous trust of public authority and committed to Magistrates the care of enforcing obedience to the deliberations of the people.[11]

Why the magistracies men established at this point differed in character is made clear later:

The various forms of Governments derive their origin from the greater or lesser differences to be found among individuals at the moment of Institution. Was one man eminent in power, virtue, wealth or credit, he alone was elected magistrate, and the State became Monarchical; if several approximately equal among themselves prevailed over all others, they were elected jointly and there was an Aristocracy. Those whose fortune or talents were less disproportionate, and who were the least removed from the State of Nature, retained the supreme Administration in common and formed a Democracy. Time verified which of these forms was the most advantageous for men. Some remained solely subject to Laws, others soon obeyed Masters. Citizens wanted to keep their freedom, subjects thought only of taking it away from their neighbors, since it was unbearable that others should enjoy a good which they themselves no longer enjoyed. In a word, on one side were wealth and Conquests, and on the other happiness and virtue.[12]

The *Discourse on Inequality* is no less critical than the Epistle Dedicatory was of the attempt by a people to dispense with magistrates—simply or for all practical purposes—by substituting itself for them. It is a serious mistake, according to Rousseau, for a people to retain the administration of civil affairs. But it is no less serious a mistake, we learn in the *Discourse* itself, for a people not to retain the supreme administration of public affairs. Hints to this effect were not lacking even in the Epistle Dedicatory.[13] What it could mean for a people to retain the "supreme administration" of public affairs without retaining their administration pure and simple will gradually become clear in the second half of Book 3. (It should not be forgotten that in the vocabulary of the *Social Contract*

Government

"supreme administration" and "government" are equivalent expressions [3.1.7]).

In the elective aristocracy praised by Rousseau magistrates are chosen for their virtue and wisdom, whereas in the one he had mentioned previously they were chosen for their power and wealth. Considerations of wealth, however, are not absent from the elective aristocracy Rousseau favors. Some inequality in wealth is assumed by him to be present. Some families will be wealthy enough to permit their members to be educated when young and to devote themselves to public affairs when mature. Neither condition can be assumed to be within everyone's reach in the kind of economy Rousseau presupposes. An elective aristocracy of the kind Rousseau desires would be one in which those among the wealthy who are preeminent in wisdom and virtue will, for the most part, be elected to government. Wealth is important in both the elective aristocracy Rousseau prefers and in the one he mentions earlier. The essential difference between the two is found in the qualities on the basis of which those who govern are elected. This again draws attention to the importance of those by whom they are elected. The kind of elective aristocracy Rousseau favors supplies the closest approximation, on the level of civil society, to the natural aristocracy of the first societies in the state of nature. That is why he calls elective aristocracy the "best and most natural" governmental order (3.5.7).

We saw earlier why Rousseau denied that natural aristocracy is properly speaking an aristocratic government. The reason was that natural aristocracy is not a government properly speaking. We must now face the question of why Rousseau makes the same denial regarding hereditary aristocracy as well as why he labels it the worst of all governments. The second question would be easier to answer if one understood hereditary aristocracy to refer to a kind of sovereignty. An explanation is given in *Letters Written from the Mountain* why an aristocratic sovereign is even more to be feared than a despot. Rousseau describes the situation that would result, in Geneva, if the aristocratic council were permitted to fulfill its ambition to be sovereign:

> In a small state where no one can hide himself in the crowd, who will not live in eternal dread then and not feel at every moment of his life the misery of having his equals for masters? In large States private individuals are too far from the Prince and from chiefs to be seen by them, their

smallness saves them, and provided the people pays one leaves them in peace. But you will not be able to take a step without feeling the weight of your chains. The relatives, the friends, the protegées, the spies of your masters will be your masters more than they will; you will not dare either to defend your rights or to lay claim to your possessions for fear of making enemies; the most obscure corners will not be able to screen you from Tyranny, it will be necessary to be a satellite or victim: You will at one and the same time feel political slavery and civil slavery, you will barely dare to breathe freely.[14]

The same view was expressed by Voltaire in the article of his philosophical dictionary entitled "Tyranny":

> If I have only one despot, I am rid of him if I lean against a wall when I see him pass by, or prostrate myself, or strike the ground with my forehead, according to the custom of the country; but if there is a company of a hundred despots, I must repeat this ceremony a hundred times a day, which can be a very boring business, after a while, especially if you don't have supple hands. If I own a dairy farm in the vicinity of one of our lords, I am crushed; if I file a suit against a relative of a relative of one of our lords, I am ruined. What is to be done? I am afraid that in this world we are reduced to being anvil or hammer; happy the man who escapes this choice![15]

The temptation to understand hereditary aristocracy as a form of sovereignty is strengthened by the way in which Rousseau summarizes his discussion of it in the *Letters Written from the Mountain*:

> The different forms which government can assume can be reduced to three principal ones. After having compared them in the light of their advantages and disadvantages I give preference to the one which is intermediate between the two extremes and which bears the name of aristocracy. One should remember here that the constitution of the state and that of the government are two very distinct things and that I have not confused them. The best of governments is aristocratic [government]; the worst of sovereignties is aristocratic [sovereignty].[16]

Rousseau reaffirms this view regarding aristocracy in another work where he calls aristocracy "the worst of sovereignties" and appends the following note to his remark: "I would bet that a thousand people will find yet another contradiction here with the *Social Contract*. This proves that there are still more readers who ought to learn how to read than authors who ought to learn how to be consistent."[17] The contradiction to which Rousseau is referring would arise if one overlooked the distinction between government and sovereignty and if one failed to pay attention to the difference between elective and hereditary aristocracy. The conclusion to which we are led is that when Rousseau calls elective aristocracy the best of all governments he is thinking of government in his special sense of the term, whereas when he calls hereditary aristocracy the worst of all, he is thinking of hereditary aristocracy as typically a form of sovereignty. That would explain why hereditary aristocracy is not aristocracy properly speaking. The reason would be that it is not a form of government properly speaking but rather a form of sovereignty.

In the second note to the chapter on aristocracy Rousseau makes it clear that "hereditary aristocracy" can refer to an illegitimate species of sovereignty: The "republic" of Venice is mentioned as an example of both a hereditary aristocracy and of a "dissolved state." By a dissolved state Rousseau means in this context a society in which sovereignty has been usurped (3.10.5–6). Venice is typical of the situation that results from a failure of the sovereign to enact laws requiring magistrates to be elected and to determine how that election will take place. Leaving this undetermined means leaving the selection of new magistrates in the hands of those who are magistrates already and leads to hereditary aristocracy and, ultimately, to the usurpation of sovereignty. Here Rousseau introduces an interesting qualification, however. While the way of Venice is understood to be typical of hereditary aristocracies, exceptions to it are possible, though rare. Berne is mentioned as such an exception; owing to the extreme prudence of its senate it is not a "dissolved state" like Venice. He calls Berne a "dangerous" exception because if the fact that it is an exception is overlooked one might be tempted to imitate it and unwittingly prepare the way for the worst kind of sovereignty.

Rousseau did not wish readers of the *Social Contract* to conclude that, since democracy is the only legitimate form of government, all undemocratic regimes should be overthrown. Since he was no believer in progress, he did not think that, as a rule, overthrowing undemocratic regimes would give rise to democratic ones. It is his view that a certain kind of democracy is the only legitimate form

Chapter Four

of government and that the subjects of illegitimate rulers are under no obligation to obey them. What subjects could do, as a matter of strict right, however, was different from what he thought it sensible for them to do. He tried to expose his teaching in the *Social Contract* in such a way as to prevent men from drawing erroneous practical conclusions from it. Some examples of his efforts to do this were described previously. In the present case one sees him, on the one hand, cautioning a free people as strongly as he can against the danger of permitting a hereditary aristocracy to form, while, on the other hand, he refrains from pronouncing all subjects of hereditary aristocrats free from their obligation to obey their rulers; he leaves open the bare possibility that, in a given case, what confronts one is an aristocracy like Berne, and that one's obligation to obey its laws remains intact. Whether such a possibility is strictly speaking compatible with his teaching remains to be seen. But it is eminently compatible with the effect that he wishes his teaching to have.

At the time Rousseau first expounded his view of law, no limitation on what the sovereign could will, as long as its decisions were general in content and spirit, were in evidence. Turning to political laws in particular, and first of all to those by which governments are established, Rousseau again permits no limitation on what governmental arrangements are admissible. The first impression one is made to receive is that all forms of government are good under some circumstances and bad under others. Rousseau has worded his teaching in such a way that he can claim to be perfectly open to all forms of government. As one proceeds with the discussion of the three main forms of government, however, exclusions begin to appear. We learn that the directly democratic administration of public affairs would be undesirable, even if it were possible, because it would destroy the impartiality of the sovereign. We learn next that a law instituting a hereditary aristocracy would be an invitation to disaster. For unlike strictly democratic "government," hereditary aristocracy is far from being impossible: active measures must be taken to prevent it from coming about. The direct administration of public affairs by the people is to be avoided, and so is an arrangement under which the people play no role whatever. Laws instituting a hereditary aristocracy cannot be good. It remains to be seen what Rousseau will think of laws instituting a hereditary monarchy.

The professed compatibility of Rousseau's principles with governments of all kinds is, to say the least, not confirmed by his chapters on democracy and aristocracy and is all but openly abandoned in the chapter on monarchy. That chapter, from start to finish, is a merciless analysis and condemnation of monarchy. A number of careful students of Rousseau have found it difficult to believe, after reading that chapter, that he seriously thought a monarchical regime could be republican, and hence legitimate. They have noted that, in that chapter, monarchies and republics are explicitly contrasted on two occasions (3.6.8; 3.6.13). The analysis of monarchy makes no use of any of the distinctions made in the *Social Contract* that might mitigate its force. Earlier Rousseau had at least suggested a distinction between a monarch who is subordinate to a legitimate sovereign and one who is not (2.6.9 note). Later, when he has to face the practical question of at what precise point subjects of a monarch regain their right to do as they please, he will carefully distinguish between a monarch, a tyrant and a despot, each of which words will acquire a special meaning (3.10.9, 10). The chapter on monarchy ignores all these distinctions. A sovereign legislative assembly with a will of its own is nowhere in sight: the very word "sovereign," which occurs as a matter of course in every other chapter concerning one of the various kinds of government, is absent from the chapter on monarchy. The kings as well as the royal government of which Rousseau speaks in that chapter are what one would normally understand by kings and by monarchies. Rousseau ignores in the chapter on monarchy not only his own but even the traditional distinction between kings and tyrants. He speaks as if, for all practical purposes, there were no difference between legitimate and illegitimate monarchs. The only "kings" mentioned by name in the chapter are the notorious tyrants Dionysius of Syracuse and his son of the same name, whom Rousseau tempts one to call Dionysius the Second; the anecdote told about them is intended to illustrate the nature of hereditary "kings" (3.6.11).

The kind of monarchy found in the world—Rousseau had earlier referred to monarchy as the most common form of government—is admittedly efficient and powerful. Its power, however, depends on the inability of the people to offer any resistance to it. Their impotence is one of the major sources of its power. The interest of even "the best of kings" as kings and the public interest are necessarily in conflict (3.6.5). The efficiency of monarchical rule, while undeniable, serves the interest of the monarch. It does not, cannot, and never will serve the interests of the people.

114

0

114   *Chapter Four*

Rousseau had argued earlier that monarchical government is suited to large states. He does not withdraw that assertion now. But whereas earlier he had spoken of all governments as best under certain circumstances and worst under others, he now makes clear that the fact that only a monarch can rule a large state by no means implies that he can do so well. The fact that monarchical government is unavoidable under some circumstances—perhaps under most circumstances, it would appear—does not prevent it from being unavoidably bad. The enlargement of the commonwealth makes it ultimately necessary to decrease the number of supreme magistrates to one. As the difficulties confronting government increase to unmanageable proportions, the number of supreme magistrates available to cope with them diminishes to one. This is sufficient to guarantee that public affairs will be managed poorly. The king will be obliged to appoint others to assist him. In making these appointments, Rousseau argues, the king will not be able to step outside the circle of flattery, intrigue and hypocrisy which surrounds him. Here we learn for the first time that there is an essential difference between the way in which magistrates are named in a "republic" and in a "monarchy." In a republic "the public voice" elevates them to their places (3.6.8). The public voice can be assumed to have more eyes and ears than a king. The king is easily deceived. He can judge how matters affect him, and in that respect it can be presumed that his appointees will be careful to satisfy his wishes as far as possible. However, he cannot judge how matters truly stand with his subjects since his information regarding them comes from his appointees.

Republics and monarchies were commonly understood to be mutually exclusive regimes. Rousseau had earlier claimed that a monarchy could also be a republic (2.6.9 note). The republican monarchy is nowhere in sight in Rousseau's analysis of monarchy. From a certain point on, that analysis not only presupposes the dichotomy between republics and monarchies but has that dichotomy as its chief subject. The first three paragraphs of the chapter on monarchy describe the power of monarchical government on the basis of results that had been arrived at previously. The body of the chapter deals with the extent to which the public interest is served by monarchy, and from the very outset of that discussion the issue is clearly stated to be peoples versus kings and republics versus monarchies. Machiavelli's *The Prince*, for example, is said to be a book for peoples, not for kings, and Machiavelli himself is called a partisan of republican, not monarchical, government.[18] The remainder of the chapter repeatedly contrasts government by a senate which has been selected by "the public voice"—and which typifies republican government throughout this chapter—with the rule of a king and his advisors. The contrast is always favorable to the publicly elected senate. Its members are able. It is a continuing body the character of which does not change, as does that of every monarchy, with every succession to the throne. Because it is a continuing body, the regime in which it functions is spared the always more or less turbulent transitions from one king to another. Rousseau reverses the commonplace regarding the instability of republics and the stability of monarchies: contrary to what is sometimes said, it is republics that are constant and stable, if they are properly constituted, and monarchies that are capricious and inconstant.

It is a mistake to assume that the criticism of monarchy in the *Social Contract* is simply in conflict with the praise of monarchy by Aristotle and Plato. Rousseau assumes the absence of the kind of superiority which Plato and Aristotle presuppose in their strongest utterances in praise of monarchy. Rousseau does not question that individuals possessing a superiority of that magnitude are to be found, but only whether one will ever find them occupying the throne (3.6.15). The monarchies he attacks are different from the ones that Plato and Aristotle praise. According to Rousseau, lack of merit in a king tends to occasion insolence rather than modesty.

In the chapter on aristocracy, Rousseau had said that the best and most natural order is one in which the wisest govern the multitude, provided one can rely on their governing it for its profit and not for their own. He does not despair of finding aristocratic governments in which that takes place. Why should he despair of finding monarchical governments in which something similar is to be found? Let us remind ourselves of the one king named in the *Social Contract* whose natural superiority was commensurate with his rank. That king was Lycurgus. Precisely because of his superiority, he preferred being a legislator to being a king, and in order to become a legislator abdicated his throne. The true king, the king who deserves his title, can only find scope for his abilities by becoming a legislator and thereby ceasing to be a king.

The chapter on mixed governments is brief. It is almost as if it is there chiefly because one would expect a discussion of it after the simple forms of government had been dealt with. The possibility of so subdividing a government that one part of it is administered monarchically and another aristocratically, for example, had already been mentioned when various kinds of governments were classified (3.3.6). The present chapter (3.7) makes interesting additions to what had been suggested earlier.

Rousseau begins by affirming that strictly speaking there are no simple governments. He explains what he means by this by pointing out that a king cannot rule unless he names others to assist him and that even the assembly of the people has to be presided over by a head. Yet it is not in the sense in which even democracy and monarchy are not simple that he will proceed to speak of mixed government in the remainder of the chapter. The appointees of a monarch serve at his pleasure. They are dependent on him, not he on them. The same holds true of the head of a popular assembly. Mixed government, in the sense in which he will discuss and approve of it in the remainder of the chapter, is government divided into parts none of which is totally dependent on the others and none of which is totally independent of the others. The example he cites with approval is the government of England, no part of which can do its work without the cooperation of the other parts. An example of what one should avoid in mixed governments is the Polish Diet, where too much authority is wielded by the parts into which government is divided. The degree to which mixed government means government divided into mutually dependent but different parts is clear from the way the chapter ends. The last sentence of the chapter speaks, like the first, of simple governments, but unlike the first it *contrasts* simple governments with mixed governments: Extreme force and extreme weakness are to be found in simple governments, while governments of moderate strength are mixed.

The sentence with which the chapter on mixed government ends is silent about aristocracy. The sentence with which it opened was also silent about it. While affirming that, strictly speaking, no simple government is simple without qualification, it proceeded to show this only of monarchy and democracy. One can understand what this means if one bears in mind that the only kind of aristocracy of which Rousseau approves is elective aristocracy and that in an elective aristocracy the electors are no less part of the government than those whom they elect. In other words, an elective aristocracy is a mixed government with a democratic and an aristocratic component. Simple aristocracy, if one were to understand by that a regime in which the governing few chose their own replacements, is rejected by Rousseau as being only one step from hereditary aristocracy and the dissolution of the state. But simple democracy is also rejected by Rousseau. The only kind of democracy he approves of is one in which the people delegate important executive functions to committees of individuals. As regards monarchy, he rejects it in all its forms, hereditary or elective. One is left wondering whether, in the final analysis, any governments other than some one of the many possible democratically elected aristocracies are acceptable to Rousseau. If one bears in mind that the only kind of aristocracy of which he approves is, properly speaking, a mixed government, his pairing of governments of moderate strength with mixed governments—a pairing that silently passes over unmixed aristocratic governments—becomes intelligible.

The preceding analysis of government had explained that governments acquired strength as their size diminished and that their strength had to increase as the state grew larger. Nothing was said, however, to indicate how the sovereign would acquire the new force it would need to keep government obedient to itself. Nor did the prospects for doing so seem good. How could a sovereign whose sway over its individual subjects has weakened, and which therefore needed a stronger government, hope to increase its sway over the individuals in that government? We argued earlier that it would be a mistake to declare this problem simply insoluble although we did not deny that it might well become insoluble in large states, a suspicion that Rousseau's treatment of monarchy would tend to confirm. We now learn of two ways in which one can deal with this problem when it is not insoluble. When the executive power has enough authority over the subjects, but does not depend sufficiently on the sovereign, one can remedy this disproportion by dividing the government. According to Rousseau, doing this will weaken it vis-à-vis the sovereign without weakening it vis-à-vis the subjects. Rousseau did not think that the problem of at the same time setting the government over subjects and setting the sovereign over the government would always be insoluble or always soluble. Up to this point we had been informed of the means by which government can be made stronger. Now we are also told how it can be weakened vis-à-vis the sovereign without impairing its strength. As regards the sovereign, a general analysis was offered of one of the causes which diminish voluntary compliance with its commands. Nothing has been said explicitly, as yet, of how the sovereign, taken by itself, acquires additional force vis-à-vis the government, however. That theme will not be neglected.

Dividing the government does not always have the effect of weakening it. It can also serve to strengthen it where the authority of government over subjects is too weak while its subordination to the sovereign is what it should be. This is a disproportion typical of democratic governments, according to Rousseau. The proposed remedy for it is to assign governmental powers of various kinds to various committees. This "concentrates" the powers of government. How many committees there should be as well as how permanent they are and how long any individual can be permitted to serve on them are questions which he does not settle and which varying circumstances, one may assume, would largely decide. Since these means are designed to facilitate democratic administration, the committees would, in some way, be answerable to the people as a whole in the people's capacity as chief magistrate. It is important to note that the formation of committees to render efficient the democratic administration of public affairs is also given as an example of divided or mixed governments.[19]

To divide a democratic government in the manner indicated is to mix it with aristocracy. There does not appear to be any clear dividing line between a mixed democracy of this kind and the elective aristocracy Rousseau had earlier praised. There are many ways, to be sure, in which either the democratic ingredient or the aristocratic one could be strengthened. But on both sides there is an absolute limit to which this process can be carried without transgressing one of Rousseau's prohibitions. Those who hold office in an aristocratic government must be chosen to it, it would appear, by the "public voice." Their choice is not left to their predecessors. On the other hand, no democratic government can dispense with establishing special bodies for the prompt management of public affairs. Within these limits a great variety of arrangements remains possible. The only question is whether anything not within these limits would be acceptable to Rousseau. On the basis of what has gone before it is difficult to see how it could be.

As we follow Rousseau in his analysis of forms of government, we note that the sequence of subjects discussed and the titles under which they are discussed are much more traditional in character than are the conclusions that are reached. The difference between the titles of the chapters and their contents continues to be manifested by the last two chapters which apparently conclude the discussion of government (3.8 and 3.9). The remainder of the book at first glance deals with a different theme, namely, maintaining legitimate sovereignty. The subjects announced in the titles of the last two chapters on government—that every form of government is not suitable to every country and the signs by which a good government can be recognized—seem appropriate for bringing the discussion of government to its conclusion. One need not read the two chapters with great care to see that free government is in fact their true theme: the first discusses conditions necessary for free government while the second proposes a simple quantitative sign of its beneficence. The theme "free government" provides a link to the second half of Book 3 in which the threats to free government and the best way to meet them are discussed.

In one sense, the relation between the title and the content of the chapter on various countries and their suitability to various forms of government remains what it has been throughout the discussion of government and, indeed, throughout the *Social Contract*. Rousseau made clear at the outset that his intention was not to produce a comprehensive treatise on politics but rather to set forth the principles of legitimate rule. Legitimate political life, not politics simply, is his subject. Other subjects are discussed only to the extent that they shed light on that one. His discussion of government is first and foremost a discussion of what kinds of governmental arrangements are compatible with legitimate rule. His discussion of what countries are suited to what governments is first and foremost a discussion of which conditions favor free or republican—that is, legitimate—government and which do not (3.8.6, 7).

In considering what makes a given country and climate require a government of a certain kind, Rousseau concerns himself primarily with the amount those who govern consume and with the surplus that the country and climate produces. The less remote government is from the people—in a democracy the two are united—the less it consumes, he affirms, while the more remote government grows the greater the burden of supporting it becomes. The most ravenous governments, he says, are monarchies. Only opulent nations which produce a vast surplus can afford them, although, he will go on to add, opulent nations are benefited by having monarchies consume the vast surplus that is produced in them. Aristocracies are appropriate only where a much more moderate surplus is available, while democracies are suited to poor and small states.

The foregoing classification, which distinguishes between the three kinds of government and the circumstances to which they are suited, is almost immediately abandoned in favor of a slightly different one in four parts. Unfruitful and barren places which cannot be cultivated are suitable for savages alone. Places where only the bare necessities are produced are for barbarous peoples. Since there is no surplus to be had, no political order is possible. A moderate excess suits free peoples. An abundant and easily produced excess suits monarchies. In the second classification not only are free peoples contrasted with peoples ruled by monarchs, but they are held to differ from each other as much as savagery and barbarism differ from each of them.

Rousseau is aware that the correspondences he speaks of are not always to be found. He knows that governments can exist in circumstances and climates for which they are not suited. His interest is drawn not to free peoples in opulent circumstances but to monarchical or despotic governments in places that do not readily yield a large surplus. The entire contrast between the South and countries like Poland, England, Germany, and France draws attention to the fact that the more northern countries are not as fertile, that far more exertion is needed to cultivate them, that the food they produce is less nourishing, and that their inhabitants consume more of it. Everything points to the conclusion that only republican regimes are suited to Europe. There simply is no surplus to support a monarchy there. Yet monarchy is what one most commonly finds there. Nothing that Rousseau says encourages one to believe that he thought European monarchies were any less wasteful than Oriental ones. On the basis of his assertions one can understand somewhat better the mysterious passage in which he accused the kings of Europe of weakening it to the point where it would collapse if confronted by a new wave of barbarians. From Rousseau's analysis it follows that the more northern parts of Europe are suited for republics, not monarchies. The more general statement that republics are at home in the moderate zone extends this observation to Mediterranean lands as well (3.8.8). The fact that freedom is not to be found in a climate that calls for it means, for Rousseau, that sooner or later revolutions will occur to restore it to them (3.8.8). (It should be noted that France is mentioned more frequently in this chapter than it is in any other chapter of the *Social Contract*.)[20]

Rousseau's final observation regarding climate and government concerns the density that is required to support life in various

Government

climates. Because southern lands, as compared to northern ones, are easier to cultivate and can grow more nourishing food, it takes fewer people to produce what the population needs in these lands. The surplus beyond what it needs is consumed by the despot. In a comment which is extraordinary for him, because he finds something good to say about despotism in it, Rousseau praises that regime for consuming this surplus. That praise cannot be extended, however, to the monarchs of Europe. In Europe what kings consume is not a surplus but the very substance of their subjects. In climates suited to despotism a stable population can result from it. In climates requiring a high degree of population density for the support of life, monarchy is inimical to the self-preservation of its subjects. The effect of monarchy in Europe is the depopulation of Europe, a process described by Rousseau at great length elsewhere and which he does not omit to refer to later.[21]

The impression first created by Rousseau is that despotism is the worst of all political orders. Further study reveals hereditary aristocracy to be even worse. Finally, we learn that, in one respect at least, European monarchy is also worse than Oriental despotism. Rousseau's analysis of European monarchy permits one to speak, without anachronism, of there being an antagonism between the productive forces of Europe and the political orders that are superimposed on them. In Europe, the effect of monarchy on what he thought of as the productive forces of the nation—its agriculture—leads necessarily to the decline of agriculture and to a corresponding decline in the population the country can support. If one reminds oneself of what he had affirmed to be the end of the social order—self-preservation—one would have to say that European monarchy is destructive of the end of political society. Rousseau did not believe, however, the productive forces belong to an order of being that is in some way prior to or more fundamental than the political order. As we will soon learn, political circumstances can "demand" a monarchy with even more urgency than the land and the climate "demand" a republic. All one can say, according to him, is that under such conditions no sound solution is possible.

The theme of the closing chapter of the first part of Book 3 is closely linked to the theme of the immediately preceding chapter on climate. The closing remark of the chapter on climate is that the least populated lands are those most suited to tyranny. The suggestion of the closing chapter is that whether a people is fruitful and multiplies under a given government should be taken as a certain

Chapter Four

sign of whether its government is "infallibly the best" or the reverse (3.9.4). It is Rousseau's conviction that, measured by this standard, free republics would reveal themselves to be the best, the absolute monarchies of Europe to be the worst, and Oriental despotism to be better than the one and worse than the other. That Oriental despotism should rank higher than the absolute monarchies of Europe is not surprising in view of the foregoing: without being any less ravenous, the despot consumes the superfluous while the king consumes the necessary. The despot keeps the body politic from being diseased. The king and the court, as described by Rousseau, are a disease on the body politic, a disease that consumes the patient and would destroy him if a foreign enemy did not do so first.

Rousseau arrives at his suggestion of a clear, quantitative expression of how good or bad a government is by seeking to derive it from an agreed upon end of the political association. That end he affirms to be the preservation and prosperity of its members. We met with preservation earlier in the discussion. Prosperity might seem to introduce a new consideration. By prosperity, Rousseau does not mean luxury. In the preceding chapter he had praised the monarchical regimes for consuming luxury where it is readily produced. Elsewhere he explicitly distinguishes prosperity from riches. Prosperity means that there is enough for all and enough work for all. Where there is prosperity, families are not afraid to have children because they are not afraid of being unable to feed them. He did not believe that this criterion would lead to results different from those he had already arrived at independently, because he was sure population would flourish where there was freedom and that it was declining in the absolute monarchies of Europe. The final chapter of his account of government sets forth a new, simple, and precise quantitative criterion for good and bad government. In the chapter immediately preceding the last one, and in a note to the last one, we learn of the results to which this new criterion will lead.

The last chapter of the section on government (3.9) is clearly linked to the preceding one by its opening words ("when one asks therefore . . ."). Rousseau denies that there is any one answer to the question, What is the best government? In making this remark he is simply repeating something he had affirmed earlier: no one government is best suited to all peoples under all circumstances or even to the same people under all circumstances. This point had been a major contention of the chapter on climate (hence the "therefore"). Having said this, he goes on to propose a sign on the basis of which one can determine which government "is infallibly the best" and which "is infallibly the worst." The two statements are not in contradiction with one another because in the first he is denying that any one form of government can be suitable under all circumstances. In the second he is considering the question from the standpoint of how well governed the people are. We had learned in the chapter on climate that there are conditions for which despotism is suitable. The fact that a government is good in the sense of being suitable does not mean that it is good in the sense that its subjects are well governed. When he reopens the question of the best government after having apparently closed it, what he is looking for is the government under which the people are best governed (and that under which they are governed worst). Before proposing his simple solution he enacts a debate between "subjects" and "citizens." The first of the two alternatives that follow reflects the preferences of the "subject" of the kind of absolute monarch favored by Hobbes, not as that monarch is described on the pages of Hobbes but as he is almost certain to be according to Rousseau. The second alternative reflects the preferences of the citizen of the free commonwealth which Rousseau favors. The "subject" chooses public tranquility over individual freedom, security of possessions over security of persons, severe over gentle government, the punishment of crimes over their prevention, being formidable to one's neighbor in preference to being ignored by him, and having money in circulation— that is, commerce and luxury—in preference to seeing to it that people have enough to eat. The choice of the "citizen" is in every case opposed to that of the "subject." Rousseau seeks to sidestep the interminable dispute to which, according to him, any attempt to settle these questions to the satisfaction of both parties would inevitably lead. Instead he proposes the internal increase in the number of members of a society—the greatest self-preservation of the greatest number, so to speak—as the manifestly adequate criterion of good government, a criterion which he says manifestly follows from the purpose of political society and which he assumes both parties to the dispute would have to accept. In the note which he appends to the conclusion of this chapter, it becomes apparent that this criterion is not neutral regarding the debate he had set aside in its favor. The repudiation, in that note, of the "apparent repose" of strong governments, the conclusion he reaches there that "freedom" rather than "peace" is what promotes an increasing population, and that political agitation of the kind one finds in republics is not all that bad for the soul, show that his criterion settles the debate between the "subject" and the "citizen" in favor of the "citizen."

Rousseau was obviously pleased to have found a simple formula for determining how good a government is. The result of applying that formula would only confirm, he thought, the superiority of his principle, freedom, over Hobbes's principle, peace, as a means to what both acknowledged to be the end of political society, self-preservation. It is clear from Rousseau's entire exposition, however, that this simple formula is not the source of the principle he espouses or of the profound differences between him and Hobbes but at best only a derivative and external indication of its soundness. The simple formula does not express the core of his disagreement with Hobbes. Moreover, despite the fondness for it that Rousseau displays in this chapter, that formula, upon reflection, proves to be in need of serious qualifications. In a note to *Emile* Rousseau concedes that China is an exception to his rule. In his *Letters Written from the Mountain* he also speaks of the absence of a declining population in the Oriental despotism of China and attributes it to the fact that the despot makes it a rule to side with the people against high officials. In any event, how can one describe as "infallible" a mark of excellence which would force him to conclude that the Chinese are well governed, when he viewed their social order with loathing?[22] Rousseau, to be sure, qualifies his assertion that increasing population is an infallible sign of good government. He only says that it is such a sign "other things being equal." This qualification, however, robs his criterion of much of the conclusiveness which makes him value it. Whether or not the population increase took place in an extremely fertile country or in an extremely poor one, would presumably have to be a pertinent consideration. The exception of China would still not alter the fact, or what Rousseau took to be the fact, that republics in the difficult conditions of Europe had succeeded in increasing their population in spite of these conditions and to that extent ranked higher than the despotism of China. Nevertheless, Rousseau refuses to concede to China even the mitigated degree of merit to which it would seem to be entitled by his criterion. Nor is that reluctance surprising in a thinker who preferred the proud and independent American Indian to the slavish subject of a despot. However that may be, we are dealing here with the periphery and not the core of Rousseau's thought, and it is perfectly possible that this is a matter he simply did not think through.

In the first half of Book 3 Rousseau does not fully state his views regarding the important role that the people must play in any sound government. This helps produce at least the impression that his principles are compatible with governmental arrangements of all kinds. All vagueness on Rousseau's part concerning this point is removed by the second half of Book 3, in which he elucidates the decisive role of the people in the exercise of governmental authority as well as of sovereign authority.

The Sovereign People and Government

The second half of Book 3, like the first, consists of nine chapters. It opens by setting forth the end that awaits every political order as unavoidably as premature death or old age and death await every human being. The metaphor is Rousseau's. It aptly illustrates the two kinds of degeneracy he speaks of as well as the inevitability he ascribes to degeneracy. Death corresponds to the dissolution of the state by the government. Old age corresponds to the contraction of government. Both are referred to as examples of degeneracy. If a city ages, its government will decline in the normal course of things from democracy to aristocracy and from aristocracy to monarchy and the city will ultimately die when the government ceases to be legitimate (as we will see there will be some question as to the precise point at which this happens). A city does not have to die of old age, however. It can also die prematurely. If it should die during its initial, democratic phase, rule by the legitimate sovereign is replaced by mob rule. Rousseau was aware, as we have seen, of the possibility that the people, acting as the government, can usurp its own sovereignty. This would mean the end of sovereignty and of the sovereign people as Rousseau understands them. Instead of rule by legitimate laws one would have illegitimate rule by the mob and its decrees. If the body politic dies while it is in its second phase, that is, if the aristocratic government possesses itself of sovereign authority, oligarchy results. Rousseau had already made known his conviction that permitting those who govern to choose their own replacements would rapidly lead to the oligarchic usurpation of sovereignty. Finally, monarchy is replaced either by tyranny or by despotism, a distinction to which we will return. If the commonwealth dies prematurely, the drift to monarchy or despotism is not arrested: Rousseau marveled at the fact that Venice, which he had called a dissolved state, was not a monarchy yet. Where climate does not draw political orders to despotism other causes do, whether despotism is appropriate to the climate or not. All paths, it would appear, lead to despotism, although they may not end there. The political world of the *Social Contract* is no different from the political world of the *Discourse on Inequality*. In both works, good governments are and must be political exceptions.[1]

The most surprising thing to be found in the first chapter of the second half of Book 3 concerns the status of democracy. In the first half, democracy had been declared to be too high for man, monarchy was tacitly shown to be unacceptable, while aristocracy, if only of a certain kind, was pronounced the best form of government. Now, however, aristocracy is presented as a degeneration of democracy and monarchy of aristocracy. Democracy tacitly replaces aristocracy as the best form of government. As if to confirm this change, the Roman republic, to which no reference has been made in the first half of Book 3, now reappears in the discussion.[2] Rome will continue to be referred to until the end of the work. Rome, it now appears, was a genuine democracy (3.10.3 note, ¶3). The Roman people are said to have been "not only sovereign but also magistrate and judge." Though Rousseau will find much to criticize in the Roman constitution,[3] those criticisms will not nullify the impression created by the fact that his most exalted political example, republican Rome, was a "genuine democracy" according to him. The rejection of democracy pure and simple will not be retracted. The status of democracy, however, will appear enhanced. This appearance will be strengthened as one progresses through the second half of Book 3. Rousseau, as we will see, will require democratic government as an important component in the solution he will finally propose. The change in the status of democracy does not entail, for Rousseau, a change in the status of hereditary aristocracy or, more generally, in the ranking of the legitimate regimes. Hereditary aristocracy, he repeats, is the worst of legitimate governments and nothing is said that might lead us to alter our earlier views as to why it has that rank. A new distinction, however, that between tyranny and despotism, is to be found in this chapter. It is not immediately apparent what the relation is between tyranny and despotism, as now defined, and the bad regimes that were ranked previously.

Both despotism and tyranny are declared to be specimens of dissolved states. In both, the social contract has been violated and the sovereign is oppressed. The difference between them is that the despot arrogates to himself the right to make new laws, whereas the tyrant is content to govern by those already in effect, with the exception, of course, of the law he violates by exercising governmental authority. The despot would appear to be the worse of the two. Does this not render questionable the result we arrived at earlier according to which Oriental despotism was superior, if only from one point of view, to the absolute monarchies of Europe?

The earlier result was the outcome of contrasting one-man rule in a "climate" such as that of Europe, which called for republican government, with one-man rule in a climate which calls for one-man rule. In that chapter, the voracity peculiar to government by one is far more important than the shades of difference between monarchy, tyranny, and despotism: in fact, these three terms were employed interchangeably, and monarchically governed states were continually being contrasted with free states and free peoples. The two kinds of one-man rule which are now contrasted are tyranny and despotism. Both are illegitimate. They differ in that in one the ruler defers to the laws whereas in the other he sets himself above them. Sylla and Caesar are referred to as "genuine kings" and are distinguished from the "despot" Tiberius. Later in the work—to say nothing of his other writings[4]—Rousseau declares that Sylla and Caesar *seized* the authority they exercised and implies that they enslaved Rome (4.6.8: "chains"). In the chapter on monarchy Rousseau ascribed "a secret intention" to Machiavelli's *The Prince*, an intention that revealed itself in the choice of Cesare Borgia as an example intended for peoples of what rule by kings would mean (3.6.5 and note). By choosing two tyrants, Dionysius the First and Dionysius the Second, to illustrate what hereditary monarchy is, Rousseau does the same thing more openly: he abandons the view according to which hereditary monarchy can be a legitimate form of government. By calling the tyrant Caesar a "genuine monarch," he is drawing the reader's attention to the fact that the distinction between (legitimate) monarchy and (illegitimate) one-man rule has been replaced in his argument by the distinction between (illegitimate) tyranny and (illegitimate) despotism. The shift from the distinction between monarchy on the one hand and tyranny or despotism on the other to the distinction between tyranny on the one hand and despotism on the other leads to an important change

129   *The Sovereign People and Government*

in Rousseau's declared views. Only one of the two kinds of government referred to in the first distinction was illegitimate. In the second distinction both kinds of rule referred to are illegitimate. If Caesar is declared to be a monarch, as he is in the note to this chapter, the suggestion, given the first distinction, is that he was a legitimate king and that the citizens of Rome had an obligation to obey both him and Augustus: accordingly, the note dates the dissolution of the Roman state from the despotism of Tiberius. If Caesar was the usurper and tyrant he is declared to be in this chapter, if he did, as is affirmed elsewhere, enslave his country, then he ruled over subjects who had no obligation to obey him, that is, the state was already dissolved in his time. However, an illegitimate ruler who does not act as if he were above the law appears to be preferable to one who does, just as Berne is preferable to Venice. If that ruler owes his throne to some "law" regulating succession, that may serve as an inducement for him to be a "tyrant" rather than a "despot" as well as for his subjects to prefer illegitimate rule by him to the illegitimate rule of a complete newcomer.

The inevitability that government will degenerate in the long run is traced by Rousseau to the very reasons that made government necessary in the first place. Government is necessary because the will of private individuals and the general will are not the same. Yet the very waywardness of the particular will that makes government necessary reappears within government itself. It would be a mistake, as we have already argued, to conclude from this that Rousseau thinks good government is therefore impossible. Love of country and love of freedom, if embodied in the customary life of a people, can reinforce the general will sufficiently to make good government possible, if proper political measures are taken. What he concludes from the foregoing is that sooner or later good government will become impossible because sooner or later the particular wills embodied in government will succeed in oppressing the sovereign. The efforts of those who govern to usurp sovereignty are said to be always present and to be always ready to take up any slack that results from any decrease in the resistance to them.

One student of the *Social Contract* has raised the question of whether Rousseau is not contradicting himself in the way in which he explains why the conflict between the government and the sovereign is incessant.[5] The explanation given is that there is no other body with a will capable of counteracting the will of the prince in order to make it conform to the general will. Had Rousseau forgotten his own discussion of this point in his chapter on mixed government? Must the will of government be left unchecked? What about the intermediate magistrate spoken of in that chapter and discussed at length later in the work in the chapter devoted to the tribunate (3.7.5; 4.5)? The answer to this question is to be found in the long note regarding Rome that is appended to this chapter. One learns there that the tribunate in Rome, which serves as an imperfect model for Rousseau's later discussion of how to temper government, was not immune to the influence of the particular will, and that from a certain moment on, the prerogatives of the tribunate were one of the weapons employed by the particular will in its struggle with the general will (3.10.3 note, ¶3; 4.5.5). The bodies instituted to check the encroachments of government can themselves become part of those encroachments. They are not immune to abuse. Since Rousseau's point here is the eventual success of the efforts to encroach, rather than the fact that they can be retarded, he can afford to ignore, for the time being, the fact that some of the vehicles of that success had, in other times, served to retard it.

It is plain that, according to Rousseau, government should be subordinate to the sovereign people. He believes, however, that sooner or later the sovereign people will be stripped of its rights by the government and will be subjected to it. Why does he think that this must inevitably happen? At first it might appear, from the way in which he had previously spoken of a people growing old and of its civic spirit wearing out, that this was the effect of a process comparable to aging in human beings: as the laws and morals of a people grow old, they weaken. As they weaken, government grows stronger, both because it wishes to and because it must if it is to do its job. The dissolution of the state, to which the concentration and strengthening of government ultimately leads, would have resulted even earlier if government had not been made stronger. The degeneration of government not only cannot be avoided but, up to a certain point, one has no right to take issue with it. The concentration of government in one way retards and in another way hastens the dissolution of the state. But what sets the decline in motion is the gradual weakening of good laws, unwritten or written.

However, in the chapter immediately following the one we are discussing, Rousseau denies that the legislation of a people necessarily weakens with age, or, perhaps one should say, necessarily weakens because of age. While strongly reaffirming the mortality of every political society—"If Sparta and Rome perished, what state can hope to last forever?" (3.11.1)—he denies that the mortality of political constitutions is comparable to the mortality of the human frame. He moreover denies that laws must weaken through age. On the contrary, he affirms that in well-constituted commonwealths, laws gain force as a result of age. What strengthens law, in turn strengthens morals. "Although the law does not regulate morals," he will later tell us, "it is legislation that gives birth to them: when legislation weakens, morals degenerate" (4.7.4). On the one hand, the right kind of customary morals and opinions, if properly established, "day by day acquire new strength." They "revive or replace the other laws when they grow old or extinguish." They "preserve a people in the spirit of its original institutions"(2.12.5). The mutual reinforcement we have mentioned was discussed by Rousseau earlier. He did not find it paradoxical. We need not follow his analysis to the end in order to see that the mere lapse of time does not explain why the decline and fall of every good commonwealth is inevitable.

Unwritten laws are declared to be the keystone of the social order. These laws contain and reveal themselves in what Rousseau calls "public opinion," "public judgment," or the habitual beliefs of a society regarding what is honorable and despicable. Such beliefs are all-important for the well-being of a republic, but adherence to them cannot be decreed by law. However, they are very far from being sheltered from change or immune to it. On the contrary, "public opinions, although [they are] so difficult to govern, are still very unsettled and changeable in themselves. Chance, a thousand fortuitous causes, a thousand unforeseen circumstances do what force and reason cannot do: or rather, it is precisely because chance directs them that force can do nothing."[6] To borrow an example from Montesquieu, an extraordinary victory, as well as an extraordinary defeat, can lead to a slackening of the morals of a people. Every slackening in morals, in turn, plays into the hands of the propensity on the part of government to increase its power. It furnishes that propensity with a justification against which Rousseau himself finds it impossible to argue. Sound morals make for sound government. And the vulnerability of morals cooperates with the tendency of government to degenerate.

But if everything depends on morals, and these, in turn, depend on public opinion; and if public opinion is as fluid and as exposed to external influence as Rousseau says, does this not mean that the very foundations of political life are so unstable as to make

lasting and strong political orders like Sparta and Rome verge on
the miraculous? What is said of the exposed nature and susceptibil-
ity to change of public judgment and hence morals has to be taken in
conjunction with Rousseau's other contention that in a free commonwealth unwritten as well as written laws acquire fresh strength
with time.[7] Both sets of views are affirmed by Rousseau. They are
not in conflict with each other. The strength of laws written and
unwritten in a free society may well undergo increase through age
and concurrently undergo a weakening through the impact of un-
foreseeable events and circumstances. Sooner or later the social
order will undergo a sequence of shocks which will weaken its
morals. This in turn will necessitate a stronger and hence more
concentrated government. A people's morals do not disappear
overnight. The process Rousseau is describing is a gradual one. Its
chief beneficiary is the particular will embedded in government.
Can government, however, be said to be the cause of the weakening
of morals?

In the note immediately preceding the second part of Book 3,
Rousseau refers to the "secret object" of those who foster the
cultivation of arts and letters. He quotes from a description by
Tacitus of how Agricola reconciled the Britons to the servitude he
had imposed upon them by fostering a taste for Roman civilization
and refinements among them, a taste the acquisition of which led
the Britons to look down on their own customs. Healthy morals and
highly civilized refinements were incompatible for Rousseau. He
had declared himself regarding this point in his first important
writing, the *Discourse on the Arts and Sciences* and in the controversies which stemmed from it. He returned to this topic in the
Letter to D'Alembert, a work in which he sets forth the danger to the
morals of Geneva that he believed would result from accepting the
proposal to civilize the city by establishing a theater in it. He
declares the civilizing efforts of Agricola to be part of a calculated
plan and he ascribes similar intentions to kings, princes, and even to
republics seeking to strengthen their hold on subject colonies.
However, even though the plan to establish a theater had the
approval of the highest circles in Geneva, Rousseau nowhere, to my
knowledge, ascribes that plan to a conspiracy on the part of the high
or even on the part of Voltaire himself. The propensity to degenerate need not be a conspiracy. Magistrates who are annoyed by
the inevitable checks on their authority in a sound republic need not
see where the road down which they are traveling leads and might

well shrink from what they would find there. This is true even if these magistrates are more susceptible to the cosmopolitan influences that undermine sound republican morals than are other members of the social order. What was perceived by the classics to be a disproportion between civilized refinement and wisdom on the one hand and society on the other becomes in Rousseau an unmitigated antagonism between the requirements of the city at its best and the requirements of the individual at his best. It was precisely when both were at their best that the classics thought the disproportion need not be an antagonism. That solution is unavailable to Rousseau given his determination to take his bearings by "men as they are."

The difference of which we are speaking manifests itself in the difference between Rousseau and the classics regarding the virtue both regard as necessary for a sound political order. When Rousseau speaks of virtue as the principle of every well-constituted society he indicates that he is elaborating on the analysis of Montesquieu. By virtue Rousseau means republican virtue or public-spiritedness. Such virtue was rare in the Europe of his time, he thought, but it was much more common when political societies in Europe largely consisted of republics. Requiring such virtue was not requiring more than one could ever expect of "men as they are." By virtue Rousseau does not mean the moral and intellectual virtues portrayed by Aristotle in the *Nicomachean Ethics*. A man of Aristotelian moral virtue is open to philosophy and defers to it. A public-spirited and pious people of the kind Rousseau desires is not one among which the arts and sciences could be expected to flourish. Rousseau claims that one must choose between freedom and civilization. A passage from one of his later works indicated to his successors one way in which the need to make that harsh choice could be avoided, even though it was not a way that Rousseau himself took. Rousseau speaks with admiration, in his writing on Poland, of "the poems of Homer recited to the Greeks in solemn assembly . . . in the open air and in the presence of the whole body of the nation" as well as of "the tragedies of Aeschylus, Sophocles and Euripides, which were then performed before them." He indicates that these performances and the Greek athletic games were all part of the national religion of Greece, a kind of religion that he will declare in the *Social Contract* to be no longer possible. Nevertheless, this example suggested to his successors that, contrary

Chapter Five

to Rousseau, civilization and republican freedom need not be incompatible.[8]

The life span of an individual human being is limited by nature. The same is not true of the life span of a good commonwealth. Rousseau wishes the state to be built so as to last as long as possible, just as one might erect a public building so as for it to last as long as possible without imagining that it could last forever. Until now the most significant way mentioned of retarding the degeneration and dissolution of the commonwealth is sound republican morals. But morals are not the only means for retarding degeneration and death. There are also political institutions of various kinds by which this can be done. These institutions are the chief subject matter of the second half of Book 3. They will prove to be components of what Rousseau calls the constitution of the state.

In setting forth the social compact, Rousseau affirmed that its content was determined by the nature of the act. One could at least in principle decide against enacting it, but if one chose to enact it there was only one way in which one could do so. The laws and regulations discussed in the second half of Book 3, do not afford one much more leeway than the social compact itself does. They are presented as no less indispensable to the preservation and hence to the very being of the state than the social compact itself is, even if they are, in a sense, derivative from it. That sovereign authority must be exercised by assemblies of the sovereign people in person, that governments must be instituted partly by the sovereign and partly by the people acting as a democratic government, and that periodic sovereign assemblies of the people must be held are rules that admit of no exception. They are principles of political right.

In distinguishing between despotism and tyranny, Rousseau appeared to leave open for a moment the possibility that rule by usurpers does not necessarily entail the dissolution of the state. If the usurper rules in accordance with the preexisting law and claims no right to enact new laws, he would retain a valid claim on the obedience of his subjects, according to what is at least one possible interpretation of Rousseau's words (3.10.9, 10). This concession to relatively law-abiding monarchs is now revoked by implication. Yesterday's law we now learn "is not binding today: but tacit consent is presumed from silence, and the sovereign is assumed to be continually confirming those laws which it does not abrogate, having the power to do so." In order to be a tyrant rather than a

The Sovereign People and Government

despot a usurper would have to permit the legislative authority of the people to continue in being. Unless the sovereign is intact and free to declare its will, there can strictly speaking be no laws, hence no rule of law, and hence no tyrant as distinguished from a despot (3.11.4; 3.15.8).

What it would mean for the sovereign to remain free to declare its will is stated with full clarity in the three chapters that immediately follow (3.13–15). They are devoted to the preservation of the sovereign authority and all bear the same title: "How Sovereign Authority Maintains Itself." Only on one other occasion in the *Social Contract* do we find three consecutive chapters with the same chapter heading: Book 2, Chapters 8 to 10. There is a connection between the two sets of three chapters. In Book 2 the subject of the three chapters is the people. In Book 3 the subject is assemblies of the people. Nothing can become a law unless the assembled people in person enact it. All other legislative authority is illegitimate. Rousseau makes perfectly clear in the present context just how uncompromising he is regarding this point and his uncompromising stand is affirmed to be the direct consequence of his principles. The general will is inalienable. It cannot be represented. It can only reside in the assembled people. Not only are popular assemblies necessary for a law to become a law, but a law cannot even remain a law unless popular assemblies continue to be the effective legislative authority of the society. That is one of the reasons why, even after all important laws have been enacted, "it is necessary for there to be fixed and periodic assemblies [of the people] which nothing can abolish or adjourn" (3.13.1). These assemblies are required by the very being of the laws and of the sovereign. Without them the being of the sovereign would be altogether fleeting. In endowing the sovereign with the power to endure, the laws establishing these assemblies at the same time protect the sovereign authority against what Rousseau views as the greatest threat to its continued existence, governmental usurpation. In a later writing he will wonder at the fact that this way of protecting the legislative authority should have occurred to no one before him. Fixed and periodic assemblies of the people are the necessary institutional embodiment of the sovereignty of the people, and as such they protect the sovereignty of the people against usurpation.[9]

The frequency with which popular assemblies should be held cannot be determined in advance according to Rousseau. Nevertheless, the general rule he gives regarding this point—the stronger the

government the more often the sovereign should show itself—
guarantees that their frequency will not fall below a certain level.
Either the people will be assembling often because they take part in
government to a great extent, or they will be assembling often
because they do not.

The sovereign people would have to assemble most frequently
of all in a monarchy, according to Rousseau's rule. Yet monarchies
were said by him to be suited to large states, generally speaking.
How could he have thought it possible for the people of a nation like
France to assemble even once, let alone for them to do so repeatedly
at frequent intervals? Rousseau had previously tried to show that
his claim that sovereignty could only be legitimately exercised by
the people in person is not incompatible with political practice by
pointing to the ancient city and in particular to the city of Rome with
its huge citizen body. But while he does suggest that what is true of
the Roman republic may even have been true of some European
peoples in an earlier period, he does not even attempt to show that
anything comparable would be feasible in the hereditary monarchies of his own time. Instead he says, "One must not advance the
abuses of large states as an objection against someone who wants
only small ones." That the principles he puts forward are incompatible with monarchy and with the situation that typically calls for it is
now acknowledged. That his principles are incompatible with anything but a mixed government with a strongly democratic component will become increasingly apparent (3.11.5; 3.13.6).

The only way in which a large state could fulfill the requirements of Rousseau—now that he has made clear that a single
meeting of the people at the dawn of society is not sufficient to do
so—would be to transform itself into a confederation of small states
each of which would be able to fulfill the requirements. He is willing
to relax his requirements to the extent of permitting smaller groups
of the people to meet in succession in various regions of a country.
When the point is reached at which this becomes too burdensome,
the formation of smaller states out of the larger one is dictated by his
principles. The success of the project contained in his later writing
on Poland depends, in his opinion, on the success of Poland in
transforming itself, in the long run, into a confederation of small
states governed by the principles of the *Social Contract*.[10] Representative government as a device for enabling large states to have a
republican form of government in spite of their size is repudiated by
Rousseau for reasons we shall consider as soon as what is meant to

The Sovereign People and Government

take place at the periodic meetings of the sovereign people has been elucidated.

Rousseau's initial description of the periodic assemblies he desires has puzzled some of his commentators (and was criticized by Voltaire): "the moment the people is legitimately assembled as a sovereign body, all jurisdiction of the government ceases, the executive power is suspended, and the person of the humblest citizen is as sacred and inviolable as that of the first magistrate: because where the person represented is to be found, there no longer is any representative" (3.14.1). He later explains that the sovereign people, which cannot be represented in the enactment of the law, not only can but must be represented in the execution of that law (3.15.8). It is true that he appears to qualify this utterance almost immediately by referring to the fact that in the Greek city the people did everything for itself and remained continually assembled in the public square. "Everything" suggests a people that acts as sovereign and as government, or a democracy in Rousseau's strict sense of the term. *Must* a people be represented in the execution of the law, as had been formerly asserted? Is democracy as impossible as he had earlier claimed? The practical bearing of the Greek example is diminished considerably by the dependence of Greek democracy on slavery. The unavoidability of representation in government would thus appear to be indirectly confirmed. Even republican Rome, which he calls "a true democracy" because in it the people were "not only sovereign but magistrate and judge," found it necessary to establish a "subordinate commission"—the senate—to make government effective and in doing so followed a practice which no sound democracy can avoid.[11] Much more remains to be said about the issues raised by the chapter in which Rousseau describes and rejects representative democracy. We will return to them presently. For the moment we will limit ourselves to asking what light his distinction between the respect in which the people cannot be represented and the respect in which it must be represented sheds on the requirement for the suspension of the executive power. Rousseau says that, while the sovereign people were assembled, the senate was "nothing at all," although the tribunes and the consuls continued to have a role to play in facilitating the business of the assembly. But to whom does the executive authority that is suspended revert? Is it to "the people . . . assembled as sovereign body"? How could it revert to them if the sovereign is forbidden to exercise the authority? These questions are not idle. They lead to

Chapter Five

the nerve of Rousseau's argument in the concluding chapters of Book 3.

We learn more about why the relationship between the sovereign people and the government by which it must allow itself to be represented is especially problematic in the light of Rousseau's principles, when he turns to the question of how government is established. Regarding this point, he breaks radically and completely with all his predecessors for whom the right to rule originated, as it does for him, in a voluntary agreement or contract. The notion that those who are to govern acquire the right to do so in virtue of a contract to obey them entered into by those whom they are to rule is rejected by Rousseau as false and incompatible with the principles he has laid down. The sovereign people would forfeit its authority by being party to any such agreement. Moreover, according to Rousseau the establishment of government requires that certain individuals be assigned to govern. Such assignments are a particular act. Yet every act of the sovereign people must be a universal law. The establishment of government therefore cannot be an act of the sovereign people. The last-mentioned argument proves too much: taken by itself, it would point to the conclusion that government cannot ever come into being legitimately because in order to do so it would have to be before it can begin to be. Nevertheless, although Rousseau does not accept the conclusion that results from this argument, he takes the problem underlying it very seriously indeed. His solution to that problem will at the same time supply him with the one and only way in which to establish a government legitimately according to his principles. In some respects the situation at this point of his analysis is comparable to what it was before the social contract was unveiled by him. There too the reader was faced with what seemed to be a hopeless difficulty: the only reliable way of surrendering one's natural freedom to a sovereign seemed illegitimate, while the only legitimate way to do so seemed unreliable. A way—the only way—out of this difficulty was finally proposed and it involved the establishment of a democratic sovereign. A way—the only way—out of the present difficulty will also be found and it will entail the establishment of a mixed government that is more democratic, in Rousseau's sense, than his explicit utterances would have led one to expect.

The only way in which a government can be legitimately instituted, according to Rousseau, is the following one. First the sovereign must enact a law determining what the form of government shall be. Next, the citizens who make up the sovereign must transform themselves into a provisional democracy. According to Rousseau, a provisional democracy is an unavoidable stage in the transition from the decision to form an aristocracy, for example, and the choice of those who are to hold office in it. Naming magistrates is an act of democratic government. Democracy is the only form of government that can be brought into being by a simple act of the general will, because where all govern no decisions need be made regarding who is to govern. Democratic government does not have to already be before it can begin to be (3.17.7).

That the subordination of government to the people as sovereign and to the people as magistrate is not a temporary condition of the body politic at the dawn of political society becomes clear from the final chapter of Book 3. There we learn what business will be transacted at the periodic assemblies through which the people maintain its sovereignty:[12]

> These assemblies, whose only object is the maintenance of the social treaty, should always be opened by two propositions that can never be omitted and that are voted on separately.
> The first: *Does it please the sovereign to preserve the present form of government.*
> The second: *Does it please the people to leave the administration in the hands of those who are currently responsible for it* (3.18.6–8; cf. 3.17.1–3).

The assemblies described above periodically reenact the original institution of government. The first question is addressed to the people as sovereign. It gives them an opportunity to change the form of government if they want to. The second question is addressed to the people as government. In the act of putting the second question, the provisional democracy through which government was originally established is again reconstituted and all officers of the established government are subordinated to it. The people as government can, if they so desire, replace those in office with others. The extreme subordination in which government finds itself at its inception is to remain a permanent feature of its being. In this way alone, can the government be prevented from supplanting the sovereign as it has almost everywhere done. In keeping with this extreme subordination of the government to the sovereign, Rousseau subtly but revealingly modifies the way in which he describes the government which the people institute. In the preceding chapter, while speaking of the democratic government which is a necessary stage in the legitimate institution of every kind of government, he had called it "provisional government" in contrast to the form of government that is finally established (3.17.7). Now he speaks of that finally established government as "a provisional form which [the people] gives to the administration [of public affairs]" (3.18.2). Strictly speaking, all forms of government which the people institute are provisional. On the other hand, the provisional democracy through which it is necessary to pass temporarily in establishing any form of government is now revealed to be a permanent part of the government of every legitimate society, a part that is superior in rank to the magistrates of the established government.[13]

We can now understand somewhat better the strange opening sentence of Chapter 14 of Book 3, in which Rousseau, describing periodic popular assemblies, declares that "the moment the people is legitimately assembled in a sovereign body, the whole jurisdiction of government ceases [and] the executive power is suspended." These measures might seem far more drastic than the purpose of the periodic assemblies requires. Only in the light of the last chapter in Book 3, where we finally learn what is to take place at these assemblies, can we see why these measures are necessary for Rousseau. At these assemblies the continued existence of the prevailing form of government as well as the continued exercise of executive authority on the part of those wielding it are called into question. If the form of government is pronounced satisfactory by the sovereign, the continuation in office of the magistrates who have exercised governmental authority under that form is subsequently called into question before the people, now sitting as the supreme government. Meetings which call into question the continuation of the established government as radically as do those described by Rousseau are meetings in which one can say, without overstatement, that "the executive power is suspended." This need not mean, despite the fears expressed by Voltaire in his comments on this passage, that one must also suspend the fire department or the policeman on the beat. The routine work of government can continue while the fate of the relatively higher magistrates and of the form of government are being decided.

Up to this point of our exposition we have omitted considering Rousseau's chapter on representative government. That chapter repudiates the large commercial republic which Montesquieu

The Sovereign People and Government

admiringly portrayed in the *Spirit of the Laws*. The arguments Rousseau advances against Montesquieu's England force one to wonder whether he thought it possible for sound political orders to come into being in modern times.

Rousseau's disparaging analysis of the large, commercial republic and its representative institutions is not due to an understanding of their origin different from that supplied by Montesquieu. Rousseau regards England as a political order peculiar to modern times. One of England's roots is the feudal institution of representative government—an institution unknown to the ancients—while another root is the modern governmental system of finance of which the ancients were also ignorant. This lack of awareness on the part of the ancients was not regarded as a defect by Rousseau. Acquisitiveness, as we have seen, could not be a substitute for public-spiritedness in Rousseau's eyes because of his understandable reluctance to rely, in matters political, on invisible hands, or, to put it more precisely, because he believed that preventing a drift away from what is politically sound had to remain a matter of public concern. A bond stronger than interest was needed for political society, he thought, a bond that was irreducible to interest even though, on the whole, it was not in conflict with interest. If acquisitiveness ever became the only concern of the members of a society, the needed bond would be effectively prevented from forming. Active participation in public affairs is an essential ingredient of that bond, as Rousseau conceives it. Just how active that participation is meant to be has become a good deal clearer in the second half of Book 3. If public-spiritedness is to be effective from day to day and not only during emergencies, citizens must take part in public life from day to day as well. Rousseau's intention is for as much of the citizen's life as possible to be lived as part of the life of the city, thereby extending the transformation undergone by the individual when he is part of the sovereign assembly to his existence beyond it. Representative government as presented by Rousseau means that one permits someone else to be publicly active on one's behalf. It therefore readily harmonizes with the indifference to public affairs to which the single-minded pursuit of gain gives rise. Active participation in the life of the city by its citizens and an intense public concern for the public good were linked by Rousseau. He did not expect to find one without the other. In attempting to explain the success of American democracy many decades later, Tocqueville attached great importance to the

Chapter Five

way in which the American regime allowed for and encouraged active self-government on the level of the township and the county. When reading Rousseau's descriptions of representative government in the *Social Contract*, we must bear in mind that he understands by such government a substitute for and not a complement to self-rule on a small scale. We should also remember that the England of which he is thinking is the England in which the bribery of members of Parliament by the Court had become, in the opinion of many, a permanent feature of political life there. England's reputation in France had suffered a sharp decline generally, and not only in Rousseau's writings, during the second half of the eighteenth century.[14]

Rousseau's analysis implies that he thought patriotism and popular government required one another and could not be found apart. This may well strike the contemporary reader as an odd assertion given the success, since Rousseau's death, of regimes that are not at all democratic in arousing patriotic sentiments. To follow Rousseau's reasoning on this point one must bear in mind that he is thinking of patriotism as a permanent principle of political life. He is thinking not of wartime patriotism but of everyday peacetime patriotism and he is thinking of it as the keystone of political society. Patriotism in that sense may well be what it was held to be up to Rousseau's time as well as by Rousseau, a preserve of those societies whose members actively participated in civic life. Patriotism in this sense would be at its peak in a sound democracy, to use the word in its usual sense.

Rousseau's most exalted example of what patriotic morals can and should be is Sparta rather than Rome—the egalitarian Sparta whose founding is described in Plutarch's *Life of Lycurgus* rather than the corrupt regime analyzed by Aristotle. Rousseau's Spartan had no life apart from the life of his city. What made Sparta unique was not the fact that its citizens were immersed in public affairs— such immersion was typical in Greek cities, according to Rousseau—but rather the fact that in Sparta this immersion was carried to its limit and put to proper use, with prodigious results. These results confirmed Rousseau in his belief that good political morals or everyday patriotism went hand in hand with the active participation by citizens in the life of their city.

From the foregoing it would seem to follow that political morals at their very best, or the peak of political virtue, will be found only in a pure democracy. Earlier in the *Social Contract* pure democracy had been declared impossible: "One cannot imagine the people remaining continuously [*incessamment*] assembled to attend to public affairs." We learn, however, that this is not, after all, unthinkable: "Among the Greeks everything the people had to do it did by itself [and not through representatives, not even in government]: it was constantly [*sans cesse*] assembled on the public square. It lived in a mild climate; slaves did its work, its most important business was its freedom." Ancient morals and pure democracy are no longer possible in Rousseau's time, it now appears, not only because of the prevalence of representative institutions and of the spirit of commerce but also because of the disappearance of slavery.

The requirements of democracy are incompatible with the requirements of Rousseau's egalitarianism. Rousseau proceeds to force an awareness of this conflict on the reader in a passage immediately following the one cited above:

> No longer having the same advantages, how can the same rights be preserved [by you modern peoples]? Your more severe climates increase your needs; during six months of the year, it is impossible to stay out in the public square; your indistinct languages cannot be heard outdoors; you are more concerned about your profit than your freedom; and you fear slavery far less than poverty.
>
> What! Freedom can only be maintained with the support of servitude? Perhaps. The two extremes meet. Everything outside nature has its disadvantages and civil society more than all the rest. There are some unfortunate situations when one cannot preserve one's freedom except at the expense of others, and when the citizen can only be perfectly free if the slave is completely enslaved. Such was Sparta's situation. As for you, modern peoples, you have no slaves, but you are slaves. You pay for their freedom with your own. You boast of this preference in vain; I find more cowardice than humanity in it (3.15.9, 10).

Given the impossibility of Sparta without slavery, what determines which of the two Rousseau will choose to forego?

For a moment, it may even be unclear whether Rousseau thinks he has any choice in the matter. The remarks he addresses to modern peoples may make one wonder whether he thought legitimate political orders of any kind to be possible among them, with slavery or without. If one presses this doubt one might begin to wonder, as some readers of the *Social Contract* have done, whether

Rousseau, in describing the city that conforms to his principles, is any more serious about the likelihood of its being realized than Plato is with his just city in the *Republic* or Aristotle with his regime sketched in the last two books of the *Politics*. From this point of view, the desirable city sketched in the *Social Contract* would be a standard which could be approximated without there being any serious expectation that any given city could fully live up to it.

What makes the interpretation we have mentioned impossible to accept is the fact that it overlooks the difference between the question to which Rousseau addresses himself and the question to which Plato and Aristotle address themselves. Rousseau's question is not what the best political order is but what can make political society legitimate. For Plato and Aristotle a political society can be imperfect without ceasing to deserve the allegiance of its subjects. It can be argued that the justice of even the best cities of Plato and Aristotle is imperfect by the very standards that they themselves lay down. For Plato and Aristotle imperfect justice does not entail imperfect legitimacy and is a very different thing from it. For a city not to live up to Rousseau's norm, however, would mean for it not to be legitimate. Rousseau's theme, like that of Hobbes and Locke before him, is the *legitimate* regime, not the best regime. Because what is at stake in the *Social Contract* is the legitimacy of political rule, Rousseau declares it to be his intention to consider "laws as they can be" only insofar as one can imagine their being obeyed by "men as they are." The restriction to "men as they are" is meant to guarantee the possibility of the norms of legitimacy established by Rousseau.

Rousseau's conclusion is not that moderns are incapable of legitimate government, or that the prohibition against slavery makes legitimate political orders unattainable in modern times. The passages that immediately follow those quoted above make this clear:

> I do not mean by all this that it is necessary to have slaves, or that there is a legitimate right of slavery, for I have proved the contrary. I am only stating the reasons why modern peoples who think themselves free have Representatives, and why ancient peoples did not. However that may be, at the moment that a People gives itself Representatives, it is no longer free; it no longer exists.
>
> All things considered, I do not see that it is possible henceforth among us for the Sovereign to preserve the ex-

ercise of its rights unless the City is very small. But if it is very small, will it not be subjugated? No. I will show later how the exterior power of a large People may be combined with the smooth-running administration and good order of a small State (3.15.11, 12).

Rousseau, as we see, reaffirms the thesis that slavery is illegitimate. The absence of slavery among modern peoples shows them to conform at least to that extent to Rousseau's norms. The practical consequence of its absence is not that legitimate political society is no longer possible but that it is possible only if the city is very small. The restriction to small political units is the price one has to pay, under the principles set forth by Rousseau, for the abolition of slavery and the prohibition against representative government. This does not necessarily mean that legitimate societies are doomed to impotence in foreign affairs. Confederations of the right kind can render them formidable to other powers in spite of their size.

If Rousseau's view had been that the aim of political society is to foster political virtue, in his and in Montesquieu's sense of the term, it would not have been easy for him to repudiate the solution exemplified in his thought by Sparta, despite the slavery on which it was based. The end of the social contract, however, was said to be the preservation of those who enacted it. That preservation in turn, was enlarged to include security of life, person, and property and the freedom from dependence on another's arbitrary will. The attainment of that end required public-spirited participation by all citizens in political life, which, in turn, required political virtue and fostered it. It was as a means to the embodiment of the principles of political right that virtue made its appearance in the discussion, not as an end in itself.

The fact that the conditions necessary for republican virtue at its peak are incompatible with the principles of political right does not mean that virtue in a somewhat less exacting sense is incompatible with those principles. Indeed, Rousseau had affirmed it to be necessary in some measure for every well-constituted social order.[15] The greatest degree of republican virtue was required by pure democracy, a form of government Rousseau had already declared to be impossible. In the light of what we have learned in the present chapter, it is not surprising that it was. Citizens who must work for a living have no leisure, Rousseau affirms, for the intense education in citizenship that the young Spartan was given, and they cannot be expected to devote all their time to taking part in their city's life.

Chapter Five

Rousseau's city is capable of only a mitigated approximation to Spartan virtue, but that mitigated virtue must be present if his city is to exist. For although the requirements of virtue and of legitimacy do not coincide, they do overlap to a considerable degree.

Our discussion has thus far been governed by Rousseau's use of the example of Sparta. The example of Rome, a city Rousseau admired even more, forces one to reconsider the conclusion we have reached. If morals at Rome were not what they were at Sparta, the laws of the Roman republic and the manner in which obedience was rendered to them were without equal, according to Rousseau. He thought at least as highly of the citizen of Rome and his attachment to his republic as of the Spartan's love of his city. Yet Rousseau does not attribute Roman virtue to the presence of slavery in Rome. The good citizen of the republic before its corruption, as he appears in Rousseau, was a hard-working farmer in addition to being a soldier and a citizen, not a man whose work was done for him by his slaves (4.4.8, 9). Rousseau expects his citizens also to be farmers and soldiers in addition to being citizens. Why, then, should the disappearance of slavery make impossible a closer approximation to Rome than Rousseau seems prepared to envisage?

Slavery is not the only condition of ancient patriotism mentioned by Rousseau. A different condition, and indeed source, of patriotism was found in Rome, no less than in Sparta and in all other ancient peoples. It is what Rousseau calls "national religion" and it

> unites divine worship and love of the laws, and by making the fatherland the object of the Citizens' adoration, it teaches them that to serve the State is to serve the tutelary God. It is a kind of Theocracy, in which there should be no other pontiff than the Prince, no other priests than the magistrates. Then dying for one's country is to be martyred, to violate its laws is to be impious, and to expose someone who is guilty to public execration is to deliver him to the wrath of the Gods (4.8.18).

Judaism was also, in a way, a religion of this kind, according to Rousseau. Another example which could be given is the religion embodied in the noble lie of the *Republic*: even today countries that are ruled by atheistic regimes have something that they appear to feel compelled to call their "sacred" soil. For reasons we will have to discuss later, national religions will be declared to be a thing of the past by Rousseau, who will not find this to be a simply bad thing. Though he recognizes the political advantages that national religions can confer, he blames them for being "based on error and deceit" and for fostering cruelty and hatred. The civil religion he will substitute for national religion will be free of these defects but it will also be far less effective as a cause of patriotism. Our conclusion once again is that while the kind of social order demanded by reason, humanity, and self-preservation cannot exist without patriotism, it is incompatible with patriotism at its peak. Insofar as future republics will be based on Rousseau's principles, they will be more enlightened but less heroic in virtue than the great republics of the past. The republics that Rousseau hopes will some day return to Europe will resemble Geneva in more respects than they will resemble Sparta or Rome.

An objection to what has been said might be raised on the grounds that the foregoing discussion, while attempting to do justice to the exemplary status of the republican virtue of Rome and Sparta in the *Social Contract*, has ignored the important example of Corsica. Yet Corsica is the only country mentioned in the work which is said to be fit for a new founding. Now it is precisely the Corsicans of whom Rousseau says in his *Confessions* that their nascent virtues already give promise of one day equalling those of Sparta and Rome. Does this not suggest that there is not so great a gulf with regard to virtue between the republics Rousseau seeks to found and those of ancient times, in spite of what he affirms in the present chapter and what we have suggested in seeking to understand his remarks?

In order to meet this difficulty, we must remind ourselves of the distinction that was previously made between emergency patriotism and everyday patriotism. At the time Rousseau wrote his brief paragraph about it in the *Social Contract*, Corsica was experiencing the enthusiasm resulting from a victorious struggle for freedom. That enthusiasm, however, is not enough to keep the Corsicans free, in Rousseau's opinion. For this, "good laws and a new constitution" are needed, and the question is to what extent they can help preserve that enthusiasm. It is sufficient to note that the Corsicans are advised to imitate the rural cantons of Switzerland at their incorrupt best rather than Sparta or Rome. Simplicity, self-reliance, and a sturdy and independent love of freedom, rather than patriotism in the Roman or Spartan sense, are the most striking features of that model. In a word, Rousseau's remarks about the Corsicans in the *Confessions* are to be understood as his enthusiastic response to their victory and to the enthusiasm which their victory aroused among them. Rousseau's unfinished writing on Corsica does not lead us to revise our conclusion that in the absence of the means employed in the ancient city, it is not possible to keep patriotism at the pitch at which it was kept in that city. If future republics follow Rousseau's advice, their citizens will never equal the heroes of Plutarch.

In the second half of Book 3, Rousseau tries to show that popular assemblies of the people are necessary if the sovereign is to maintain itself, that is, to exist, in spite of persistent efforts to usurp its authority. The discussion of popular assemblies continues through the first half of Book 4 (Chapters 1 to 4). The best way to conduct these assemblies in order to assure the supremacy of the general will is the chief subject of this set of chapters as it was of the chapters in the second half of Book 3 (Chapters 10 to 18). (We will try to show that this is true even of the chapter on elections [4.3]). The second half of Book 4 (Chapters 5 to 8) continues to discuss ways of preventing the destruction of the state by making it stronger, but the institutions dealt with are no longer popular assemblies.

A people is also subject to decay. Holding government in check is not enough. One must also check the decay of what holds government in check. Rousseau does not assert that the decay which makes great concentrations of governmental power necessary makes the oversight needed to balance that concentration impossible. Many things can make stronger government necessary without making the people incapable of overseeing it. Relations with foreign powers can become more involved. An increase in population may occur. Extremes of wealth and of destitution may become less and less exceptional. None of these changes necessarily brings about the disappearance of republican virtue, although some of them may contribute to its decline by ending an earlier and simpler way of life. The elective aristocracy with democratic oversight is Rousseau's eventual answer to the question of the best form of government. Accepting that answer means settling for less republican virtue than is necessary for and fostered by a simply democratic order. Rather than meaning the end of legitimate government, virtue on a diminished scale is typical of it. The election of public officers to administer public affairs may mean reduced participation in them and reduced participation may in turn mean reduced public spirit, but reduced public spirit is far from being the same as no public spirit.

The Sovereign People and Government

Rousseau illustrates what he believes to be the inevitable decline in the effectiveness of the general will by contrasting three distinct kinds or periods of self-government. The first is one in which simple, sturdy peasants deal with public affairs in open-air meetings, and deal with them well. Here the general will manifests itself without any difficulty. In the second, the resistance of private interests and of the coalitions formed to advance them has the effect that the general will makes its voice heard only with difficulty and after a struggle. In the final stage, which is reminiscent of the last days of the Roman republic, the general will falls silent and is without effect on public life. Its silence, Rousseau argues, does not mean that it has been destroyed. Those guilty of violating it continue to be somehow aware of it in a way that he will explain. Measures of the right kind could put this awareness to use and lengthen the period during which the general will continues to influence public life.

What distinguishes the three situations described by Rousseau is the condition in each of them of the bond that unites society. In the first, the social bond is strong and clear. The general will is declared with ease because the members of society are alike and because each, looking within himself, is able to see the others. This is not sufficient to account for the health of this kind of society, however, because just prior to the death of the state all members again become alike in seeking their own advantage at the expense of the common advantage while pretending to do the reverse. The difference is that in the healthy city men consider themselves as one body and seek their advantage as parts of that body rather than at its expense. The general will requires for its formation, not that one cease to be swayed, in one's deliberations on the common interest, by one's own interest but that the effort to determine the common advantage should be genuine and not a pretense. Men's looking on themselves as one body is a condition for the genuineness of that effort. Men's being direct, upright, and alike assures that effort of ready success. A unified and homogeneous citizen body is the optimum condition for the manifestation of the general will. It manifests itself readily and distinctly in such circumstances. These are not, however, the only circumstances in which it manifests itself.

The example Rousseau gives of a people in the optimum condition, which is also the simplest condition, is not Geneva. By the happiest people that can be seen "now" Rousseau is generally thought to mean the people in the rural cantons of Switzerland. Their government, as it appears on these pages of the *Social Contract*, would have to be called democratic in any but the perfectly rigorous sense which would exclude any government from being called democratic. The other extreme in this context, if one limits oneself to legitimate regimes, is the state on the verge of collapse, which is represented by the Roman republic in its last days.

In the simple peasant democracy the general will is easiest to discern and strongest. In the middle condition the social bond has loosened. The city is no longer as unanimous. Unity and homogeneity had made the unanimity of the peasant democracy possible. Here, however, the city is no longer simply one. Men are now part of associations, coalitions, or factions different from the city and seek at times to advance the interest of these factions at the expense of the common advantage. The city is no longer the only "interest group" that there is. The citizen, looking at himself, no longer readily sees his fellow citizens. The general will's struggle to prevail in the assembly reflects the struggles within individuals. The obligation to obey the general will is no longer experienced as clearly as it was in simpler times. It is important to note that Rousseau does not despair of the effectiveness of the general will under these circumstances.

The condition immediately preceding the dissolution of the state is said to be a condition in which "the social bond is broken in all hearts." The city is no longer one body and its members no longer think of themselves as belonging to one body. Action here is determined exclusively by narrow, though not necessarily short-sighted, interest and calculation. For Rousseau this means not that the rational society is at hand but that despotism is not too far away. A kind of homogeneity reappears among the members of society. The similarity in the first condition was based on the confidence of the citizens that unanimity would result from their deliberations. The similarity here is based on the awareness that others, like oneself, are concerned exclusively with what will benefit them and their own. Appeals to the public good continue to be made, but they are understood to be not more than self-serving pretenses. Acts pretending to be declarations of the general will, but which are contrary to it, are passed in the public assembly. It is not Rousseau's view that in this condition anyone who is not a scoundrel is a fool. He did not think that Cato was either a scoundrel or a fool. Rousseau's maxim regarding the avoidance of conflicts between duty and interest would, however, have been enough to prevent him from imposing on all men the obligation to be Catos.

Just what are one's obligations under these conditions, according to Rousseau's principles of right? The answer, which is given more fully in *Emile* than in the *Social Contract*, is certainly not to promote the advantage of scoundrels at one's own expense. Nor, on the other hand, is it to get away with whatever one can until everyone else becomes good too, a position that practically speaking is equivalent to the view that nothing one can get away with is ever forbidden. The advice given to Emile is to remain on the fringes of a society that is assumed to be corrupt and to avoid both being oppressed and being vile.

The third condition is a good example of what Rousseau thought majority rule would be like under circumstances in which no one ever transcended self-interest, not even when it was in his interest to do so. Each subject seeks to exploit the city for his own benefit, each is aware that others are doing so as well and that almost all displays to the contrary are mendacious. It is Rousseau's remarkable contention that the general will continues to exist even under these circumstances.[16] He means by this that men would not evade paying their taxes if they believed doing so would mean the end of taxation and that they would not evade military service if they thought that this would mean the end of national defense. They want others to continue obeying the law that they violate. They desire the common advantage for their own advantage. If, in spite of this, they do not regard honesty as the best policy, that is because the combined advantages they anticipate deriving from the honesty of others and their own dishonesty outweighs, for them, the advantage they could expect to derive from being honest. Yet what can lead them to believe that others will not imitate their example? And if enough others do so, would this not nullify the advantage they anticipate? In speaking of the third condition, is Rousseau not assuming a state of affairs in which everyone can be counted on to try to partake of these advantages, thereby destroying them? Are the effects of dishonest conduct under the conditions described by Rousseau not precisely ones that the dishonest man would have to regard as unacceptable? To draw this conclusion would be to miss a very important point in Rousseau's account. In the condition of decay he describes, private interests rule in the name of the common good. These interests can be relied on to use their public authority to pursue the combined benefits deriving from their own injustice and from the just conduct they force on others. Almost all may desire the privilege of being unjust under these conditions, but that privilege is not extended to all who desire it. Opportunities to be unjust are a jealously guarded privilege which others are permitted to share in only to the extent that letting them do so increases one's own power to be unjust.

A lottery the winners of which are so few in number and in which it is so unsafe to be a loser is a lottery one would avoid if one could.[17] Why does this fact alone not work to prevent it from ever being permitted to take place? The situation Rousseau assumes to exist is one in which the forms of the republic are still intact. Voting still must take place. Votes still have to be bought. Why should a majority with the power to do so not prevent such a situation from arising?

The inability of a majority to act in its own interests when the social bond is broken in all hearts illustrates again Rousseau's contention that a bond transcending interest is needed in addition to interest for there to be a healthy society. His concern is to bring out the root of the paralysis that seizes a people and prevents it from doing what is in its interest and perceived to be in its interest. Perceived interest is not enough, any more than the perception, by the members of a fighting unit, that it would be in their interest to have better morale is enough to give them better morale. Once a certain kind of rottenness has set in among a people, an awareness of the disadvantages that accompany it is not enough to make it disappear. A clear apprehension of what that condition would be like can play an important role in efforts to delay its advent, however. In addition to a perceived common interest one must have mutual trust if that common interest is to be effectively pursued. It is precisely trust of this kind that is lacking once the social bond has been broken.

When Rousseau declares the general will to be indestructible, he means that an awareness of the common advantage continues to be present in subjects during the closing days of the republic. The measures Rousseau will recommend in Book 4 of the *Social Contract* will vary depending on how advanced the decay of a political society is, but the purpose of these measures in every case will be to take advantage of the fact that an awareness of the common interest continues to be available in order to increase the likelihood that it will make itself felt. To both anticipate and simplify, Rousseau will approve, for example, of open voting in a simple and vigorous republic, and he will approve of the secret ballot under circumstances in which votes are being bought and sold.

The general will is not Rousseau's definition of justice. What justice is can be discerned independently of the general will. The legislator for example, must be capable of doing so. Rousseau himself must be capable of doing so. He affirms the possibility of doing so in an important passage we discussed earlier. The general will is meant to be the reliable political embodiment of political justice, an embodiment on whose effectiveness the binding character of political justice depends. As a definition of justice, the general will is easy enough to criticize, but when one does so one is criticizing it for failing to be something it was never intended to be. As a teaching regarding the practical embodiment of political justice, Rousseau's theory of the general will is exposed to serious objections. His efforts to face them gives the *Social Contract* its richness. The light he sheds on political life results from these efforts. If Rousseau had simply equated the general will with the will of the majority, his theory would have been much easier to remember but there would have been far less reason to remember it. Like all thoughtful theorists of democracy, Rousseau found it necessary to face the possibility of an unjust majority. Doing so puts him in the company of men such as the authors of the *Federalist Papers*, Tocqueville, and Abraham Lincoln. For Rousseau only the majority can embody the general will. There are circumstances, however, in which not even the majority can do so. In these circumstances, *nothing* can embody the general will. Rousseau is not unique in holding that a just society is not always possible. The difficulty in his teaching lies elsewhere. In seeking to make Hobbes's sovereign incapable of abusing its authority, Rousseau brings the legitimate political society closer to what the classics meant by the best political order. The price Rousseau pays for doing so is high however. He finds himself compelled to declare—however softly—that most political orders are and will be illegitimate, even when they happen to be the best possible political orders under the circumstances.

Rousseau's doctrine of the general will is a political doctrine. Because it is a political doctrine, restrictions and qualifications which would have been fatal to it if it were a definition are, in fact, a condition of its being taken seriously by political men. Rousseau does not have to be taught that mathematical precision (*la précision géométrique*) has no place in moral quantities (3.1.16). The doctrine

Chapter Five

is intended to permit one to distinguish a legitimate from an illegitimate social order. Rousseau supplies one with a paradigm for doing so. The unanimity of the simple peasant democracy described in the opening paragraph of Book 4 is that paradigm. The question arises of what value that paradigm has once that simple condition and its unanimity are no longer to be found. Rousseau does not say that it is impossible to ascertain the health of a political community once its early days are past. Even when political matters become more complex, when the members of the legislative assembly no longer see in advance, as those in the simpler condition did, what the outcome of their deliberations will be, when considerable resistance has to be surmounted before the best view prevails, what one may call unanimity at one remove continues to remain possible, at least among the large majority of the citizens. Rousseau appeals to this possibility in his efforts to establish that laws, that is, determinations of the general will, achieved by a majority vote are the will of those who voted against them no less than of those who voted for them. Since his argument regarding this point is not easy to follow and has been denounced as sophistical, it might be advisable to quote it in full:

> Apart from this original contract, the vote of the greatest number always binds all the others; this is a consequence of the contract itself. But it may be asked how any man can be free and [yet] compelled to comply with wills which are not his own. How can the opponents be free and subject to laws to which they have not consented?
>
> I answer that the question is badly posed. The citizen consents to all the laws, even to those which are passed in spite of him, and even to those which punish him when he dares to break any one of them. The constant will of all the members of the State is the general will: it is through it that they are citizens and free. When a law is proposed in the assembly of the People, what is asked of them is not precisely whether they approve the proposition or reject it, but whether or not it conforms with the general will which is their own. Each by giving his vote states his opinion on that point, and the declaration of the general will is found by counting the votes. Thus when an opinion contrary to my own prevails, that proves only that I was mistaken, and that what I thought to be the general will was not. If my particular opinion had prevailed, I should have done something other than what I had willed, and it is then that I would not have been free (4.2.7, 8).

This passage will almost certainly be misunderstood if it is considered apart from the one that immediately follows it and that explicitly states the assumption on which it is based:

> This assumes, it is true, that all the characteristics of the general will are still [to be found] in the majority; when they cease to be there, whatever position is taken there is no longer any freedom (4.2.9).

To enter political society means to abandon the right to act however one thinks best. In Rousseau's language, it means to abandon natural freedom. It means to be guided by the general will rather than by one's own will. This substitution is only acceptable because only the general will can be as relied on to be directed to one's preservation and security—if not to one's happiness—as one's natural will had been. The fairness of the general will, where that fairness is understood as derivative from its equal directedness to the preservation, security, and freedom of each citizen, and the perception of that fairness by the members of the city, are at the center of Rousseau's teaching regarding the sound political order. The right to vote is an indispensable ingredient of that fairness and of one's perception of it, although it is not the only important ingredient. Rousseau holds that it is not necessary for the outcome of the vote to coincide with the way one voted in order for that outcome to be perceived as fair. What makes subordination to the general will an acceptable substitute for natural freedom in the first place, what makes it possible to rely on its fairness, are those features of it which safeguard it against always coinciding with the particular will of any one citizen. What makes the general will immune to control by the particular will of any man also makes it unlikely that it will always be what one thinks it should be. That in some cases the vote determining the general will will not coincide with one's own vote is what one might expect to happen from time to time given the very nature of the general will. As long as most citizens understand the differences between themselves and the majority, when they occur, in this manner the general will is still intact despite the absence of the simple unanimity one can find in certain peasant democracies.

How is that simple unanimity to be understood, given Rousseau's assertion that the general will cannot permanently coincide with the particular will of any citizen? No such coincidence is implied by that unanimity. Where a simple coincidence between the common advantage of all and the private advantage of each is found, no law is needed to insure that men will act as their common advantage requires. It is to the advantage of the city and its citizens for them to breathe, but no law is needed to get them to do so. The unanimity in the peasant democracy is conditional. It takes the form of a willingness to act in a certain manner provided that others do so as well. It results not from a coincidence between the general will and the particular will but from the ease and clarity with which the law needed to secure the common advantage is visible to all. In the simple city, the outcome of the general will is successfully anticipated by every citizen. As political life becomes less simple it ceases to be possible for all to anticipate what law the sovereign assembly will enact. Varied and conflicting interests begin to influence the citizens' perceptions of what that law should be. The outcome is no longer anticipated by all. Its being anticipated by all is not a condition, however, for its being fair and its being perceived as fair.

The fact that the particular will and the general will do not coincide does not make disagreements between citizens regarding what laws to enact inevitable. Under all but the very simple conditions described by Rousseau at the beginning of Book 4, however, such disagreements are the usual result of differences between the general will and the particular will. The general will is easiest to discern in a simple peasant democracy. In a more complex republic which has retained its soundness, the citizen must await the verdict of the majority before he can be sure of what the general will is. Here a difficulty presents itself. If the above is correct, how can Rousseau assert that the general will is "indestructible"? How can he affirm that the citizen, who sells his vote under conditions in which the buying and selling of votes is rampant and in which the majority no longer reflects the general will, nevertheless succeeds in discerning what the general will is? How can a citizen in a republic in which the majority vote no longer reflects the general will succeed in seeing what a citizen in a sound republic cannot see until the decision of the majority has been declared?

Rousseau does not ascribe to every corrupt member of a corrupt city a clear perception of what the laws most appropriate to its diseased condition are. He ascribes to him an inclination to the common advantage which is a subordinate part of his inclination to his private advantage. But can that inclination be divorced from any perception whatever of what is in the common advantage? The most

The Sovereign People and Government

important advantage afforded by the general will is that it enables one to benefit from the cooperation of others—a cooperation without which one cannot survive—without becoming the victim of an oppressor. The general will, according to Rousseau—and this is one of his more extreme doctrines—alone affords security against oppression. The corrupt subject is assumed to know at least that much about the general will. He is also assumed to be aware of how the vote that he has sold will benefit a certain individual or party to the detriment of the common good. Neither of these perceptions presupposes a clear understanding of what laws the city needs now.

When Rousseau declares the general will to be indestructible he does not mean that the general will of a city outlives that city. The general will endures as long as the state does. The death of the body politic must be dated from the usurpation of sovereignty and the dissolution of the state. What continues to exist after the social contract has been violated and the obligation on the part of subjects to obey their rulers has been destroyed may pretend to be a political society, but it no longer is one. It is no more than a herd consisting of a master or masters and their slaves. In that condition citizens no longer have any liberty or any will (4.2.3). The existence of the general will is coeval with the existence of the body politic. This result may appear to be disappointingly trivial, given the fact that the body politic is defined by the sovereignty of the general will. What is not at all trivial is the assertion that the general will continues to exist even during the transition period in which it no longer determines the outcome of public deliberations but in which sovereignty has not yet been usurped. If one does not limit oneself to legitimate social orders, Rousseau contrasts four different conditions of a people in Book 4, Chapter 1: the people of a simple peasant democracy, those of a somewhat more complex republic, those of a republic just prior to its death, and those of Paris or London. It is with reference to the third of these conditions that he makes his observation regarding the continuing presence of the general will despite the fact that citizens are no longer guided by it. His purpose in doing so is to show that there is something healthy to which one can appeal even in that desperate situation. Throughout Book 4 he will discuss measures for strengthening that healthy thing as far as possible.

Rousseau ends the first chapter of Book 4 with some remarks about subjects that are worthy of attention but that he will not be able to treat in the *Social Contract* because they demand a treatise to themselves. His remarks have occasioned some perplexity. He clearly declares that the right to vote on laws is an essential part of sovereignty. He has been believed to hold further that the right to bring a new law before the sovereign assembly and to state one's opinion of its merits or disadvantages must be the preserve of government. In the *Letters Written from the Mountain*, however, while he continues to favor reserving to the governing councils of Geneva the right to submit new laws to the sovereign he complains of their denying the sovereign the right to debate them.[18]

Rousseau undoubtedly affirms that the right to vote on laws cannot be taken from the citizens. He undoubtedly makes no such affirmation about the right to propose laws and debate them. He does state that government seeks to reserve these rights to itself. His precise words are, "government takes great care to leave [these rights] only to its members" (4.1.7). These words do not amount to an enthusiastic endorsement of the practice they describe. We must remember that Book 4 immediately follows the book of the *Social Contract* in which government appears as the chief threat to freedom and that one of the major tasks of Book 4 is to find ways of protecting a people against the harmful consequences of its own decay, ways other than those which would have the effect of making government stronger. Rousseau's remarks suggest that there are many possible arrangements regarding the right to propose and to debate laws compatible with his principles. He does not claim that under his principles only the government can ever have the right to propose and to enact new laws, nor does he say that his principles exclude it from ever reserving that right for itself. In the peasant democracy in which "the first one to propose [new laws] only says what all have already felt" and in which there is no need for "intrigues or eloquence to pass into law what everyone has already resolved to do as soon as he is sure that others will also do likewise," there is no need for any restriction of the right to propose new laws. In a republic that is so corrupt that the buying and selling of votes is rampant, it would be dangerous even to permit new laws to be debated in the sovereign assembly.[19]

The introductory chapter of Book Four closes with an allusion to Rousseau's distinction between the government and the sovereign and to his views regarding the potential tension between them. The difficulty created both by the indispensability of effective government and by the threat that government poses is the background against which Book Four must be understood. Rousseau began preparing the way for the understanding of this difficulty early in the work. His account of how the particular will is transformed into the general will (2.3) draws attention to the danger of partial associations with a kind of general will of their own, one which will substitute itself among the associates for the general will of the body politic. The best protection against partial associations, where one cannot prevent them from arising is "to multiply their number and prevent their inequality." After alluding to the need to secure the cooperation of the more able members of society who have the perspicacity to discern the common advantage but who may not prefer it to their own, and after turning to the legislator to meet that need, Rousseau takes up, in Book 3, a partial association with a "general will" of its own which will enlist, if it does its job properly, the cooperation of the ablest members of society and which cannot help being superior to any other partial association. He turns to government. He is not unaware of the fact that commonly the sovereign and the government are not distinguished. That fact merely confirms, in his eyes, the validity of his analysis regarding the propensity of the government to usurp sovereignty and its success in usurping it sooner or later. Since he thinks that government is indispensable despite this danger, he tries to keep it in check by means of popular assemblies. As a people decays, government must grow stronger. As government grows stronger, the importance of these assemblies and the frequency with which they must meet increases. Yet, how can these assemblies do their work well, given an advanced state of the decay which made it necessary to strengthen government in the first place? Ultimately they will fail to do their work and government will usurp sovereignty. Still, the advantages of public freedom are sufficiently manifest to a sufficiently large number of citizens for their ability to be effective watchdogs of government not to decline precisely in proportion to their ability to govern themselves. A moment does arrive, however, at which citizens cannot rely on each other to perform that function for their mutual advantage, because the advantage, or at least the relative advantage, to be gained by selling oneself to those who aspire to illegitimate authority seems to be even greater. While beliefs and customs are sound, the reciprocal awareness on the part of citizens that they can rely on each other to seek their private advantage as part of the common advantage strengthens the effectiveness of the general will. In the last days of the republic, the reciprocal awareness, on the part of citizens, of the desire of each one to seek his advantage at the expense of the common advantage speeds the dissolution of the state. That dissolution is like a rout. Before it has taken place, it is contrary to the interest of the soldiers for it to take place. After it has taken place, each soldier is thrown back on his own resources. Book 4 sets forth the various measures by which such a rout can be delayed if not prevented.

The three chapters that follow the opening chapter to Book 4 continue to deal with the proper conduct of popular assemblies. The succeeding chapters do not deal with sovereign assemblies only. One of them deals exclusively with governmental acts. Rousseau had linked the fate of the popular assembly as sovereign to its success in exercising its authority over government, an exercise of authority that turned out to be itself governmental. The governmental tasks which the assembly of the people performs are indispensable for the effectiveness of the general will. Rousseau's discussion deals with the role of popular assemblies in government as well as in the exercise of sovereign authority. Both had been present in the analysis of popular assemblies with which Book 3 closed. Both are still present in the treatment of popular assemblies with which Book 4 opens.

The discussion of popular assemblies in Book 4 deals to a large extent with voting procedures. The opening chapter arrives at the conclusion that the purpose of the arrangements governing popular assemblies is less to preserve the general will from destruction— Rousseau argues that it is "indestructible"—than to see to it that it makes itself heard. What follows deals directly or indirectly with the kind of voting arrangements which permit this to happen. A comprehensive analysis of such arrangements is not attempted. Rather, Rousseau indicates within what limits a choice of arrangements is possible as well as what considerations should govern that choice.

The first of the three chapters that follow 4.1 is devoted to determining how large a majority is necessary for a declaration of the general will. Only in one case is this question fully answered in advance by the principles which Rousseau has been enunciating: the social contract itself requires unanimous consent. That requirement is inflexible. The difficulty of meeting it is not as great, however, as it might at first seem to be. Rousseau overcomes it in the same way Hobbes and Locke had done before him: those voting against the social contract do not neutralize those voting for it since the two groups are not members of one and the same society; nothing forbids those voting for the social contract from forming a political society even if others do not wish to join it. The rule of the majority begins only within a society that has been unanimously formed. Unanimous consent to the social contract makes it binding on the members of the political society it creates. However, Rousseau does not limit himself to affirming that this is so. He declares in addition that the social contract is the only law requiring unanimous consent and that, in virtue of that consent, a majority suffices to pass all subsequent laws. By a majority Rousseau does not necessarily always mean a bare majority. It is the point of the chapter on voting to show that the answer to the question of how large this majority should be is not the same under all circumstances (4.2). That answer depends on how difficult it is for the general will to make itself heard, that is, on how far the decline of the state has progressed. Precautions that would have been unnecessary in the simple peasant society described earlier must now be taken in order to be sure that the general will "is always questioned and that it always answers." One such precaution would be to require a large majority for the enactment of important laws. In the simple peasant society this requirement would not be needed because it would be met as a matter of course.

At the end of Book 3, Rousseau asserted that the sovereign should periodically pronounce on the desirability of retaining the established form of government. He admitted that it was dangerous to make changes in that form except when it was absolutely necessary to do so, but he stated that what was at issue was the right of the sovereign and not the wise exercise of that right. Here we see one of the ways in which the instability inherent in keeping the form of government provisional can be mitigated. The abolition of the prevailing form of government and the establishment of a new one would be an important law. A bare majority, the foregoing discussion implies, might not be enough to pass it. On the other hand, the majority needed to remove someone from office would not have to be great, since such removal would be an act of government, not of legislation. These are not rigid rules, however. They indicate the latitude available to practical wisdom and the considerations by which the use of that latitude should be governed.

If unanimous consent is needed for the social contract itself, the question may arise why anything less than that should ever be binding. In addressing himself to this question, Rousseau takes up explicitly an objection that grows out of the way he had himself stated the problem which the social contract is meant to solve. That problem is to find a way in which each, united himself to all, nevertheless obeys only himself, and remains as free as before. How can someone who is subject to a will which can be at variance with his own, as the will of a majority can be, be said to obey only himself and to be free? Rousseau does not have available to him the way out of this difficulty that Hobbes propounds. For Hobbes the whole point of instituting a sovereign is to assure that "in those necessary matters which concern peace and self-defense, there be but one will of all men." Hobbes's very definition of a city is "one person, whose will, by the compact of many men, is to be received for the will of them all." The subjects of a Hobbesian commonwealth agree, for the sake of security and peace, to allow the will of the sovereign to represent their own will.[20] If one of the chief ends of political society were freedom, according to Hobbes, it would have been open to him to argue, however unpersuasively, that since I have willed that the will of the sovereign is to be taken for *my* will, everything I do in accordance with his will I also do in accordance with my own, and hence freely. While a somewhat less crude version of this argument can be found in the writings of some successors of Hobbes, it would be a serious mistake to attribute this argument to Rousseau. He flatly denies that the will can be represented. His novel teaching regarding what a legitimate sovereign must be depends on that denial. He holds that an agreement to represent the will must be invalid because one can perfectly well promise to do something, and one can be compelled to fulfill one's promise, but one cannot be compelled to *want* to fulfill it. A promise to *want* to do something is absurd. Hobbes is well aware that "the will itself [is] not voluntary," that "we will not to will but to act," and that the will "therefore falls least under deliberation and compact." This does not, however, lead Hobbes to deny the validity of compacts in which the will is represented.[21] The strong will to peace which the state of nature generates keeps Hobbes from believing that the difficulty he raises invalidates his construction. For Rousseau that difficulty becomes an impossibility. The will cannot be transferred or represented. No agreement to transfer or represent it can be valid. Sovereignty is inalienable for Rousseau precisely on these grounds.

If the will cannot be represented or transferred, how is the relation between the will of an individual subject and the general will to be understood? They are clearly not one and the same according to Rousseau. Nor is the one the representative of the other. Rousseau understands the relation between the two as the relation of whole to part. But the whole in question is of a peculiar character. If one is speaking of Rousseau's sovereign as distinguished from, say, his governments, one is not speaking of an "organic whole," that is, of a whole consisting of parts that are essentially different in character and rank. The whole which is the sovereign body in Rousseau consists of parts which are, as far as possible, and as far as it is concerned, equal and alike. The formation of that whole is described in terms like these: a man finds it necessary—vitally necessary—to remove a certain obstacle to his survival. He is not strong enough to remove it by himself. All others find themselves in the very same predicament. What each lacks the strength to do by himself, all have the strength to do if they act together. This sketch enables one to see, in part, how Rousseau conceived the relation between the individual will and the general will. That relation is not one of representation, in which one will comes to be substituted for another. It is one of participation, in which the will of private individuals gives rise to something other than each of them, something for whose continued existence each of them remain indispensable. The general will is an "all of us" composed of "each of us" (1.6.9).

The fact that the relation between the individual and the general will can be described as one of participation does not completely remove the difficulty which Rousseau invites the reader to face. Rousseau lays stress on the difference between the general will and the particular will. He even says that they tend to be at variance with each other. While admitting the difference between them, he requires the social contract to leave those who enact it as free as they were before they enacted it. Since he has deprived himself of the right to say that the general will represents the will, or the true will, or the higher will, or the rational will of the individual and that in obeying it he is therefore free, since he insists on the impossibility of representing the will, how can his requirement be met? If the general will is not the same as my will and does not represent my will and I am bound to submit to it, in what sense am I as free as I was when I was bound to submit to no will but my own?

Rousseau seeks to overcome this difficulty without renouncing his prohibition against representing the will by arguing for yet another sense in which the general will can be said to be my will. He had said that the social contract required and received unanimous consent. The will by which the social contract was adopted was the will of each and every member of the society. Rousseau now ex-

Chapter Five

tends to the general will the unanimity he claims for the social contract. "The citizen consents to all laws, even those that are passed in spite of him, and even those which punish him when he dares to break any one of them. The constant will of all the members of the State is the general will." (4.2.8).

There are solid reasons, according to Rousseau, why every citizen would wish to see the general will obeyed. These reasons were given earlier and they are briefly restated in this chapter. It is thanks to obedience to the general will, that is, to equitable laws that the members of the state are free citizens rather than slaves at the mercy of the whims of their masters. It is thanks to rule by the general will, that is, by equitable laws, that they enjoy the security, which includes security against oppression by those who govern them, for the sake of which they entered political society. The key assumption of Rousseau's argument here is that *the majority embodies the general will and is perceived to do so by the citizen body*. As we have already seen, this requirement is not met merely by taking a majority vote. Only a majority can embody the general will, but not any and every majority does so. The outcome of a vote may be influenced by secret arrangements of various kinds. In a sound social order, such arrangements are either prevented or neutralized. In explaining how there can be a unanimous desire to see the majority decision obeyed, even if one has voted against it, Rousseau makes two assumptions. He assumes a citizen body which accepts the belief that freedom is only secure where the majority can be trusted and which correctly holds itself to be a citizen body in which freedom is secure. There is nothing fanciful about holding that in a citizen body of this kind—as we have seen it would have to be a public-spirited citizen body to be one of this kind—the unanimity on which Rousseau's argument depends will be present.

For Hobbes, the will of the sovereign represents the will of his subjects. For Rousseau, the will cannot be represented. Instead of representation, in Rousseau the will of the individual takes part in the process through which the general will is arrived at and approves the outcome of that process in advance for the reasons indicated and under the conditions indicated. Both the participation, and the approval in advance, if they are to be of the right kind, presuppose a body made up of individuals each one of whom is what Rousseau calls a "citizen."

How great, in the end, is the difference regarding this point between Rousseau and Hobbes? There certainly is a great political difference between the kind of commonwealth Rousseau regards as alone legitimate and the kind Hobbes prefers. Our question bears rather on the theoretical account offered by each of the relations between the will of the subject and the will of the sovereign. In Hobbes, the sovereign must educate the subjects so that they will remember why sovereign authority is necessary. In this way, the sovereign's representation of the will of the subject will be less of a legal fiction than otherwise. If properly educated, Hobbes argues, the subjects will for the most part will what the sovereign wills because they see the mutual slaughter from which the sovereign protects them. Is Rousseau's argument ultimately so different from that of Hobbes, even if one takes into account Rousseau's denial that the will can be represented, a denial that has its parallel in difficulties that Hobbes had already expressed? Is Rousseau in the end not also saying that citizens obey the general will because it enables them to enjoy the benefits of social life without bullying or being bullied? Is the freedom which Rousseau's sovereign is meant to guarantee not primarily a freedom *from* the danger of enslavement and oppression? It would be another matter if Rousseau had simply equated the freedom of the citizen with public-spirited obedience to the general will and that, in turn, with moral freedom. But whatever may be true of his successors, Rousseau does not do so.[22]

Rousseau's discussion of elections in Book 4 sheds additional light on his understanding of government and in particular on his understanding of mixed government. As we saw, the initial impression Rousseau sought to create was that every form of government was compatible with his principles and that each was bad under certain circumstances and good under others. Reading on, we saw that Rousseau's argument implied more exclusions than we had been led to expect. It finally began to seem that elective aristocracy was not only what Rousseau declared it to be—the best form of government—but also that it was the only form of government which it would not be either futile or dangerous for a society to adopt. What was not treated in Rousseau's discussion of elective aristocracy was who it was who would be doing the electing. The present chapter (4.3) contributes to the clarification of this point by forcing the reader to reconsider whether what had previously been called elective aristocracy is an aristocracy properly speaking. In the course of the discussion it is denied that Venice is a true aristocracy: "its government is no more aristocratic than [is] our own [in Geneva]." Geneva's government, Rousseau's argument suggests, can be called democratic with as little or as much right as it can be called aristocratic. Its partially democratic character has nothing to do with selection of magistrates by lot since no use of this device is made in Geneva. It is partially democratic because the entire citizen body participates in the choice of magistrats, for to elect is also to govern, and where the people elect, the people take part in governing. An elective aristocracy in which the people do the electing is, properly speaking, not an aristocracy but a mixed government. But all magistrates in governments other than simply democratic ones must be elected by the people to begin with and, as we have seen, at least their right to remain in office must be subject to periodic review by the people. Contrary to the impression that the reader at first receives, Rousseau does hold that there is a best form of government as well as utterly unacceptable forms, and contrary to yet another first impression, that best form has no more right to be called aristocratic than it has to be called democratic. Not only is democratic sovereignty the only legitimate form of sovereignty, according to Rousseau, but mixed government with an important democratic component is the only legitimate form of government. This result, which emerges gradually in the course of Rousseau's argument, was in a way anticipated by him at the outset of the work when he declared his preference for the government of Geneva as he understood it or wished it to be understood.[23]

The chapter on elections is very much part of the discussion of popular assemblies with which Book 3 closed and which is continued in Book 4. It is because of the task that falls to the people in sound government as Rousseau understands it that a chapter on elections is part of his discussion of popular assemblies. That Rousseau is still dealing, in the present chapter, with the subject that occupied him at the end of Book 3 is indicated by the way in which this chapter opens. He makes it clear in the opening passage that the procedure he requires for instituting government is also required for electing those who govern.[24] Instituting government was a "complex act" in which the people acted first in their capacity as the sovereign by establishing the form of government and then as the governing body that named those who would govern. Rousseau now makes clear that the people will always continue to be the governing body by which magistrates are named. Election by the people is not something that takes place only once when a form of government is established. Election by the people, it now appears, is a permanent feature of political life. It is a feature that complements another permanent feature, the periodic reconsideration of whether to retain the established form of government, which was discussed at the end of Book 3. Taken together the two features constitute the "complex act" of which Rousseau speaks here. The form of government resulting from this act may not be a democracy; it is certainly not a democracy in the strict sense of the term, of which sense the reader is reminded here. But it is equally inappropriate to call that form of government an aristocracy or even an elective aristocracy (4.3.6). In what is his last word on the subject in the *Social Contract*, Rousseau distinguishes this form of government from true democracy and from true aristocracy as well as from monarchical government. It is a "mixed government" with pronounced democratic features.[25]

From the middle of Book 3 of the *Social Contract* up to the present point in Rousseau's argument, the popular or democratic ingredient in the governmental solution that he offers has become increasingly apparent. However, the chapter on assemblies of the people in the Roman republic does not appear to be at all democratic in inspiration. In this chapter (4.4), Rousseau discusses at length the different kinds of assemblies of the people that were to be found in the Roman republic, and how voting was conducted in them. The discussion takes the place of an explicit analysis of what is permitted and of what would be advantageous in this regard. To follow Rousseau's argument one must remind oneself again of the difficulty that we have been discussing: what can be done to prolong the life of a legitimate government after the decline of a society has set in? The previous discussion has shown that Rousseau has no intention of relaxing his requirement that the people in person exercise sovereign authority and supreme governmental authority. The argument of the first chapter of Book 4 seeks to show that popular assemblies can continue to be an important source of support for what remains sound in a social order that has advanced far down the path of decline. The thesis Rousseau affirms in that chapter is that the general will continues to remain intact and continues to be a force for the good even when the political order has decayed to the point that the survival of the state is in doubt. The whole question is how to make its voice heard in those difficult circumstances. Rousseau does not suggest that a way to do so can always be found or that the destruction of the state can always be averted. He only argues that to the extent that further decline can be arrested, popular assemblies properly conducted are an important ingredient of the effort to arrest it. Neither his principles nor his analysis of how to resist the decay of political society lead him to seek substitutes for assemblies of the people. Some of the devices he proposes for dealing with a declining republic have been discussed. Others are set forth in the chapter on Roman assemblies. None of them contemplates the replacement of popular assemblies by representative assemblies. All the devices advanced by Rousseau presuppose that popular assemblies will continue to exist. These assemblies are the heart of the constitution of the state, and the measures under discussion in Book 4 are ways of strengthening that constitution.

The chapter on the kinds of assemblies that Servius established and reformed takes the place of an explicit statement of precepts regarding how votes are to be cast and counted in assemblies of the people. Rousseau is aware that in speaking of Servius he is speaking of a mythical figure (4.1,2) who was made responsible for practices which the best scholarly authorities available to Rousseau presented as anything but mythical. It is not clear, however, what lesson Rousseau expected the thoughtful reader to derive from his account of the reforms of Servius (4.4). The centuriate assembly, in which voting is so arranged that the votes of the well-to-do preponderate, and in which the utterly destitute city dwellers have no vote at all, is expressly not intended for imitation by modern peoples. Nor is it meant for people whose political order is in decline. The strong and simple morals of the early Romans are said to have alone made the arrangements of the centuriate assembly workable. The fact that these morals and the institution of censorship were stronger than the institutions of the centuriate assembly is what corrected "the vice" of that assembly in Rousseau's opinion (4.4.19). The tribal assembly excluded senators, which robbed it of legitimacy. The curiate assembly excluded even more citizens than the tribal assembly did.

In Book 3 Rousseau began to discuss various ways in which popular assemblies could help a sound political society combat its inevitable decay. The ways considered by Rousseau in the first four chapters of Book 4 are ways of conducting such assemblies. Rousseau is not prepared to make any compromises in his demand that such assemblies be held periodically and that they be assemblies of the people. On the contrary, he argues that, properly run, such assemblies are a force for the good, that they embody the general

The Sovereign People and Government

will. At the same time, he recognizes that as a political order enters its last days, its assemblies will grow much more stormy. The buying and selling of votes will become commonplace. Those who are neither very rich nor very poor will more and more cease to be the typical citizens of the city. An increasingly large group of utterly destitute city dwellers will appear. Assemblies of the people held under these conditions might well appear to be risky affairs. Not holding such assemblies, however, would mean, for Rousseau, saying farewell to what makes a society legitimate and what can best keep it legitimate. He tries to show, therefore, what measures are available to minimize the risk one runs by holding them in this extreme condition. The discussion of Roman assemblies is meant to illustrate the degree of latitude that remains at the disposal of the statesman even after one has granted the principle that popular assemblies are not to be dispensed with. That latitude, rather than encouraging the imitation of this or that arrangement in Rome, is the subject of Rousseau's discussion.

Rousseau opened Book 4 of the *Social Contract* by contrasting a peasant people in a republic with a destitute urban mob in a monarchy. His reason for distrusting destitute urban mobs has been given more than once earlier in the work. Extremes of wealth and destitution are dangerous for the republic, he argues, because the destitute are willing to sell themselves and republican freedom to those who are willing to pay them for it. The destitute are natural allies of potential tyrants. Rousseau praises Plato for refusing to draw up a code of laws for a people among whom the equality Rousseau requires—an equality under which no citizen is "rich enough to be able to buy another and none poor enough to be forced to sell himself" (2.11.2)—is absent. This equality, however, is one of the first casualties of decline.[26] Late in the life of a healthy republic one is likely to find the extremes of wealth and poverty which, had they been present at the outset, would have made it impossible for it to be founded. Rousseau's whole point in the opening chapter of Book 4 was that this situation need not be utterly hopeless. The general will can still make its presence felt if the proper devices are employed. By reading Rousseau's chapter on Roman assemblies and by studying his judgments on the various arrangements he describes, one can discern what some of the devices he recommends are.

Three points emerge clearly from an examination of Rousseau's discussion of Roman assemblies. Voting arrangements which limit the franchise to soldiers and former soldiers are not incompatible with his principles, even if a modest property qualification is attached to the right to be a soldier. The resulting exclusion of the utterly destitute from the centuriate assembly did not nullify the legitimacy of its decisions, in Rousseau's opinion (4.4.34). Voting arrangements in which votes are counted by tribe and in which the influence of the urban dwellers is restricted because there are more rural tribes than urban ones are also acceptable for Rousseau. In the assemblies of tribes convened by the tribunes, votes were counted precisely in this way. Those officers and friends of the people, the tribunes, were the ones who checked the influence of the urban tribes in the manner indicated, until membership in a tribe became something citizens could change at will. Finally, while the exclusion of those not qualified to serve as solders did not nullify the validity of the centuriate assembly, the exclusion of the patricians from the assembly of the tribes was incompatible with the principles set forth by Rousseau. His principles do not determine a set of precise minimum conditions for being a citizen any more than they determine after how many years and under what conditions a resident alien may become a citizen. What they do require is that no citizen who meets these conditions may be denied a vote. The exclusion of patricians from the tribal assembly, once that assembly had acquired the right to legislate, is an example of what it means to violate the generality that Rousseau requires of every valid law. The law that determines membership in the sovereign assembly need not admit everyone, but it may not leave out anyone who meets the minimum requirements it lays down.

As one can see, some latitude remains at the disposal of the statesman even within the limits on which Rousseau insists in the *Social Contract*. A variety of arrangements with regard to voting is possible. There may even be several different councils of the people, each with its own set of rules.

Rousseau's concern with the assemblies he discusses is not limited to determining what makes them legitimate. He is also interested in their political effect on the well-being of the republic. A voting arrangement can be undesirable without being illegitimate. An assembly may have desirable political effects and yet may violate the principles of legitimacy. Rousseau raises no objection to the political effects of the tribal assemblies during the period in which the preponderance of the rural tribes in them was maintained. He shows how easily their violation of the principles of

The Sovereign People and Government

legitimacy could have been corrected without modifying their character. The mere fact that the centuriate assembly did not violate his principles does not mean that he wished it to be imitated. The fact that the assembly by tribes did violate them does not mean that he did not want aspects of it imitated.[27]

Rousseau's analysis of the Roman assemblies is meant to show how the institutions of the republic can be kept from degenerating into a facade. His aim is to protect the forms of the republic against the tyrannical designs of demagogues. The devices his analysis reveals to be at the disposal of statesmen are all intended to preserve the state. All these devices are compatible with the principles of political right, principles which accord a certain latitude to the prudence of statesmen. These devices are, of course, not immune to abuse. They can be employed, contrary to Rousseau's intention, to turn the republic into a facade. Rousseau could claim to have made every effort to warn against such misuse of them as well as of the other devices discussed in the first half of Book 4.

Institutional Supports

Book 4 as a whole is concerned with strengthening the constitution of the state. In the first four chapters, the ways of doing so that are discussed determine how the sovereign itself would be constituted and what the extent of its authority will be. They determine who will have the right to vote, how votes will be counted, what kinds of issues will be put to a vote, and how large a majority will be needed before a vote on an issue of a certain kind can count as a declaration of the general will. Differing answers to these questions are compatible with Rousseau's principles. The answer that is given ought to be adapted to the state of vigor or decay of a political society. Some answer must be given, however, if the sovereign is to exist. The four chapters we have finished discussing continue and complete Rousseau's analysis of the general will or of sovereignty. The first of these chapters has a chapter heading of the kind that one found in the first discussion of sovereignty (1.6 to 2.6). The matters we were compelled to take up in following Rousseau's exposition in the opening chapter of Book 4 revealed that we were still engaged in a discussion of the nature of the social compact, of the general will, and of sovereignty. What occurred in the course of our analysis of the second half of Book 3 has also occurred in our analysis of the first half of Book 4: an exposition which might have appeared at first to be concerned with another subject proved, on reflection, to be an essential part of Rousseau's analysis of the nature of sovereignty. The thirteen chapters stretching from Book 3, Chapter 10, to Book 4, Chapter 4, are a second treatment of sovereignty. The first treatment was followed by a discussion of the legislator, that is, of someone who is different from the sovereign and in a way higher than the sovereign. The second treatment of sovereignty is followed by a discussion of the tribunate, of dictatorship, of censorship, and of civil religion. All four are distinct from the sovereign and all are, in a way, higher than the sovereign. The tribunate is said to be "more sacred and more revered" than the sovereign. The dictator, named in an emergency, temporarily suspends the authority of the sovereign and is placed "above the laws." The censor is the mouthpiece of "morals" and of "public opinion," of what Rousseau had called "the most important kind of law" and "the true constitution of the State" even though it is not the kind of law that the sovereign can enact. That the divine is other than the sovereign and higher than the sovereign needs no discussion.

In the light of the foregoing, one again discerns the plan of the argument of the *Social Contract* that was set forth earlier. The work as a whole is divided into two parts. In both parts, the argument ascends from the discussion of something other than the sovereign and lower than the sovereign to a discussion of sovereignty, and from a discussion of sovereignty to a discussion of something other than the sovereign and in a sense higher than the sovereign.

The subject of the chapter on the tribunate was mentioned in the course of Rousseau's discussion of mixed government. The tribunate was one of the ways in which the proper relations between the sovereign, the government, and the people could be maintained. This was an important result because it helped show how to overcome a difficulty which strikes a reader of Book 3 and of which we have already spoken: the better the political order is, the more its population will increase; the larger the citizen body becomes, the stronger, and hence the smaller, government will have to be; but the smaller and stronger government becomes, the less obedient to the sovereign it will be. The earlier chapter showed that the situation was not utterly hopeless. It showed how the government could be made more subordinate to the sovereign without having to become any weaker in relation to those subject to its rule. It also showed how a popular government could increase its effectiveness without becoming smaller. Fuller discussion of the tribunate was left to Book 4. The chapter in Book 3 was part of Rousseau's treatment of government, and the means discussed for strengthening government vis-à-vis the people or for weakening it vis-à-vis the sovereign were all governmental means.

The tribunate is not declared to be always needed. It would be superfluous in the peasant democracy that Rousseau describes at the beginning of Book 4. It is not an essential organ of the state. Unlike the sovereign, it can be absent without the state ceasing to exist. Unlike the government, it can be absent without the state ceasing to be able to act. It is not part of the constitution of the state, but it can be a highly effective means for preserving that constitution: the tribunate is a body with the right to declare illegal a proceeding in the sovereign assembly, an act of government, or an irregular assembly of the people. If the sovereign were to try to enact as a law a measure that did not have the support of a majority as large as the law required, or if the government prevented the sovereign assembly from convening when it was supposed to meet, or if an excited crowd formed suddenly and tried to pass its decisions off as acts of the sovereign, the tribunes would have the right to nullify these acts. Not all violations of law would come before the tribunes. Ordinary judicial functions would be carried out by other bodies (4.3.8). The violations of law that concern the tribunate are violations of the constitution of the state.

Rousseau declares the tribunate to be the strongest support that a good constitution can have if the tribunate is properly moderated. Unless that is done, however, the tribunate will itself accelerate the decline of the constitution precisely when the constitution is most in need of support. It may even be the body which destroys the constitution. The power to halt or strike down any act it pleases on the ground that it is unconstitutional can make the tribunate, which is not supposed to be any part of the state at all, the most powerful body in it. Rousseau believes very strongly that the tribunes should limit themselves to safeguarding the law and that they should refrain from usurping governmental functions. The difficulty is that the tribunate cannot do its job if it is subject to any other authority but it is hard to see how it can be kept moderate if it is not. Availing himself of a suggestion that Machiavelli made, Rousseau proposes limiting in advance the period of time during which the tribunate will be permitted to function, letting it go out of existence for a definite period of time, and naming a new body which will be limited in the same way to replace it. While recognizing the usefulness of such an institution, Rousseau makes it clear why he thinks that earlier examples of it—Spartan ephors, Roman tribunes, the Venetian Ten—were dangerously defective.

Institutional Supports

On the basis of what has been said, one can understand why the tribunate—unlike the sovereign or the government—is not and should not be a part of the constitution of political society. One can even understand how not only the government but even the sovereign is subject to its authority even though it cannot enact laws or govern. In all these respects the tribunate reminds one of Rousseau's legislator. But what is one to make of the assertion that the tribunate is "more sacred and more revered" than the very sovereign who enacts the law?

To answer this question, we will have to refer briefly to Rousseau's chapter on civil religion. There Rousseau will explain his view that religion is essential to a sound political order and, without requiring all citizens to be adherents of the same religion, he will want them to agree on certain points. These points include not only beliefs regarding God, providence, and the afterlife, but also a belief in "the sanctity of the social contract and of the laws." The sacred character of the social order and of the sovereign, to which Rousseau makes reference more than once, owes its being ultimately to the civil religion. The sovereign enacts the law, but the civil religion is what endows it with a sacred character. The sovereign assembly has the right to repeal a law, but in order to do so it must obey the law it has laid down for repealing a law. The tribunate checks the sovereign assembly when that assembly is in danger of violating one of its own laws. Since that law is sacred, for the reason given, the tribunate manifests itself as the defender of its sanctity against a sovereign on the point of violating it, a role that makes the tribunate more sacred and more revered than the sovereign. For although the civil religion, as we will see, has among its tenets the sanctity of the social contract and of the laws, it does not have among its tenets the sanctity of the sovereign. The product of the sovereign assembly is endowed with a more sacred character than the assembly itself. The effect of this higher dignity is not to diminish the legitimate authority of the sovereign but to prevent the people from violating laws it has not repealed.[1]

The chapter on the tribunate deals with a temporary extraordinary body for preventing violations of law. The chapter that immediately follows deals with emergencies that would destroy the state if the law were not violated. The measures discussed until now in Book 4 have all tended to strengthen the law. But according to Rousseau, the law—and the state—must not be so rigid as to make it impossible to declare a state of emergency and to temporarily confer extraordinary, "dictatorial" power to one or more men. This can be done without undermining the state or the laws if there manifestly is a genuine state of emergency and if the extraordinary powers needed to cope with it are conferred for a very brief duration. To the argument that it would be a mistake to limit the dictator's term in advance since one cannot foresee how long the emergency he must deal with will last, Rousseau's answer would be that he is speaking of truly extraordinary powers, of powers that are exercised while the rest of the state has ceased to function. He is not speaking of emergency powers exercised in the presence of the government and the sovereign and with their continuing cooperation. Given an emergency of the kind and magnitude of which Rousseau speaks, and the powers to match it, one can see why he feels that it would be destructive of a democratic republic for these powers to be exercised for such a length of time that they cease to be experienced as extraordinary both by those wielding them and by those subject to them.

Many of the means for strengthening the republic that have been discussed in Book 4 are said to be useful for prolonging the life of a commonwealth in its late decline.[2] In the chapter on dictatorship, Rousseau criticizes Rome in its last days as a republic for not defending public liberty as effectively as it might have done if it had overcome its reluctance to have recourse to emergency powers. In the chapter on censorship, by contrast, a measure for strengthening the commonwealth is discussed that is of no help once the decline of a commonwealth is advanced. In some of the preceding chapters, an explicit reference had been made to the possible usefulness of the measures considered for a republic in its old age. But in the chapter concerned with censorship (4.7) explicit reference is made to the uselessness of censorship in such circumstances. What Rousseau means by censorship, it would appear, is effective only as long as the republic is vigorous and healthy. Once the republic loses its health and vigor, censorship cannot help restore it. Is censorship an institution which is useless provided one needs it and useful provided one does not? If so, why is it included in a discussion of ways to strengthen the state?

Censorship, as Rousseau understands it, has a contribution to make to the preservation of the state, even though censorship cannot be of any use during the final stages of the state's existence. Censorship makes its contribution not by prolonging that final stage, as do some of the other institutions and arrangements de-

177

scribed by Rousseau, but by prolonging the healthy and vigorous period which precedes it. In order to understand how censorship does this, one must grasp what kind of an institution it is, according to Rousseau.

Censorship is concerned with the unwritten law of a society. That law is embodied in the character, the tastes, the customs, the passions, and the prejudices of a people. These various ingredients of the unwritten law come together and manifest themselves in the convictions of a people regarding what is admirable or contemptible, which is what Rousseau means by "public opinion." Censors do not and cannot make this opinion be what they would like it to be. They must take it as they find it. What, then, accounts for their importance, in Rousseau's opinion?

The relation of the unwritten law to the censors is compared by Rousseau to the relation of the general will to the government. The censors give utterance to the unwritten law and they apply it to particular cases. Although they cannot bring the unwritten law into being, they confer on "public opinion" a power it would otherwise lack and make public opinion aware of that power.

At the end of Book 2, Rousseau calls the unwritten law "the true constitution of the state" and the "keystone" on which all the other laws depend. He says that "when other laws age or die out" the unwritten law "revives or replaces them" and "preserves a people in the spirit of its institution." Given these remarks, how is one to understand Rousseau's observation, in the chapter devoted to censorship, that "when legislation weakens, morals degenerate" and that once that happens, censorship cannot help matters any, or his remark that once "the laws have lost [their vigor] everything is hopeless"?

To solve this problem, one must realize that, when Rousseau speaks of laws, he sometimes refers to those that determine the constitution of the state and at other times to some other law or laws. When he speaks of the "constitution" of a people, of its "legislation," or of "the laws" pure and simple, it is the constitution of the state that he is speaking of. The claims made for "morals" at the end of Book 2 envision a situation in which some laws in particular have aged or died out, not in which the entire constitution of the state has done so, for if that were to happen morals would not only not be of any help but they would themselves have undergone corruption. It is by helping to prevent the aging or death of the constitution that the unwritten law "preserves a people in the spirit of its institutions."

The censors, according to Rousseau, cannot command public opinion. Nor can the sovereign do so. The sovereign assembly will not be obeyed if it decrees that from now on men are to admire one thing and despise another. "Public opinion" is not subject to command. However, this does not mean that it cannot be influenced indirectly. "A people's opinions arise from its constitution. Although the law does not regulate morals, it is legislation that gives rise to them." A people's morals grow out of its political constitution. Once they have developed, they strengthen the constitution. The constitution is the ground from which morals grow. Morals, in turn, gradually become the ground from which the constitution grows. The unwritten law and the political constitution reinforce each other. The one helps the other retain its vigor. The one makes the other share in its decay.[3]

It is clear from the foregoing that the "morals" and the "public opinion" of which Rousseau speaks in the chapter are republican morals and republican public opinion. They are difficult to distinguish from republic patriotism and republican love of freedom and equality. The brief remarks in this chapter are not meant to provide even an outline of Rousseau's thoughts on morals in general or on republican morals in particular. Nor is it their purpose to draw attention to the curious kind of reciprocal causation to be found in the relation between public opinion and the constitution of the republic, although they do so. In the chapter immediately preceding the one on censorship reference has been made more than once to the way in which good morals compensate for highly defective political arrangements. It was the good morals of the early Romans that kept the defects of the centuriate assembly from harming the republic. It was the good morals of Sparta that for a time kept the excessive power of Sparta's "tribunes"—the ephors—from being a threat to the Spartans. As long as the morals of Rome remained good, the Romans could appoint dictators without fear. On the other hand, Rousseau criticizes Romans such as Cicero for their opposition to taking the measures that should have been taken once Roman morals had been corrupted. According to Rousseau, Cicero should have favored the secret ballot once it had become easy to purchase votes and people were no longer ashamed to be seen voting in ways that revealed that their votes had been purchased.

Institutional Supports

The purpose of the chapter on censorship is to explain these various observations. The chapter on censorship contains an outline not of Rousseau's views regarding morals but of Rousseau's views regarding censorship.

The chief point of this chapter on censorship is to encourage its use while it can be used but to make the limits of its effectiveness manifest. Censorhip cannot legislate morals. It cannot exhort public opinion into becoming what it wishes it to be. The most it can do by way of innovation is to take a stand on a matter with regard to which public opinion has not yet declared itself. Even then, success is achieved only if the stand taken coincides with the stand public opinion was inclined to take. The limits within which censorship can be effective must be grasped clearly because of the great importance that censorship properly employed can have. Censorship properly employed is a very important, though not the only, intermediary through which a republican constitution and republican morals can be a basis for each other.

Censorship, like the tribunate and dictatorship, are institutions that are established by an act of the sovereign. In doing their work, however, they are not under its command. The most important institution of this kind, for Rousseau, still remains to be discussed. It is religion.

For Rousseau, and for the major modern political philosophers preceding him, the importance of the problem faced in the chapter on civil religion is difficult to exaggerate. The fact that two of the four books of Hobbes's *Leviathan* are devoted to it is only one indication of its importance. As long as this problem remained unresolved it was, if not the most important problem which political philosophers had to face, at least the one on whose solution the solution of all the others depended, in their opinion. The only work devoted to exposing his own views which Spinoza published in his lifetime—his *Theologico-Political Treatise*—was devoted to this very problem.

The issue Rousseau faces in his chapter on civil religion is that of determining what the relation between political and religious authority should be in a properly constituted republic. That issue derives its importance from the fact that political and religious beliefs are the beliefs over which men in large numbers are willing to wage war even against their fellow citizens. Rousseau's discussion of this issue falls into three parts. In the first (¶¶ 1-16) he gives an outline of the history of the relation between politics and religion up

Chapter Six

to his time. The second part (¶¶ 17-30) analyzes the various kinds of religion with a view to whether they benefit or harm society. Finally (¶¶ 31–35) Rousseau sets forth the principles of political right regarding the practice of religion in well-constituted republics.

The earliest theologico-political condition Rousseau describes is one in which the political order and the religion of a people are indistinguishable. Its rulers are gods, its governors are their ministers, and its laws are divine in character. In all these respects, the Hebrews were not unique but rather typical of ancient peoples, according to Rousseau. What was true of Israel was true of the ancient city. The thesis that Fustel de Coulanges was to set forth more than a century later is latent in the opening paragraphs of Rousseau's chapter on civil religion.

Rousseau traces the large number of gods that were worshiped in ancient times to the large number of peoples, each with laws peculiar to itself and each a potential enemy of the others, that these gods were believed to rule. Wars between peoples were at the same time wars between their gods. The future existence of both the city and its religion were at stake in such wars. But the purpose of these wars was not to punish the worshipers of other gods for not worshiping the gods of one's own city. This was no less true of the Hebrews than it was of other peoples, according to Rousseau. He claims to find evidence in the Bible that the God of the Hebrews, however jealous he may have been regarding the worship his own people owed him, was not jealous of the gods worshiped by other peoples. Nothing that Rousseau says suggests that the gods worshiped by pagan peoples were not equally jealous regarding their worshipers. Prosecution for impiety in the ancient city is not unintelligible in Rousseau's account. The uniqueness of the Hebrews found expression elsewhere, according to him. It manifested itself in their refusal to abandon their religion and to embrace the religion of their conquerors after they had been defeated by the Babylonians. Given the inseparability of the religious and the political, this refusal was interpreted as a refusal to accept defeat. The persecution of the Jews that followed was altogether atypical of ancient times, according to Rousseau. The later persecutions of the Christians, Rousseau says, would also be of this unusual character.

According to Rousseau, the Romans often granted legal status in Rome to the people they vanquished and to their gods as well. As vanquished peoples became part of Rome, they began to worship all its gods. The result was that "paganism in the known world finally became a single, identical religion." The first universal religion to make its appearance in the chapter on Civil Religion is Roman paganism. Like the religions previously discussed, it and the political society of which it is the religion are one.

Rousseau traces the destruction of the unity of political society to Jesus. The kingdom Jesus came to establish was a spiritual, not a political, kingdom, but it was on earth that he meant to establish it. The Romans, for whom political society and religion were one, persecuted the Christians because they were convinced that the otherworldly kingdom was meant to be a this-worldly kingdom different from the Roman Empire. Rousseau asserts that the fears of the pagans were justified by the results of Christianity's triumph: the leaders of the otherworldly kingdom began to rule over men in this world without becoming their political rulers. Men found themselves, for the first time, ruled by two kinds of rulers who stood for entirely different worlds. The result was "a perpetual conflict of jurisdiction that has made any good polity impossible in Christian states."

Rousseau uses very strong language to describe this transition. Speaking of the Church of Rome, he says that "this supposedly otherworldly kingdom became under a visible head the most violent despotism in this one." Earlier in the work he had spoken of feudalism as "that wicked and absurd government in which the human race is degraded and the name of man is dishonored." Rousseau's view of the Middle Ages is not all that different from that of many of his famous contemporaries.[4] What distinguishes him from a number of them is his conviction, which receives expression more than once in the *Social Contract* that the social order cannot be relied on to do what it is meant to do unless it is held to be sacred. Now, while self-preservation may supply political society with its purpose, it cannot make political society sacred. Civil religion is necessary for that end. But the spirit of Christianity is incompatible with any civil religion. In making these remarks, Rousseau is not thinking only of medieval Christianity or of Roman Catholicism. They are only examples of what he holds to be true in all Christian states, as his references to England and to Russia show. He holds the very same to be true, if to a lesser degree, in Moslem states like Iran (4.8.11 end), although it was not true of Mohammedanism in the time of Mohammed. In fact, he holds it to be true wherever one finds a separate priesthood with the right to determine who may and who may not be a member of the established religion of the city

(4.8.12 note). Nothing that he says can lead one to suppose that he wishes to make an exception of Protestant countries and to restore the force of what he says about Christianity to Catholic ones. On the contrary, "Wherever the clergy forms a body, it is master legislator in its fatherland. Thus there are two powers, two sovereigns, in England and in Russia just as everywhere else." Later in the chapter we learn that "everywhere else" even includes parts of Asia (4.8.16).

Rousseau praises Hobbes for discerning and proposing the appropriate remedy.[5] That remedy would consist in giving the civil sovereign the kind of authority over otherworldly matters that he already enjoys over this-worldly ones. The kings who made themselves the heads of the churches in their dominions did not gain such authority because they did not acquire the right to legislate in religious matters. As heads of the church in their dominions, their power was limited to administering the affairs of their church without making any changes in it. The power to make such changes, that is, the legislative power, effectively resided, in these postpagan religions, in the body of the clergy. In spite of his praise of Hobbes's remedy, Rousseau does not see how it could possibly win popular acceptance.

Rousseau makes clear in his survey of the history of the relations between religion and politics that he believes religion to be not only useful but indispensable for political society and that Christianity has made it impossible for religion to perform this function. It is therefore not surprising to learn that, according to him, the civil religion cannot be Christian. To avoid being misunderstood, Rousseau proceeds to compare three different kinds of religion with regard to the benefit or harm each does to political society. In the course of this comparison, a new kind of Christianity makes its appearance, a kind unmentioned in the preceding historical survey—the "pure and simple religion of the Gospel." Even without meeting that religion in the survey, a reader of Rousseau would have come to know it from the profession of faith of the Savoyard Vicar in *Emile*. Rousseau's consideration of the true religion of the Gospel, however, which he also calls "true [*vrai*] theism" and "true [*véritable*] religion," does not lead him to modify the conclusion about Christianity at which he had arrived previously. Eleven of the sixteen paragraphs in the second section of this chapter are devoted to arguing that pure Christianity is no less opposed to a sound political order than the historical Christianity which he had earlier

Institutional Supports

spoken of. Rousseau's great predecessors in modern political philosophy, when they discussed the political consequences of Christianity, drew a distinction between a false Christianity, which had bad consequences, and a true Christianity, which they held to be perfectly compatible with their understanding of the requirements of political society. Rousseau also distinguishes a true and genuine Christianity from the spurious Christianity "of today," but he draws the distinction only to condemn the political consequences of genuine Christianity no less strongly than he condemns the political consequences of spurious Christianity. He appears to wish to leave no doubt in the reader's mind that the requirements of political society are incompatible with the requirements of Christianity, whether at its worst or at its best. Since Rousseau himself, or at any rate his Savoyard Vicar preaches the simple and pure religion of the Gospel in *Emile*, and since the teachings of that religion have been often taken to be an expression of Rousseau's own religious beliefs, his intention in showing it to be politically harmful is not immediately apparent.

Rousseau begins his analysis of the political consequences of religion by distinguishing between two kinds of society, general society, or the entire human race, and particular society, or the part of the human race in this or that commonwealth. The religion of general society Rousseau calls the religion of man or true theism. It is *the* universal religion. Rousseau equates this religion with the "pure and simple religion of the Gospel." The religion of the citizen is peculiar to a people. It is the kind of religion which Rousseau had described at the beginning of the chapter, a religion which is indistinguishable from the political society of which it is the religion. "[I]t combines divine worship with the love of the laws," and makes "the fatherland the object of the adoration of the citizens." To these two, Rousseau adds a third kind of religion which is neither universal nor particular in the sense in which he has now given these words. Unlike universal religion, or the religion of man, it does not submit a man to the practice of "the eternal duties of morality" toward all men without distinction. Unlike particular religion, or the religion of the citizen, it does not strengthen a citizen's love for his city. Since in every particular society there is always going to be some this-worldly and political authority in existence, according to Rousseau, the third kind of religion gives men "two systems of legislation [*deux législations*], two heads, and two fatherlands, subjects them to contradictory duties and prevents them from being, at the same time, devout men and citizens." Rousseau calls the third kind of religion the religion of the priest.

One can easily find the passages in Rousseau's historical survey in which he discusses the religion of the citizen. It is not at all easy, as we noted earlier, to find the passages in which he discusses the religion of man. The Christianity he describes in that survey is the religion of the priest rather than the religion of man. Moreover, as described in that survey, it was never anything other than the religion of the priest as distinguished from the religion of man. The religion of man is a religion "without temples, altars, or rites." Above all, it is a religion without priests. Rousseau will find much to criticize in it when he considers its effects on political society. For example, he will disapprove of the fact that the religion of man makes it difficult to love one's own people more than one loves other peoples, or at least that it makes it difficult to do so with a good conscience. But whatever his criticisms of the religion of man may be, causing divided sovereignty will not be one of them. Now, causing divided sovereignty is precisely the mark of the religion of the priest. And causing divided sovereignty is also precisely what Rousseau criticizes Christianity for doing in his historical survey. It is by no means clear that Rousseau intends to exempt Jesus from this criticism. "Jesus," according to Rousseau, "intended to establish a spiritual kingdom *on earth*" (4.8.8; emphasis added). Divided sovereignty is presented as a consequence of his success. In another writing, Rousseau suggests that divided sovereignty was a consequence of the failure of Jesus rather than of his success. The pagans' distrust of the Christians' claim that they had no intention of wielding any this-worldly authority is said to have been confirmed by what took place after Christianity triumphed.

The religion of the priest requires a separate priestly body (4.8.12). That body is what Rousseau calls the sovereign of that religion. Because the religion of man has no priests, it does not lead to the establishment of a sovereign different from the civil sovereign. It is not because it gives men two different sets of rulers in this world that Rousseau says that he knows of nothing more contrary to the social spirit than the religion of man. The religion of man gives men an otherworldly spiritual fatherland which includes all men, past, present, and future. It is to that fatherland that the true adherent of the religion of man, whom, following Rousseau, we will call the true Christian, belongs heart and soul. Because he belongs heart and soul to that city, he cannot belong heart and soul to an earthly one. He cannot, without ceasing to be a true Christian, love anything this-worldly as passionately as Rousseau requires the citizens of a well-constituted city to love it. Even if there is no conflict of duties, there cannot help being a conflict of loves between the true Christian and the good citizen.

Rousseau does not leave matters at a presentation of the conflict between the city and the society consisting of the entire human race. He sides with the city. He prefers the soldiers of Fabius and their passion for victory to any army composed of genuine adherents to the religion of man. "As for me, I admire the oath taken by the soldiers of Fabius [*c'étoit un beau serment à mon gré que celui des soldats de Fabius*]; they did not swear to die or conquer; they swore to return victorious, and kept their oath. Never would Christians have taken one like it; they would have thought that it was tempting God" (4.8.27). What is remarkable about this passage is that in it Rousseau explicitly sets himself apart not only from Christianity but even from the pure and simple religion of the Gospel.[6]

Rousseau's chief reason for siding with the city is his belief that life in a free republic is incomparably better for men than life in the unjust and oppressive societies that one finds where free republics are absent. He knows that the patriotism he requires of his citizens will lead to less humane attitudes toward men who are not members of the city than true Christianity would regard as proper. But the essential thing, he affirms, is to be good to those among whom one spends one's life and this, he believes, is brought about more effectively by a good city than it is by the religion of man.

The only kind of religion that Rousseau does not find utterly unsatisfactory from a political point of view is the religion of the citizen. That religion is characterized by the fact that its divine laws are political laws. It is also characterized by the fact that its priests are citizens rather than a body separate from them. It is the only one of the three kinds of religion discussed by Rousseau that strengthens the state. Yet it too is found to have serious defects. It is based on error and falsehood. It makes men superstitious and keeps them so. In its extreme forms, it can degenerate into bloodthirsty fanaticism.

In the third part of the chapter on civil religion (secs. 31–35), Rousseau lays down the principles of political right with regard to religion. These principles are based on the assumption that the sovereign has the right to require citizens to love their duties and therefore to believe in a religion that will lead them to do so. The sovereign can require the love of duty as a condition of citizenship and can also demand the acceptance of certain dogmas without which the love of duty would not be possible. In setting forth this demand, Rousseau is making his own conclusions that had already been advanced by Spinoza and by Locke. The religious dogmas in question are general and simple truths on which all the religions tolerated by the commonwealth would agree. Each citizen and each religion has a perfect right to interpret these dogmas in its own way.[7]

The civil religion is an established religion.[8] It is instituted by a positive law. The rules determining the content of that law are principles of political right. Because it is an institution established by law without which the state would not exist (4.8.14), the civil religion is said to be part of the constitution of the state.[9] The civil religion is not likely to be the only religion of a citizen, but its tenets are so chosen as to be compatible with the beliefs of every other tolerant religion found in the city.

The religious situation favored in the third part of the chapter on civil religion differs from any of those discussed in the first two parts. How can that situation, involving an established civil religion that coexists with a number of different religions, each with its own distinctive rites and many with their own separate priesthoods—religions which tolerate each other and a civil religion whose beliefs seem little different from those of pure Christianity—be a satisfactory response to the difficulty analyzed by Rousseau? When Rousseau spoke of divided sovereignty, he made it clear that the sovereign authority which rivaled that of the civil sovereign was the separate priesthood. The solution Rousseau finally sets forth does not eliminate such separate bodies. Since the day of exclusive national religion is over, according to Rousseau, the religions that these bodies rule transcend the boundaries of a given political society and lend no support to it. The religion of man, since it has no separate priesthood, was not accused by Rousseau of fostering divided sovereignty. Its transpolitical otherworldliness, however, was said to detach a citizen from this world and from the part of this world that his own city is. Does not the solution Rousseau finally proposes combine features to which he objected in both the religion of man and the religion of the priest?

Toleration is what distinguishes the situation envisioned by Rousseau from what he calls the religion of the priest. In declaring the solution proposed by Hobbes to be "good," "true," and "correct" (4.8.13 and note) and in proposing toleration as the way to make it workable, Rousseau makes his own a path on which he was

Institutional Supports

preceded by Spinoza, whose analysis of the theologico-political problem in the Christian West is the same as Hobbes's and who finds the embodiment of divided sovereignty in the separate priesthood of the nonnational Christian religion. Rousseau's adoption, in this chapter, of Spinoza's suggestion on how to reunite the two heads of the eagle—by toleration—does not explain how the transition from intolerant to tolerant religion takes place. For light regarding that point one must turn to Spinoza and to other authors who preceded Rousseau. But it is possible to understand without difficulty why Rousseau thought that the sovereign had nothing to fear from the tolerant God of tolerant priests, as long as the sovereign too is tolerant. The threat of divided sovereignty arises only when the adherents and the priests of a religion ascribe the highest importance to beliefs and practices peculiar to themselves, when they make them life-and-death matters, and when they claim the right to decide which commands of the sovereign are compatible with these all-important beliefs and practices and which are not. An outlook of this kind is altogether incompatible with the kind of outlook that toleration fosters. From the tolerant and even from those who initially only pretend to be tolerant the sovereign has nothing to fear. If they are willing to live on friendly terms with those whose peculiar beliefs and practices are different from their own, they have, whether or not they are aware of it, broken decisively with the intolerant outlook.

But even if the sovereign has nothing to fear from the tolerant religion of the priest, how much support can political society expect from it or from the civil religion? Are the tenets of the civil religion not exposed to the very same objections which Rousseau raised when discussing the religion of man? Is not the central tenet of the civil religion, as set forth by Rousseau, the afterlife? Does not the predominant concern with the afterlife lead to a depreciation of this life and, since political life is part of this life, to a depreciation of political society as well? To understand Rousseau's answer to this question, one must bear in mind that his discussion of what a society of true Christians would be like was explicitly based on the false assumption that such a society is humanly possible (4.8.22). The adherents of the tolerant religions will not be true Christians. No people, not even a people that adheres to true Christianity, can be a people of true Christians. What we are speaking of is the well-known truth that religions are often far more otherworldly than their adherents are. This is true of intolerant religions for which, in moments of crisis, men may sacrifice important worldly interests. It is no less true of tolerant religions. The impure adherents of pure religion may be better citizens because of their impurity than pure adherents of pure religion would be, if they could exist. The theoretical incompatibility between the religion of man and the requirements of political society is not a practical incompatibility. The imperfect adherents of true Christianity, just because they are imperfect adherents of it, can perfectly well combine a concern for the afterlife with a belief in the sanctity of the social contract and the laws. The natural religion espoused by the Savoyard Vicar, for all its otherworldliness, does not lead Emile to repudiate sexual desire—any more than it leads the Savoyard Vicar to do so—but contributes to making Emile a better husband and father.[10] Similarly, the civil religion, for all its otherworldliness, helps make the members of political society good citizens. The insurmountable gap between the religion of man and political society is theoretical rather than practical but Rousseau wishes to contribute to a theoretical understanding of the relation between religion and political life no less than to help establish a sound practical relation between them.

Even if the civil religion is not exposed to the most obvious objections that could be raised against it, given Rousseau's own analysis, the question still remains of whether something has not been irretrievably lost, according to Rousseau, in the transition from the period in which exclusive national religions were typical to the present period in which such religions are no longer possible. Even if the tolerant civil religion and the tolerant religions of the priest do lend support to political society, can they lend it anything like the support which exclusive national religions once did? The answer would have to be that they cannot. But Rousseau does not unequivocally praise national religions. He is aware of the powerful love of country they instilled but also of the high price that was paid for the benefit they conferred. The following passage, from Rousseau's first draft of the present chapter, forcefully states this:

> Now if pagan superstition, despite this mutual tolerance and in the midst of literature and a thousand virtues, engendered so many cruelties, I do not see how it is possible to separate those very cruelties from that very zeal, and reconcile the rights of a national religion with those of humanity; it is better, then, to bind the citizens to the State by weaker and gentler ties, and to have neither heroes nor fanatics.[11]

Institutional Supports

One is reminded by this passage of the earlier discussion in which Rousseau showed that a more democratic and more public-spirited political life was made possible by slavery in ancient times than is possible now or than it would be permissible to institute now, given the radical injustice of slavery which Rousseau reaffirms in that very discussion. Ancient national religion as well as ancient slavery made possible a republican spirit far more powerful than any spirit one could hope to establish in their absence. A political life based on Rousseau's principles of political right will be more just and more humane than political life in ancient times but it will not be as heroic. Something that it would be wrong to even try to recapture is therefore irretrievably lost to political life in modern times according to Rousseau.

The *Social Contract* concludes with the only chapter in the work that contains only one paragraph. In that paragraph, Rousseau claims to have completed the task he set himself in the work and announced in the subtitle to it. He claims to have succeeded in setting forth the true principles of political right and to have attempted to found the state on the basis of these principles. He outlines the matters that still remain to be treated concerning the relation of a state to other states. He declares in closing: "But all this forms a new object too vast for my weak sight [*courte vue*]; I should have *always* kept it fixed closer to me" (emphasis added).

How is Rousseau's closing statement to be understood? What can the touch of regret voiced in it mean? For a moment it might almost seem as though Rousseau felt that the matters he treated in the *Social Contract* were as much beyond his limited powers of vision as the subjects he now lists. But a little reflection suffices to make one realize that this cannot be what he means since in the immediately preceding sentence he affirmed that he had completed setting forth the true principles of political right. Could the regret have another source? Did something in Rousseau begrudge the time and effort he lavished on setting forth the principles of political right, time he could have spent on more important matters closer to himself? The work opened with a forceful statement of the tension between the individual and society. Its close reminds one of that tension. The last word of the work is "me" (*moi*) just as its first word was "I" (*je*).[12] Every chapter since Book 4, Chapter 5, has dealt with something that is other than the sovereign and that is in some sense higher than the sovereign. One wonders whether Rousseau thought that his individuality, his "self," which is other than the sovereign, was also in some sense higher than the sovereign. It is not of himself as legislator that this could be the case. As legislator, he would fulfill himself, in at least one sense, *by* setting forth the principles of political right. His doing so could not, therefore, be an object of regret to himself as legislator. There remains the question of what it could possibly mean for something in Rousseau's self to be in some sense even higher in dignity than the social order or than his activity as a legislator. The answer to this question is beyond the scope of the *Social Contract*. To learn what it is, one would have to turn to the writings of Rousseau the subject of which is Rousseau himself.

Abbreviations

P   Jean Jacques Rousseau, *Oeuvres complètes*. Ed. Bernard Gagnebin and Marcel Raymond. 4 vols. Paris: Gallimard, Bibliothèque de la Pléiade, 1959–. Numerals preceding P refer to volumes of this edition. Numerals following P refer to pages in these volumes.

CS   Rousseau: *Du contrat social*. References to this work are by book, chapter, and paragraph. In references to particular editions, the name of the editor is given in parentheses.

Abbreviations of other works by Rousseau

D'A	*Lettre à d'Alembert sur les spectacles*
B	*Lettre à M. de Beaumont*
C	*Les Confessions*
CS^1	Early draft of *Du contrat social*
D1	*Discours sur les sciences et les arts*
D2	*Discours sur l'origine et les fondements de l'inégalité*
EP	*Discours sur l'économie politique*
E	*Emile, ou de l'Education*
GP	*Considérations sur le gouvernement de Pologne*
LM	*Lettres écrites de la montagne*
R	*Les Rêveries du promeneur solitaire*

References to particular editions of these works give the name of the editor in parentheses.

Notes

Chapter One

1. Cf. Leo Strauss, "On the Intention of Rousseau," *Social Research* 14, no. 4 (December): pp. 485–87.

2. This is not to deny Robert Derathé's well-documented claim that in the *Social Contract* Rousseau attempts to supply valid principles of what one might call natural constitutional law in place of the invalid ones contained in the inadequate and, Rousseau suggests, far from disinterested teaching of such jurists as Grotius, Pufendorf, and Barbeyrac. According to Derathé, Rousseau "owes these jurists more by what he rejects than by what he retains of their teaching." The debt to Hobbes and to Locke, as Derathé brings out, is a good deal more substantial. Cf. *Jean-Jacques Rousseau et la science politique de son temps* (Paris: Vrin, 1950), pp. 25f., 51f., 107f., 174f., 200ff., 333ff. In the *Social Contract* Rousseau generally indicates when he is discussing the teachings of these jurists by referring to the views of Grotius, whom he regarded as their master (E, 4 P 836): cf. CS 1.2.4; 1.4.2; 1.4.7; 1.5.2; 2.2.5. For the peculiarly modern character of *jus publicum universale seu naturale* and its origin, cf. Leo Strauss, *Natural Right and History* (Chicago: University of Chicago Press, 1953), pp. 190ff.; hereafter cited as NRH.

3. Derathé, *Rousseau et la science politique*, p. 131. In the Epistle Dedicatory of *The Prince*, Machiavelli claims that despite its brevity his book incorporates the highest knowledge he possesses in its entirety. The Foreword to the *Social Contract* as well as its conclusion draws attention to the omission of important matters from the work.

4. In the *Social Contract* Machiavelli's *The Prince* is cited for the light it sheds on kings as they are (3.6.5 and n.), Plato's *Statesman* for the light it sheds on kings as they should be and on how rare they are (2.7.2; 3.6.15).

5. CS¹, 3 P 309 (emphasis added); cf. 3 P 328–29.

6. LM, 3 P 812. See below, pp. 38ff., 112f., 129f.

7. E, 4 P 837.

8. CS¹, 3 P 309.

9. LM, 3 P 806–9.

10. E, 4 P 266, 537, 836–39. The Aristotelian gentleman who is intended to lead the life of moral excellence is also not assumed to be uncommonly gifted (cf. *Nicomachean Ethics* 1143b6–14). In spite of the different conclusions they come to, both Aristotle and Rousseau are interested in the best that the right kind of upbringing can accomplish for human beings of ordinary abilities. Aristotle thought that men would be most likely to receive the right kind of upbringing in a good city. It is by no means clear that Rousseau was of a different opinion. (The projected sequel to *Emile* describes the destruction of Emile's marriage [C, 1 P 57; cf. 4 P 881–924]. A sound political order would have protected it against what destroys it.) One of the many important differences between Emile and the Aristotelian gentleman is that the latter can somehow see what is humanly highest (philosophy) and defer to it. While Emile could defer to his teacher, to Cato, to Jesus, and, were he to ever become an actual citizen, to the great founders of free cities (E, 4P 596, 625ff., 841), what access could he have, as potential citizen, to the ecstatic sentiment of existence of the solitary walker (E, 4 P 249; CS 2.7.3; D2, 3 P 192–93; R, 1 P 1046ff., 1065ff.)? In Plato and Aristotle the citizen at his best is somehow aware of the best way of life and defers to it though it is different from his own: there is or can be some common ground between the two. In Rousseau there cannot be any. See above, pp. 4, 9ff., 190f. It is therefore far more difficult for Rousseau to account for his genuine, if not unmitigated, esteem for republican virtue than it is for Plato and Aristotle to account for the rank of its counterpart in their teachings.

11. Cf. Michel Launay, "L'art de l'écrivain dans le Contrat social," in *Etudes sur le contrat social de Jean-Jacques Rousseau* (Paris: Société les belles lettres, 1964), pp. 353ff., 365f., 371; Ronald Grimsley, Introduction to *Du Contrat social* (Oxford: The Clarendon Press, 1972), pp. 1–3, 88; hereafter cited as CS (Grimsley).

12. For the conditional character of the natural law in post-Hobbesian political philosophy prior to Kant, see Leo Strauss, *The Political Philosophy of Hobbes* (Oxford: The Clarendon Press, 1936), pp. vii–viii. My translations from the *Social Contract* are very much indebted to the English versions of Cranston, Crosby, Masters, and Watkins.

13. 1 P 56. For the "strong soul" of his father, who serves as the example for this maxim, see 1 P 55.

14. Rousseau's own note to one of the autographed copies he made of the *Confessions* enables one to determine that he is speaking of writings he published previous to 1765. See 1 P 1260, var. (a) to 1 P 56.

15. 1 P 404–5. Rousseau is speaking of his visit of 1754.

16. C, 1 P 395, 581.

17. See Derathé, *Rousseau et la science politique*, pp. 200ff.

18. Cf. Strauss, NRH, pp. 254–55.

19. 1.2.2; 1.6.3, 4; 1.8.2; 2.4.10.

20. 1.8.1 (emphasis added).

21. Translations from the *Discourse on the Sciences and Arts* and the *Discourse on Inequality* reproduce, with occasional minor changes, Roger D. Masters, ed., *Jean-Jacques Rousseau: The First and Second Discourses*,

trans. Roger D. and Judith R. Masters (New York: St. Martin's Press, 1964). Numbers in brackets following the references to the pages in the Pléiade edition refer to pages in the Masters translation—D2, 3 P 170 [149–50].

22. D2, 3 P 171 [150–51]. In the *Discourse on Inequality* Rousseau distinguishes three different periods in the state of nature and three different periods in the state of civil society. Each period is separated from its successor by a "revolution." The "first" or "pure" state of nature is terminated by the appearance of fixed dwellings; this has an effect that Rousseau calls a "revolution" because it leads to the establishment and the distinction of families (3 P 167). This period is terminated by another "revolution" characterized by the division of labor and the introduction of property (3 P 171). The three periods in the state of civil society, each separated from its predecessor by a "revolution," are (1) laws without government, (2) government under law, and (3) lawless government (3 P 187). It is in the second period of both states that the greatest happiness is to be found (3 P 171, 186), although it is declared to be typical of the human condition only in the second period of the state of nature. It should be remembered that the typically happy period in the state of nature belongs to the part of Rousseau's account that is hypothetical from every point of view (D2, 3 P 162–63). Cf. below, n. 29.

23. Derathé, *Rousseau et la science politique*, p. 106.

24. E, 4 P 687; GP, 3 P 1004–5.

25. Cf. Launay, "L'art de l'écrivain," p. 358 n. 36. Each of the first three books ends with a chapter which sharply exposes the limitations of the chief subject under discussion in that book. The last chapter in Book 1 discloses an important limitation upon the justice that is brought into being by the enactment of the social contract: a people's claim to its territory cannot be established by the social contract, and may well be disputed by other peoples with perfect justice, unless conditions are met which one cannot reasonably expect any people to meet. (Apart from all other conditions, a people would have to be not the present, but the first, occupant of the territory it inhabits, and even this could not oblige another people to respect its claim if the self-preservation of that other people were at stake). The second book, which is devoted to law as the central act of the general will, as well as to what the legislator must do to bring into being a society in which law *is* the act of the general will, ends by describing as "most important of all" a kind of law which never comes up for discussion in the assembly of the people and which is never submitted to the people for its ratification, but "which the great legislator occupies himself with in secret." The chapter which ends the book that is devoted to government makes clear that, strictly speaking, every government is provisional. Although the fourth book does not exhibit this pattern, its last substantive chapter brings out clearly the extent to which the political order, which originates from the human will, depends on men's convictions concerning an order which by definition cannot originate from the human will.

26. In the course of the discussion, rules for framing these "political" laws emerge, rules which one must also acknowledge to be principles of political right. See 3.17.7; 4.8.31.

27. *On the Social Contract*, ed., with introduction and notes by Roger D. Masters, trans. by Judith R. Masters (New York: St. Martin's Press, 1978), p. 21; the *Social Contract*, ed., with introduction and notes by Charles M. Sherover (New York: New American Library, 1974), p. 174. These editions hereafter cited as CS (Sherover) and CS (Masters).

28. Roger D. Masters, *The Political Philosophy of Rousseau* (Princeton: Princeton University Press, 1968), p. 406 n. 205.

29. In the *Social Contract* it is taken for granted that mankind was once in the state of nature. Rousseau professes not to know how the transition from it took place, not whether it did (1.1.1). For the question of whether this conflicts with the allegedly hypothetical character ascribed to the state of nature in the *Discourse on Inequality*, cf. Marc F. Plattner, *Rousseau's State of Nature* (De Kalb: Northern Illinois University Press, 1979), pp. 17–30. Plattner makes a convincing use of note J to the *Discourse on Inequality*—the note deals with whether orangutans are human beings who never left the state of nature—in support of the view that Rousseau believed the state of nature to have truly existed.

30. *De Cive*, chap. 1, secs. 7–10. Rousseau's vehement disagreements with Hobbes did not prevent him from warmly admiring him. He called him "one of the finest geniuses who ever existed" (3 P 611 and n. 1). He credits him with being the only Christian author to understand correctly the theologico-political problem in Europe as well as to require what the solution to it must achieve. In the *Discourse on Inequality* he acknowledges that Hobbes grasped "the defect of all modern [i.e., medieval and post-medieval] definitions of natural right" (3 P 153 [129]). Rousseau exhibits much more respect for Hobbes than for Grotius, in contrast to what he thought was the common view of their relative merits (E, 4 P 836).

31. Strauss, NRH, pp. 185–86, 297–98.

32. Derathé (*Rousseau et la science politique*, pp. 200ff.) shows that this reasoning is present in Locke. Derathé even speaks of "freedom" as a "prolongation" and "juridical expression" of the right to self-preservation in Locke and Rousseau. The passage in Locke to which Derathé refers, however, is not part of Locke's discussion of the relation between parents and children. Rousseau, one should add, was not aware of any essential difference between his principles and those of Locke; he claims that his principles are "exactly the same" as those of Locke (LM, 3 P 812).

33. *De Cive*, chap. 6, sec. 13n.

34. The author intends to set forth the response Aristotle could make to this objection in a future work on Aristotle's views regarding the right to rule.

35. Defoe, *Robinson Crusoe* New York: Signet-New American Library, 1961), p. 147 (cf. pp. 128–29, 236). For the novel as a whole, cf., Thomas S. Schrock, "Considering Crusoe," *Interpretation* 1 (1970): 76–106, 169–232.

36. Hobbes is discussed in this chapter rather than in the chapter concerned with slavery and sovereignty resulting from voluntary agreements because of his teaching that the sovereign's practically unlimited right over his subjects derives entirely from nature and not from any agreement between the sovereign and his subjects.

37. Cf. the remark concerning Otho in the quotation on p. 35.

38. Jean Jacques Rousseau, *Rousseau juge de Jean Jacques*, 1 P 864.

39. Derathé (*Rousseau et la science politique*, pp. 182–92, 195) points out that the jurists whose views Rousseau disputes in 1.4 modeled their account of the compact of sovereignty on the compact of slavery; Derathé also notes that the topics discussed in 1.4 and the order in which they are discussed are the same as those found in the jurists whose views Rousseau is rejecting.

40. Cf. Masters, *Political Philosophy of Rousseau*, p. 323. Also cf. 3 P 1443, n. 3 to p. 359.

41. Translations from *Emile* reproduce, with occasional minor changes, *Emile*, trans. Allan Bloom (New York: Basic Books, 1979). Numbers in brackets following the references to the pages in the Pléiade edition refer to pages in the Bloom translation. E, 4 P 838 [460]; emphasis added.

42. Derathé, *Rousseau et la science politique*, pp. 333ff.

43. Raymond Polin, *La politique de la solitude* (Paris Editions Sirey, 1971), p. 113.

Chapter Two

1. Cf. 3 P 1443, n. 1 to p. 360.

2. In CS¹ (3 P 322) Rousseau speaks of "the impossibility that great geniuses will succeed one another continually in government."

3. Cf. Charles H. McIlwain, *Constitutionalism Ancient and Modern* (Ithaca: Cornell University Press 1940), pp. 30–37; T. A. Sinclair, *A History of Greek Political Thought* (Cleveland: The World Publishing Company, 1968), pp. 173–84; and above all Leo Strauss, "Plato," in *History of Political Philosophy*, ed. Leo Strauss and Joseph Cropsey, 2d ed. (Chicago: University of Chicago Press, 1972), pp. 42–51, as well as Strauss, NRH, 140ff.

4. 1.6.7; emphasis added. Compare "common superior" in the passages from *Emile* quoted above on p. 27.

5. Stephen Landsman, Donald McWherter, and Alan Pfeffer, *What to Do Until the Lawyer Comes* (Garden City, N.Y.: Anchor-Doubleday 1977), p. 18.

6. EP, 3 P 248; emphasis added.

7. LM, 3 P 841f.; cf. D2, 3 P 112, GP, 3 P 974. Emphasis added.

8. LM, 3 P 807.

9. Cf. above, p. 4; C, 1 P 404–5; EP, 3 P 248–9; Derathé, *Rousseau et la science politique*, p. 229.

10. I am indebted for this formulation to Charles Sherover.

11. Leo Strauss, *The City and Man* (Chicago: University of Chicago Press, 1964), p. 33 n. 46.

12. Cf. Masters, *The Political Philosophy of Rousseau*, pp. 301 ff.

13. CS¹, 3 P 297.

14. See Derathé's note to the chapter on monarchy (3 P 1479–80), as well as his article on the subject, cited in that note.

15. Cf. below, chap. 5 n. 1.

16. E, 4 P 468; GP, 3P 954; D2, 3 P 187. Cf. Strauss, NRH, pp. 259–60.

17. Cf. below, chap. 4 n. 21.

18. Derathé, *Rousseau et la science politique*, pp. 151–71.

19. Strauss, NRH, p. 286; Masters, *Political Philosophy of Rousseau*, pp. 316ff.

20. D2, 3 P 125–26; cf. CS¹, 3 P 329.

21. Cf. Strauss, NRH, p. 276f; Alfred Cobban, *Rousseau and the Modern State* (London: George Allen and Unwin, 1934), p. 169.

22. 2.12.2; LM, 3 P 890–91.

23. Cf. R. A. Leigh, "Liberté et authorité dans le *Contrat social*," in *Jean-Jacques Rousseau et son oeurve* (Paris: C. Klincksieck, 1964), pp. 249–62.

24. Cf. above, p. 10f.

25. 2.6.6; 3.18.2.

26. 1.9.6; 2.4.9; 1.9.8 and n.; 2.8.1; 2.11.2 and n.; 3.5.10; cf. E, 4 P 524 n. For the society Rousseau seeks to establish as a predominantly middle-class society, cf. CS (Sherover), pp. 36, 84.

27. D2, 3 P 177 [159].

28. John Plamenatz, *Man and Society* (New York: McGraw-Hill, 1963), 1: 394.

29. Masters, *Political Philosophy of Rousseau*, p. 326. CS(Grimsley), p. 25. 3 P 1453, n. 1 to p. 368. Cf. EP, 3 P 247.

30. Cf. above, n. 3.

31. In the best regime described in the last two Books of the *Politics*, the demos is replaced by slaves who can be promised their freedom as a reward for good conduct, that is, whose enslavement is not by nature right. If one disregards the dawn of political life, in other regimes, concessions must be made to claims to rule other than those deriving from virtue and practical wisdom (1282b 14–1283a 3). I do not believe this observation to be in disagreement with Strauss, NRH, pp. 140–43, 156–57.

32. Plamenatz, *Man and Society* 1: 393.

33. LM, 3 P 807; CS¹, 3 P 310; CS, 4.1.1,2.

34. Strauss, NRH, pp. 276f.

35. Cf. Richard Fralin, *Rousseau and Representation* (New York: Columbia University Press, 1978), p. 86.

36. Masters, *Political Philosophy of Rousseau*, pp. 389f.

37. Cf. CS¹, 3 P 327.

38. EP, 3 P 244.

39. Cf. Strauss, NRH, pp. 286f.

Chapter Three

1. Masters, *Political Philosophy of Rousseau*, pp. 366 ff.

2. E, 4 P 526–27 [237–38].

3. Cf. the fragment on Moses, 3 P 500 (no. 26).

4. The passage from Montesquieu quoted in 2.7.2 implies, in its original context, that a succession of individuals can be a "legislator" as well. Cf. 2.8.5.

5. CS (Grimsley), p. 85.

6. For Corsica, see 2.10.6. For Poland, see GP, 3 P 961, 969–70.

7. GP, 3 P 1024, 1027. Cf. below, chap. 5 n. 17.

8. Hobbes, *Leviathan*, ed. Michael Oakeshott (Oxford: Basil Blackwell, 1960), p. 241; emphasis added.

9. Hobbes, *The Elements of Law*, Epistle Dedicatory.
10. Strauss, NRH, pp. 169ff.
11. Ibid., pp. 198ff.
12. D1, 3 P 19, 21.
13. D1, 3 P 3, 6.
14. Cf. above, p. 40f.
15. E, 4 P 676 [343].
16. C, 1 P 62; see *Lettre à Lecat*, 3 P 102.
17. Cf. GP, 3 P 955 (last paragraph), 3 P 969 (beginning of last paragraph), and 3 P 957–58 (Numa).
18. See chap. 1 n. 30.
19. By "motion and will" in 2.6.1 Rousseau means "action" (cf. 3.1.2, 4).
20. As Derathé finely observes (3 P 1474, nn. 2 and 4 to p. 396), whereas the words "sovereign" and "sovereignty" distinguish the function from the body that exercises it, in the case of "government" one word expresses both. The general chapter on government (3.1) supplies separate definitions of the function (3.1.7) and of the governing body (3.1.5).
21. LM, 3 P 808–9.
22. LM, 3 P 703, 809.
23. The law recommended in 4.5.7 reinforces but does not form part of the constitution of the state.
24. There is also a sense in which the state (in its imprecise sense) or the republic or the body politic can be simply equated with the sovereign (cf. CS, 1.6.10; GP 3 P 985) in which case the state would have no component parts that the sovereign body as sovereign body does not have. But this is not the usual sense in the *Social Contract* of the term "constitution of the state" (cf. 4.5.1, 2).

Chapter Four
1. CS¹, 3 P 296; emphasis added.
2. On Rousseau's mathematical language, see Derathé, 3 P 1472–73, n. 2 to p. 395.
3. Masters, *Political Philosophy of Rousseau*, pp. 382, 386.
4. D2, 3 P 186–87.
5. Fralin, *Rousseau and Representation*, p. 93.
6. CS (Grimsley), p. 161 n. 2.
7. LM, 3 P 811.
8. Fralin, *Rousseau and Representation*, p. 94.
9. Masters, *Political Philosophy of Rousseau*, p. 398; Fralin, *Rousseau and Representation*, pp. 94–95.
10. D2, 3 P 113–15.
11. D2, 3 P 180 [163].
12. D2, 3 P 186 [171]; (emphasis added).
13. D2, 3 P 114–15.
14. LM, 3 P 894.
15. "Tyrannie," *Dictionaire philosophique*, ed. J. Benda and R. Naves, p. 412. We have quoted the translation by Peter Gay (New York: Basic Books, 1962), pp. 481–82.
16. LM, 3 P 808–9.

17. *Jugement sur la polysynodie*, 3 P 645 and n.
18. 3.6.5 and n.; cf. 3.8.6.
19. 3.7.6; cf. 3.4.3, 4.
20. For what precedes and what follows, see John B. Noone, Jr., *Rousseau's Social Contract* (Athens, Ga.: University of Georgia Press, 1980), pp. 64–71.
21. 3.9.4 n.; 3.13.8; D2, 3 P 206–7.
22. D1, 3 P 11; E, 4 P 1694, var. (a) to 4 P 851; LM, 3 P 843.

Chapter Five
1. Rousseau was accused of contradicting himself in the *Discourse on Inequality* on the grounds that the denunciation of political life in the body of the *Discourse* was incompatible with the praise of Geneva contained in its Epistle Dedicatory. Rousseau replied that in the Epistle Dedicatory he had congratulated his fatherland for having one of the best governments that can exist, while in the *Discourse* he found that there could be very few good governments; he denied that this was an inconsistency requiring an explanation (*Lettre à Philopolis*, 3 P 235).
2. The reference in 3.3.5 was to the Roman Empire.
3. 4.4.24 ("usurpé"); 4.5.5; 4.6.9; cf. LM, 3 P 880.
4. Cf. GP, 3 P 959: each of the large states surrounding Poland is called a "despotism."
5. Rousseau, *Du contrat social*, ed. Georges Beaulavon (Paris: Armand Colin, 1938), p. 256 n. 1.
6. D'A, ed. M. Fuchs, p. 99; cf. Masters, *Political Philosophy of Rousseau*, p. 385.
7. 3.11.5; 2.12.5; D'A, ed. Fuchs, p. 89.
8. 4.8.35; GP, 3 P 958.
9. GP, 3 P 978; cf., however, Hobbes, *De Cive*, chap. 7, sec. 5.
10. See above, chap. 3 n. 9. This is not the place for an extensive discussion of Rousseau's writing on Poland. The following should be borne in mind, however. Rousseau makes two kinds of proposals in his work on Poland. Some are intended for immediate adoption. The more far-reaching and profound ones are meant to be introduced gradually, "without a perceptible revolution": they include the emancipation and enfranchise-ment of the serfs, the extension of citizens' rights to townsmen, and the transformation of Poland into a confederation of small states (3 P 971, 973–74, 979, 1024–28). Understanding Rousseau's work on Poland would require seeing the connection between his suggestions for immediate action and the long-range changes on the need for which he insists. The political result of these changes is not manifestly in conflict with the *Social Contract*, which is quoted throughout the work on Poland. Rousseau never elabo-rated his views concerning what rights a federation of free states would have over its members. The *Social Contract* calls for such a federation (3.15.12 and n.) and at two points provides a footing for it. In the first place, the conduct of foreign policy is not a function of sovereignty (2.2.3). The federation could conduct the foreign policy of its members without infring-ing on the sovereignty of its members. Moreover, the sovereign, which cannot incur obligations to itself, can incur obligations to foreigners, pro-

vided these do not conflict with the social contract: It could incur the obligation to obey the decisions of the federal diet by which the federation is ruled. The chapter attacking the exercise of sovereignty by deputies or representatives is the one that makes the need for federations of free states clear (3.15.12. and n.), federations whose affairs are managed by what one can only call a kind of representative rule. It is because the exercise of sovereignty by deputies or representatives is inadmissible that a certain kind of representative rule becomes necessary. What remains undeveloped by Rousseau is his answer to the question "how far the right of confederation can be extended without jeopardizing that of sovereignty" (E, 4 P 848 [466]).

11. 3.4.3; 4.3.7; 3.10.3 n.; 3.7.6.

12. Cf. Fralin, *Rousseau and Representation*, pp. 105–12.

13. 3.1.6; 3.18.1. Cf. LM, 3 P 840 on "provisional government in my sense of the term." Fralin (cf. n. 12 above) sees the importance of this but does not do justice to its permanent implications.

14. Derathé, *Rousseau et la science politique*, pp. 270ff.

15. 2.11.2; 3.4.5, 6; 3.5.9.

16. Cf. LM, 3 P 878: the very need to buy votes proves that freedom still has not been extinguished.

17. I am indebted to Melvin Richter for making me aware of the importance of this metaphor.

18. Cf. Derathé note on the end of 4.1 (3 P 1492, n. 1 to p. 439).

19. The quote concludes, "But this important matter would require a separate treatise, and I cannot say everything in this one." Rousseau draws the reader's attention to the fact that he has not declared his views concerning these points. One should therefore not read the concluding paragraph of 4.1 as if he had. In a later work (LM) Rousseau makes his views better known. Legislative initiative is to be reserved to a governmental body (3 P 872). The apparent superfluity of such a measure in a simple peasant society does not detract from its usefulness as a precaution against worse times. The right to debate matters brought before the assembly of the people is *not* to be reserved to government, however (3 P 830).

20. *De Cive*, chap. 5, secs. 6–9.

21. *De Cive*, chap. 5 sec. 8. Cf. Strauss, NRH, p. 190 n. 30.

22. Strauss, NRH, p. 277, 280f.

23. Derathé, in a note to CS, 4.2.11, points out that it follows from it that the people must exercise part of the functions of government in addition to those of sovereignty (3 P 1494, n. 2 to p. 441). This makes the final paragraph of 4.2 a transition to 4.3.

24. 3.17.1; 4.3.1. Cf. n. 22 above.

25. This interpretation is opposed to that offered by Fralin in *Rousseau and Representation*, pp. 108–12.

26. 2.11.2 and n.; cf. 1.9.8 n.; LM, 3 P 890.

27. Fralin (*Rousseau and Representation*, p. 114) suggests that, according to Rousseau, the population of the urban tribes in Rome was greater than that of the rural tribes. The only passage that seems to support this contention—4.4.15 end—does so only if one ignores the distinction between the "inhabitants of Rome" and "the entire Roman people" as well

as the distinction between the "inhabitants of Rome" and the "inhabitants of the countryside" (4.4.7; cf. 4.4.12, 13, 14, 23, 27, 31, 34).

Chapter Six

1. The foregoing is not intended to deny that the sovereign is sacred according to Rousseau—it is affirmed to be sacred in 3.7.9; cf. 3.14.1; 4.1.5—but only to account for the differences in degree to which he points.

2. 4.2.4; 4.4.35, 36; 4.6.9.

3. See above, chap. 5 n. 12.

4. 3.15.6; 1.4.9; cf. D1, 3 P 6.

5. Cf. C, 1 P 392–93; LM, 3 P 703.

6. Cf. Cobban, *Rousseau and the Modern State*, p. 55; EP, 3 P 254, 246; E, 4 P 248–49; D2, 3 P 178.

7. For controversial points on which the civil religion deliberately remains neutral—the Trinity, the merit of good works, original sin—cf. LM, 3 P 705.

8. LM, 3 P 705.

9. LM, 3 P 703, 809.

10. E, 4 P 566–67, 604–5.

11. CS^1, 3 P 338. Cf. CS^1, 3 P 285.

12. Cf. Launay, "L'art de l'écrivain," p. 371.

Index

205

McIlwain, Charles Howard, 199 n.3
McWherter, Donald, 33, 199 n.5
Masters, Roger D., 196 nn.12, 21, 198 nn.27, 28, 199 nn.40, 12, 200 nn.19, 29, 36, 1, 201 nn.3, 9, 202 n.6
Montesquieu, 47, 104, 141–42, 146, 200 n.4

Newton, 81, 82
Noone, John B., Jr., 202 n.20

Pfeffer, Alan, 33, 199 n.5
Philo Judaeus, 20
Plamenatz, John, 50, 200 nn.28, 32
Plato, 2, 22, 31, 36, 53, 57, 77–79, 116, 145, 170, 195 n.4, 196 n.10
Plattner, Marc, 198 n.29
Plutarch, 2, 23, 89, 143, 49
Polin, Raymond, 199 n.43
Pufendorf, Samuel, 195 n.2

Richter, Melvin, 203 n.17

Schrock, Thomas S., 198 n.35
Sherover, Charles M., 198 n.27, 199 n.10, 200 n.26
Sinclair, T. A., 199 n.3
Sophocles, 134
Spinoza, 32, 180, 187–88
Strauss, Leo, vii, 18, 195 nn.1, 2, 196 nn.12, 18, 198 n.31, 199 nn.3, 11, 16, 200 nn.19, 21, 31, 34, 39, 201 nn.10, 11, 203 nn.21, 22

Tacitus, 133
Terrason, Abbé, Jean, 83
Thomas Aquinas, 3
Tocqueville, Alexis de, 32, 49, 58 142–43, 154

Virgil, 4
Voltaire, 111, 133, 138, 141, 201 n.15

Watkins, Frederick, 72, 196 n.12